GYPSY FUGUE

Caitlin Press Inc.
8100 Alderwood Road,
Halfmoon Bay, BC V0N 1Y1
www.caitlin-press.com

Text and cover design by Vici Johnstone
Printed in Canada

Caitlin Press Inc. acknowledges financial support from the Government of
Canada and the Canada Council for the Arts, and the Province of Brit-
ish Columbia through the British Columbia Arts Council and the Book
Publisher's Tax Credit.

Library and Archives Canada Cataloguing in Publication

Schiwy, Marlene Adeline, author
    Gypsy fugue : an archetypal memoir / Marlene Schiwy.

Includes bibliographical references.
ISBN 978-1-987915-59-4 (softcover)

    1. Schiwy, Marlene Adeline, —Travel. 2. Romanies—Social
life and customs. 3. Self-realization. I. Title.

DX118.S35 2018   305.891'497   C2017-
906454-1

Gypsy Fugue

AN ARCHETYPAL MEMOIR

MARLENE SCHIWY

CAITLIN PRESS

For Steve,
cherished companion on the journey,
lover of my *gypsy* soul

and for
Marion Woodman,
great soul *gypsy* of our age

Contents

Acknowledgements 9

A Book of Secrets 11

Prelude

Shimmering Darkly 18

Mother India's Forgotten Child 25

Wanderers on This Earth 49

Fugue

On Meandering 67

A Story of Red 70

Embroideries 74

Musical Body 79

Winter Music 83

Five Singing Lessons 89

You Are Flamenco 93

Deep Song 96

Beauty, Ugliness,
and the Lady from Papua, New Guinea 107

Bodies of Imagination 116

Not All Who Wander Are Lost 123

PILGRIMAGE AND LAMENTATION   126

OUTCASTS, OUTSIDERS, AND OTHERS   138

GYPSY FUGUE   142

BACH, JUNG, AND THE GYPSY   145

THE SCHOOL OF FOOLS   150

THE FIVE CHAPATIS   154

CROSSING BOUNDARIES   157

GYPSY-SCHOLAR / SCHOLAR-GYPSY   161

WRITING THE GYPSY   164

ZÜRICH DREAMS   169

FANTASIA FOR A GYPSY ANALYST   175

CARAVANS   178

O LUNGO DROM   182

NOCTURNE   185

FOLLOWING THE GYPSY   196

CODA   201

ENDNOTES   212

BIBLIOGRAPHY   229

ACKNOWLEDGEMENTS

I would like to offer my heartfelt gratitude to friends and colleagues who have expressed lively interest and encouragement for this book through the years. For their loving friendship and steadfast support I thank particularly Marketa Goetz-Stankiewicz, Sheila Langston, Lael McCall, Heather Miller, Gabi Rahaman, David and Cyndy Roomy, and Yvonne Young. My appreciation goes also to Penny Allport, Rym Bettaieb, Bonita Brindley, the late Clare Buckland, Patty Flowers, Aimee Gabor, Janice Grout, Ellen Leslie, Kate Levan, Patricia Llosa, Gail Lyons, Maureen Malowany, Maureen Phillips, Nellie Schiwy, the late Lin Stevens, Sally Turner, and Jean Way.

My writing group, the Memoiristas—Kate Braid, Heidi Greco, Joy Kogawa, Susan McCaslin, and Elsie Neufeld—offered helpful feedback and the wondrous gift of writerly friendship through the years.

Deep thanks to my Body Soul sisters in Vancouver—Sheila Langston, Heather Miller, and Margo Palmer—and the West Coast Body Soul group, for the rich journey we have shared; may it continue for many years to come.

I will always be grateful to the Body Soul Rhythms leadership—Marion Woodman, Mary Hamilton, and Ann Skinner—and the international BSR community of the Marion Woodman Foundation, with whom I began to explore the images alive in my body and soul.

Through the years I have been privileged to work with many open-hearted, creative, generous, soulful women in my workshops. In recent years this includes especially participants in the Tuesday and Thursday Morning Wild Women Writing Circles, Loon Lake and "Jung in the Yurt" Retreats, Body Soul Sundays and "Following the Gypsy" Programs. You inspire me with your trust and willingness to be vulnerable, your poignant stories and beautiful writing. Working with you is one of the great blessings of my life.

Thanks also to Murray Stein who read the original *gypsy* Symbol paper in Zürich and encouraged the book, and to the late Sonja Marjasch, who said the first time we met, "It's obvious you are a gypsy analyst." It is a gift to be truly seen.

My great appreciation to Vici Johnstone for her willingness to go in a different direction with this book. It has been a pleasure to work with her dedicated team at Caitlin Press.

As always, deepest thanks to Steve for his loving support and encouragement, generous and perceptive feedback. You are bedrock, Steve.

I would like to thank William L. Rukeyser for permission to quote an excerpt from © Muriel Rukeyser's poem "Käthe Kollwitz." My gratitude extends also to Nadia Hava-Robbins for permission to quote her poem "Gypsy Soul," and to John Stone for permission to quote an excerpt from "Road Map for a Fugue." Every effort has been made to obtain permission for quoted material; in the event of an omission please contact the author.

A Book of Secrets

Tell me for what you yearn and I shall tell you who you
are. We are what we reach for, the idealized image that
drives our wandering.

—James Hillman

Write with your breasts. It creates intimacy.

Dream fragment

There is a *gypsy* in my soul. I have felt her dark and shimmering presence in
my depths for as long as I can remember. Now I want to follow her down
the many pathways of my life and see where she will take me. I want to sing
her story.

Gypsy Fugue tells of my relationship with an inner image over many
years. I have called it an *archetypal memoir* to express my sense of connection with a broader, deeper realm of meaning and significance than my own
life could encompass, and to acknowledge the power of mythic patterns
and images that shape our lives like invisible magnets, permeating us with
particular passions, prejudices, and proclivities. The story of my outer life
cannot account for the *gypsy* in my soul, but there she is. I think she has
always been there.

"Outward circumstances are no substitute for inner experience," the
Swiss psychologist C.G. Jung wrote in the prologue to his autobiography,
Memories, Dreams, Reflections. "I can understand myself only in the light of
inner happenings. It is these that make up the singularity of my life, and with
these my autobiography deals." The imagination is another country, and there,
events, dates, and outer circumstances matter less than dreams and fantasies,
and odd affinities. May it be assumed from the start, then, that fact and fantasy are woven together here. No need to draw sharp boundaries between inner

and outer worlds because the membrane that separates them is diaphanous.

A story wants a beginning, a middle, and an ending. A memoir should focus on a specific time and place, a crisis, recurring theme, perhaps a turning point in the writer's life. There ought to be a dramatic arc and a satisfying resolution. You will find little of that here and yet I am calling this a memoir. You might say this is the story of how the *gypsy* has lived her life in me. You might call it an *imaginal* memoir because it concerns itself with the life of my imagination, or a *transpersonal* memoir, for I have always felt something coming out to meet me halfway on this journey. What's certain is that *Gypsy Fugue* has evolved out of my lifelong love of an archetypal image.

I have puzzled over the paradox of the book's title for a long time. *Gypsy Rhapsody* or *Gypsy Fantasia* would make sense, but *Gypsy Fugue*? What could the Dionysian *gypsy* possibly have in common with the Apollonian Bach and *The Art of Fugue*? I asked myself. And yet the book's title expresses the tension of these opposites in me and perhaps in all of us. The never-ending quest for serenity and balance along with the *gypsy's* recklessness and passion for life. Most often it's the former that dominates my waking hours. Caught between the Apollonian love of divine proportion and the Dionysian desire for ecstatic excess, I've often felt paralyzed, wondering how to move ahead and whether I would ever be able to *write the gypsy*.

At times I've even felt slightly apologetic, as if my writing should demonstrate how gypsy-like I am. But then I remember that it's my imagination that is the *gypsy*, not my outer life or ego. Restless and unruly, given to extremes, she brings spontaneity and exuberance to my responsible and ever-balance-seeking self. All along I've had to keep reining her in because the *gypsy* would keep wandering forever. She doesn't give a fig about writing a book.

Following my nose in service to intuition's whiffs and leaps and sparks, I've often jumped from file to file and chapter to chapter at a dizzying rate, as if the *gypsy* couldn't bear to settle anywhere for long. Exploring those intuitive leaps and following faint tracks into the darkness of the unknown, writing in circles and summoning the incantatory power of words (from *incantare*, "to sing or chant into"), I have yearned to *sing into* my story. The scholar in me wants to ensure everything fits together. My dream tells me, "Write with your breasts. It creates intimacy." I want them both.

❧

Gypsy Fugue weaves together several of my lifelong passions. Autobiography—*self/life/writing*—and the many shape-shifting forms of memoir allow me to compose stories that reflect who I am and give meaning to my life. The work of C.G. Jung, Marion Woodman, James Hillman, and other writers of the deep psyche have inspired and nourished me for decades, serving as tuning forks for my own writing. The Roma people, with all that I have discovered about them, continue to enthrall me with their unbridled lust for life and fierce determination to survive. Not least, my life has been enriched beyond words by the ineffable power of music.

Music has also provided the book's structure, that of *prelude and fugue*. The musical *prelude* unfolds and expands a particular melodic motif, while the *fugue* introduces a musical theme or subject in a single voice that is subsequently taken up by additional voices and woven horizontally in a musical texture, where it appears and seems to vanish and then reappears again.

In the *Prelude*, I explore Gypsies through a number of different lenses. Chapter 1 offers a brief account of my lifelong fascination with Gypsies and their symbolic importance in our culture. In the second chapter I reflect on common gypsy stereotypes in the Western world along with the historical realities of the Roma people. In chapter 3 we step into the archetypal landscape inhabited by the *gypsy* and her mythic family, and wander through this imaginal territory.

The *Fugue* is a series of autobiographical variations on the *gypsy* theme in my life. Its twenty-six vignettes or *fuguettes* (little fugues) interweave personal stories and reflections, dreams and fantasies, perambulations into literature and folklore, scholarly reading and writing, and other imaginal wanderings. There is no linear tale here; these are windows into my soul.

A *coda* is a closing section that rounds off a musical work and brings it to its conclusion. In the book's final chapter, I muse on a form of writing in which the deeply rooted inner realities of our lives and the soul's love of images would be the essential facts in the telling of our stories. Here I imagine archetypal autobiography or memoir as a necklace of bead memories around a central image that attracts our life stories to itself.

These pages are filled with rambunctious research and treasured quotes from many sources; my love of other people's words and images is part and parcel of this memoir. Literary bricolage belongs to the vagabond imagination and mirrors the roving soul of the *gypsy*. Reading widely and deeply, I have taken what delights me and woven it into my story.

My dearest hope is that you, the reader, may be inspired to seek out the cherished images and symbols of your own life and the mythic identifications that shape your story, and explore them for the gold they will surely reveal. Because the *gypsy* is an image of the exiled soul in all of us. Psyche is nomadic, wandering between the realms and returning from the underworld with the treasure box that holds the knowledge of life and death. *Gypsy Fugue* tells of my own journey between the realms. I hope that it will encourage yours.

◈

In any kind of autobiographical writing the essential question is always what to include and what to leave out. It's one thing to be concerned about telling one's story without hurting or betraying other people; another, to protect our own soul story, so as not to violate the inner *Others*. While writing *Gypsy Fugue* I often wondered what could be shared with a reader and what needed to be preserved within my inner holy of holies. Having loved this image for many decades, the last thing I wanted to do was destroy its numinosity. At times I was sure I would never be able to finish writing the book, and that this was as it should be.

Sacred. Scared. Scarred. I was afraid of betraying what was holy. Scared I might scar the sacred. Then I had the following dream.

There is a young Gypsy woman whose diary is held under lock and key. She is calm and quiet but it seems she's a survivor of some kind of concentration camp and torture, and I am deeply moved by her story. I see the open diary. It is a "book of secrets." I recognize a few words in it but much of it is written in a language I don't understand.

There are other people in the room and I watch as a man locks her diary in a wooden box, then puts the box away. Then Steve (my husband) tries to fit a key into the lock on the broad side of the box but the key doesn't fit. He tries a different lock on the bottom of the box and this time the key fits, so he opens the box and takes out the book.

We are all very happy and relieved to have it in our hands and gently open it. It seems to be written in a mixture of different languages and includes hieroglyphics and some colours. It's clear to everyone present that this is a precious document and we are very grateful. I have the sense that we cherish it.

The young woman is watching us quietly and I ask if this is her diary. She says yes. I begin to weep with deep emotion and she does too. There's a feeling among us all that this diary is a long-lost treasure that will provide insights and answers to some important historical questions.

Then I am walking outside with the Gypsy woman and a little girl who seems to be her daughter. We come to the end of a path and embrace each other tightly. I thank her again and again. We are both crying. She takes the little girl's hand and they turn to the left and walk up into the forest. I walk down in the opposite direction, away from them. The Gypsy woman seems peaceful and content that her book of secrets is in good hands and will be read by people who treasure her story. I wake up.

I mulled over this dream often, lived with it, and continued writing.

A NOTE ON TERMINOLOGY

Here I'd like to reflect on nomenclature. I have used the terms **Roma** and **Gypsy** interchangeably when referring to the living people, lower case **gypsy** for the cultural stereotype, and italicized *gypsy* for the archetypal image. In many instances there is considerable overlap among them; for example, the Roma's passion for music and dance is reflected in popular stereotypes of singing, dancing gypsies and belongs to the archetypal *gypsy* as well. Where this is the case, I have endeavoured to be as clear, precise, and accurate as possible.

Prelude

Shimmering Darkly

An Introduction

When the soul wishes to experience something, she
throws an image of the experience out before her, and
then enters into her own image.

—Meister Eckhart

I cannot remember a time when I was not fascinated with Gypsies. From
the time I was a little girl and heard the words of an old German folk song,
Lustig ist das Zigeunerleben—"Merry is the Gypsy life"—I was enthralled.
As a child, *Zigeuner* spoke to me of something dark and free, unruly and
exciting. When my mother referred to me as *kleine Zigeunerin*, or "little
Gypsy," I had a rare and thrilling sense of being recognized. Instead of the
mild reproach she'd intended, I took it as a secret sign that she saw who I
really was.

Who wouldn't want to be a Gypsy, I thought—proud and beautiful,
unfettered by social convention, and free to sing and dance one's way through
life? Any time I had the chance to dress up, I tied long full skirts around my
waist with the most colourful scarves I could find. I raided my mother's jew-
ellery box and bedecked myself with glittering necklaces and bracelets, then
pulled all the dark stockings I could find over my head and pretended I had
long, swinging hair. My mother had grown up with thick chestnut braids, and
decided her two brown-haired daughters would have short hair that never
got tangled up in painful knots. All my friends wanted to wear pink and be
blonde and blue-eyed so the boys would like them. I wanted curly black hair
and flashing dark eyes. No pink for me; my colour was red.

"Did you steal me from the Gypsies?" I asked my mother when she
lamented my constant desire to travel.

"Yes," she said, glancing at me sideways. "Is that what you want me to say?"

In a photograph taken at a Comparative Literature Department Halloween party years later, three young women in their mid-twenties are smiling at the camera. Colette is on the left, a glamorous witch with dimples and a seductive glance. In the middle is Mary Ann, a dashing bandit in tight black pants and matching Zorro mask that covers her eyes. And there I am, on the right, a colourful Gypsy. A glittering, beaded, crimson scarf is wrapped around my hair, with more red and purple scarves draped around my neck and waist. Shiny rings and bangles cover my fingers and wrists. I'm wearing a muslin blouse with bright red, blue, and yellow flowers and the first of my *gypsy* skirts, with its rows of sparkling beadwork and laces collected during my travels throughout the world. Even in the era of peasant blouses and hippie skirts, I couldn't find ready-made clothes that appealed to me. I didn't enjoy sewing all that much, but it was the only way I could express what I felt on the inside, something dark and shimmering, and full of mystery.

As I was caught up in the heady constrictions of academic life, that *gypsy* energy gradually went underground. But it never disappeared. Its intensity and restlessness accompanied me wherever I went. Even when I moved to England for graduate studies and stopped wearing my *gypsy* skirts in the land of Laura Ashley florals and herringbone tweed, its edgy vitality remained the ground note of my soul.

By then I had heard of the Roma people and knew that the words of the German folk song from my childhood portrayed a falsely idyllic picture of Gypsy life, a romantic fantasy of self-indulgent, childlike irresponsibility with little basis in reality. I also knew that the words *Gypsy* and *Zigeuner* were often spoken with a note of disdain toward a people perceived as begging, cheating, and stealing their way through life. The lyrics of a popular song equated Gypsies with tramps and thieves, out to get what they could without having to work for it. I had witnessed an older colleague quietly ask her office mate not to use *Jew* as a verb, but it had never dawned on me that *gyp*, which we all used freely, was just as malignant.

I'd also realized by then that I wasn't the only one fascinated with Gypsies. Far from it, it seemed that many people were. Our culture has long been captivated by visions of smouldering, dark-eyed, bearded men with violins and exotic women in flamenco dress, against a backdrop of painted, horse-drawn caravans. But beneath the romantic fantasy shimmers an archetypal experience of tremendous pathos and beauty. Violin, flamenco, and caravan evoke the possibility of life lived with a passion and intensity far removed from our goal-oriented, technologized lives. Where is the music that pulses and wails the ecstasy and anguish of our existence? Where is the dance that mirrors the primal rhythms of life in our bodies and shakes the lethargy out of our bones? Where are the spontaneous outbursts of happiness and sorrow, the belly laughter and tears, the rambunctious vitality and joy that make us glad to be alive? Where in our lives do we live in full colour?

It really *is* a different colour and tone of experience that the *gypsy* evokes. The collective may live in beige and grey but the *gypsy* lives in red and purple, mauve and gold. To use a term from alchemy, the *gypsy* dwells in the energy of the *rubedo*, that moment of greatest aliveness when the red blood of instinct and the red fire of spirit merge in a lust for life that is as sensual as it is spiritual, and both are known as expressions of the same divine energy.

I think we respond to the idealized fantasy of Gypsy life with fascination and longing because it touches our bone-deep hunger for soul. The enormous response to *Latcho Drom*, Tony Gatlif's mesmerizing film about Roma culture throughout the world, suggests just how much we yearn for reminders of other ways to live, where music and dance nurture the social body, and living ritual feeds the communal life of the soul. Both individually and as a society, we long to reconnect with a more passionate and instinctual way of being.

It's no surprise that it's the Roma who gave us *duende*, the powerful raw emotion that heralds the moment when spirit ignites matter with divine fire and the god and goddess appear. These are the moments of intensity we live for amid the humdrum of our daily lives, moments when the eternal shines through our fragile, ephemeral existence and every cell in our bodies is quickened. This is how the *gypsy* energy makes me feel—on a good day. Like every archetypal image, it also has a darker face. But that's for later.

After completing my doctoral studies I moved to New York, where I patched together a marginal income as a gypsy scholar, travelling from one university English Department to another for ill-paid adjunct teaching work. I also began offering my own women's writing workshops, which gradually included more Jungian content. It began with the work of the Canadian Jungian writer Marion Woodman—for whom too, I soon discovered, the *archetypal gypsy* was a significant inner presence. Every Wednesday evening we gathered to write and read and laugh and cry as we explored the mysteries of the *conscious feminine*. I wrote a book about women's journals, and then another book, itself a published journal. In both, the *gypsy* is present, although hiding in the shadows. This is my attempt to invite her forward.

During those years I pushed my Laura Ashley clothes to the back of my closet and began sewing *gypsy* skirts again. Then I came across Isabel Fonseca's wonderful book, *Bury Me Standing: The Gypsies and Their Journey*, and my imagination was on high alert. As I read her account of living with Roma in central and eastern Europe for four years, I began to notice how often Gypsies appeared in my dreams. If the uncanny is "the sensation of something that is both very alien and deeply familiar, something that only the unconscious knows," it seemed my unconscious knew something about my connection with Gypsies that I didn't consciously understand.

After completing a Jungian Leadership Training Program with Marion Woodman in 2004, I went to Zürich to become a Jungian analyst. During the course of study, every candidate is asked to write several essays combining scholarly research with personal associations concerning symbols of particular interest to them. For several months I read everything I could get my hands on about Roma history and culture and the archetype of the *gypsy*. The more I read, the more my fascination grew. My second essay focussed on the archetypal *dark feminine*, closely related to the *gypsy*, and the third one explored the role of song in the lives of contemporary European Roma. It didn't take my supervisor telling me for me to know I'd begun writing another book.

C.G. Jung wrote about archetypal currents forever roiling beneath our everyday experience. He was fascinated by the power of certain images to bring new energy to our bodies and souls. "The psyche consists essentially of images," he wrote. "Images are life." We're surrounded by images every day, of course, and most of them don't make a lasting impression; in fact, we learn to tune them out. But occasionally an image will seize hold of our imagination as if it has some kind of mysterious significance. It seems to me that when this happens, the image has become a personal symbol, a powerful carrier of meaning and energy, as evident in the following dream I had one summer morning, many years ago.

> I am sitting in the back of a pickup truck with several women in my writing workshop and another one is driving us. We are in England, in the countryside south of London. Suddenly we see a group of women outside on the rolling green hills, brightly clad in colourful long dresses and sitting on a stone bench. A minute later, another group appears, and I realize—these are Gypsies and we are in their territory. There are many of them, all out in the open green, laughing and talking to each other, walking and running, clearly having a good time. There don't seem to be any men. The pickup truck stops and we all climb out. There are some items for sale and our driver buys a little girl's dress sewn by the Gypsy women. The pattern is ethnic batik and it's beautiful. I wonder if the Gypsies will be friendly—they may feel we're invading their space. Are we welcome? Am I welcome? The women all speak Romany. One of them can't speak English so she calls an older woman who does. Then we have to go back to the truck and continue on our way. I desperately want to stay with the Gypsy women.

This wasn't the first dream I'd had about Gypsies, nor was it to be my last. But of those I'd remembered and recorded at that time, it had the strongest emotional tone and the sense of urgency at the end was new. In my waking life I hadn't known that the language of the Gypsies or Roma is called Romany, but something (or someone) in me seemed to know. Along with the dream, I'd recorded my spontaneous associations.

> What stays with me is the free and adventuresome spirit of the Gypsies, the beauty of their colourful clothes, and my own urgency to join them. They all had long dark hair like mine and they were wild and free and joyful. I wondered what they did for shelter at night and how they could be warm enough sitting on the stones in their beautiful dresses, but they didn't seem worried. They were living in nature and selling their crafts, daughters of the Earth Mother. And they were speaking their own language, which I recognized but couldn't speak myself.

I know this is an important dream. Exuberance. Wildness. Colour. Laughter. Dance. Nature. Community. A child. Everything I yearn for. Why a pickup truck? It's a man's vehicle, but also connected to the land. Farmers often have pickup trucks. Why was I in the back, half asleep and trying to keep warm? And why did I dutifully get back in at the end, even though I wanted so much to stay with the Gypsy women?

"A symbol does not define or explain," says Jung. "It points beyond itself to a meaning that is darkly divined yet still beyond our grasp, and cannot be adequately expressed in the familiar words of our language." Other archetypal forces have possessed me for a time and then receded in the ebb and flow of life, but the *gypsy* has made a permanent dwelling place of my soul. Over the years I have come to trust her dark gaze and to know it as my own. I have loved her radiant presence and vibrant energy, struggled with her ancient grief and burning anger, and the trickster tactics that have enabled her to survive. Her resonance has filled my dreams. Her mystery has enchanted me. Her shadows have haunted me. Her jewelled colours, plaintive strains, and earthy rhythms have dazzled me. Her vivid paradoxes are woven into the warp and woof of me. Yet even now her meaning is darkly divined at best. I wouldn't want it any other way.

But this is just the beginning. The longer I follow the *gypsy*, the richer the territory I discover. These written lines, these typographic marks on the page, can't convey the experience of the *gypsy* in my soul. These words should be embroidered onto tapestry edged with gold and glittering beads. They should be sung and danced, not trapped on paper. I want them to sparkle, glint, and glow. And always, like the mythical *gypsy*, I want to wander through this inner landscape, never needing to arrive.

It isn't the Roma's story I want to tell here. But Gypsy culture and history are filled with drama and beauty, and along the way I discovered many symbolic parallels with my own experience. One clue, intuition, synchronicity leading to another, this exploration has often felt like a treasure hunt through a territory both new and strangely familiar, where each bend in the road offers a glimpse of some unsuspected beauty and significance.

It's the story of the *gypsy*'s life in me I want to tell: how she has come to me in dreams and incarnated herself in my being. In *Gypsy Fugue,* I want to explore what it is to live with an archetypal image at the core of one's life and the mysterious, ever-evolving sense of meaning it provides. Such a mythic journey doesn't feel itself bound by outer facts or circumstances but delights in wandering into imaginal realms where opposites coexist, paradox prevails, and all things are possible.

And, while travelling through this rich terrain, I want to jump off that pickup truck at last and run into those green fields of possibility. This time I want to join the Gypsy women in my dream and dwell with them awhile, trusting I can learn to speak their language and find the words to touch on what is intimate about *gypsy* to my soul. The older Gypsy in my dream speaks English, after all.

Mother India's Forgotten Child

Gypsy Stereotypes and the Romany People

Let the Gypsies come and blossom.
We miss them.
They can help us by irritating our fixed orders.
They are what we pretend to be; they are the true Europeans.
They do not know any borders.

—Günter Grass

Who are we,
Roma without Romanes
who must read
our own history
in another tongue,
follow the butterfly
of our own being
across maps of imagination
trying to recreate
the lost structure
of our soul?

—Jimmy Story

I know I'm not the only one who yearns to run into the open fields and join the Gypsies in my dream. Many people are drawn to the Gypsy's exuberant energy and exotic otherness. Through the years Tony Gatlif's films have inspired a wide and enthusiastic following, especially *Latcho Drom*, with its captivating images of the Roma migration and diaspora. Twenty years later, I still remember the urge to dance my way down Thirteenth Street after seeing it for the first time in Greenwich Village.

"So," my friend said, looking at me as we left the Quad Cinema. "How do you feel? Did it seem familiar?" Gabi was visiting from London and knew of my lifelong passion for Gypsies.

I paused, searching for words. "It's as if they're all my cousins." The film's images and emotions felt intimately familiar to me, as if *Latcho Drom* had captured the story of my inner life in some way I couldn't account for. Gatlif has described his film as "a hymn to the universal gypsy condition." I know he's referring to the circumstances of Roma throughout the world but it seemed to me as I watched that, in some profound way, we are all Gypsies. That the Gypsy condition *is* the universal condition.

Gypsy life has been a recurring theme in folk and contemporary music throughout the years in songs such as Fleetwood Mac's "Gypsy," Cher's "Gypsies, Tramps and Thieves," Leonard Cohen's "The Gypsy's Wife," and Ann Mortifee's "Gypsy Born." And recent decades have seen a powerful renaissance of ethnic Roma music in western Europe, the Balkans, and Asia, but also in North America. Beginning with Django Reinhardt's gypsy jazz in the first half of the last century, musicians such as Esma Redzepova (known as the "Queen of the Gypsies"), the Gipsy Kings, and Kalyi Jag have enjoyed widespread acclaim throughout the world. The 2006 documentary *When the Road Bends: Tales of a Gypsy Caravan* follows five musical groups across countries and continents as they perform in sold-out concert halls to audiences clearly enthralled with their music. "We sing with fire and heart in our souls," one of the musicians in the film proclaims. "Music is God's greatest gift."

And then there's the periodic recurrence of bohemian fashion, whose colourful beauty appeals to many women, even those who aren't inclined to wear it themselves. The peasant-gypsy clothes of the flower children in the 1960s, the upmarket ethnic Gypsy and Russian designs of Oscar de la Renta during the 1970s, and the elegant bohemian motifs in the haute couture of Yves Saint Laurent and Jean Paul Gaultier all demonstrate a very different esthetic from the streamlined, minimalist sophistication that dominates so much contemporary design. Resplendent with rich colours and sumptuous fabrics, intricate beadwork and embroidery, and set off by burnished hoops and bangles, there is nothing understated about "gypsy fashion." It is *extravagant* (from *extravagari*, "to wander outside"), and that extravagance delights both our senses and the eye of the imagination.

Several years ago it seemed all of Paris was a gypsy. Every shop window was filled with vibrant bohemian colours and designs. What is the powerful appeal of this decidedly uncool esthetic in one of the most sophisticated cities of the world? I wondered as I strolled down the streets.

In the words of Giorgio Armani, "The fashion world is often one in which the romantic ideal is celebrated, rather than anything more real." For him, the gypsy look incorporates "fringing, lace, layering, decoration, multiple colors and patterns—all great tools for a designer to make an impact with." John Galliano says, "Gypsies have been able to escape from the lives that we have. The Gypsy life is one of moving from one place to the next, finding what you need, putting together a look," and Roberto Cavalli adds, "It's more than an esthetic, it's a lifestyle." The owner of Milan's most influential fashion boutique claims her customers buy Roma-inspired clothing because "Gypsies are icons of freedom, they recycle everything, mix ropes with gold, and everything works." They all agree that the lasting appeal of gypsy styles is their "undertone of nomadic escapism."

But actual Roma lives have little in common with this romantic fantasy of freedom, and Isabel Fonseca, who lived with Gypsies in central Europe for several years, offers a harsher and more realistic view. "Fashion has prettily appropriated the stereotypes," she says. "Once you can *wear* them, the strangers at the edge of town cease to seem so scary." But why do the strangers at the edge of town seem scary, and if they frighten us, why do we want to imitate them?

Shrouded in a Cloak of Mystery
The Persistence of Gypsy Stereotypes

Persecution of Roma all over the world has increased steadily over the past half century but our fascination with all things Gypsy shows no sign of waning. And throughout the Western world, the stereotypes abound. In 1986, a Boston newspaper described a local Gypsy family as "glitter and gold, decked out in the bright babushka of legend," and concluded, "the entire image is crowned with a halo of mystique, shrouded in a cloak of mystery." For many people, the word Gypsy conjures high-spirited, free-dom-loving renegades who refuse to abide by the laws of their host country and roam through the world in gaudy caravans, stopping by the riverbank at night to cook over an open fire, before bringing out violin and accordion and stirring the night air with their raucous music and dance.

Hollywood movies reflect a deep-seated ambivalence as we alternately idealize and denigrate the Roma. Films like *The Virgin and the Gypsy* (1970), *King of the Gypsies* (1978), *Angelo My Love* (1983), *The Red Violin* (1998), and *Chocolat* (2000) portray Gypsies as fiercely committed to freedom, fam-ily, and clan, and as proud and uncompromising rebels who refuse to bend to society's dictates. Sometimes there's the implication that Gypsy values are purer than those of the dominant culture, that they have preserved traces of Romanticism's *noble savage*, untarnished by industrial society. Frequently they are portrayed as exotic, dark-skinned men and women with great erot-ic appeal, and as passionate musicians and dancers in flamboyant clothing who sell their crafts and practise mysterious esoteric powers. In *Chocolat* the French River Gypsies who appear every summer are kindred to free-spirited Vianne, in opposition to the puritanical hypocrisy of the church-dominated villagers who secretly yearn for exuberance and joy in their lives.

But just as often Gypsies are portrayed as idlers and outlaws, as irre-sponsible vagrants who prey on hapless *gadje*, or non-Roma. When they don't like the laws of one region, they pack up their wagons and move on, forever evading the responsibilities of citizenship. Shunning work—so the stereotype goes—they survive by their wits and take what they want from the society around them, training their children from infancy to beg and steal in the marketplace. Shiftless and lazy, they spend all their time ca-rousing, refuse traditional morality and declare their own savage justice and primitive religion, with its sorcery, witchcraft, and black magic. In *The Red Violin* they are portrayed as grave-robbers who desecrate a young boy's coffin in order to steal his violin.

Gypsy women, so the story goes, have the power to drive men wild with their beauty and lush sensuality during the glory days of their youth. In old age they are wily and conniving shrews. The men are darkly smouldering lovers who seduce with their animal grace and musical prowess before succumbing to the ravages of alcohol and nicotine, and the children, dirty little ragamuffins whose mischievous, dark-eyed smiles charm the unsuspecting *gadjo* while their hands deftly empty his pockets.

Our ambivalence runs deep, as our language makes clear. To *gyp* someone means to swindle them, yet *gypsying* conjures carefree travel through the world, backpack in tow. "To live or roam as a Gypsy," says *Webster's Dictionary*. Nomadism, thievery, exoticism, musicality, craftiness, rebelliousness—all of these lie at the heart of our collective fantasy of Gypsy life. Could it be that this romantic projection of freedom, lawlessness, and the open road reflects a shared longing to break through the rigid boundaries and narrow constrictions of our lives into a more spacious inner landscape, where each new day might open into a vibrant new adventure?

ENCOUNTERING GYPSIES

Despite my lifelong affinity, I felt a mixture of fascination and fear during my own earliest encounters with Gypsies while travelling through Europe and the Middle East in the summer and autumn of 1979. On the first occasion, I was accompanying two American friends to the train station in Rome. As we approached the main entrance, we were swarmed by a horde of children who came at me with such force that I almost fell to the ground, and then scattered just as quickly. I was bewildered by this sudden onslaught, and so busy trying to decipher the words scrawled on a rough piece of cardboard they shoved at me that I didn't realize what was happening. As the children ran away, one of my friends saw my open purse flap and yelled at them in anger. The oldest, a girl of about twelve, whipped up her dress and pulled down her underwear to show us she wasn't hiding anything. I was shocked that she so freely exposed her pubes and naively surprised by the effective teamwork of these little thieves, about a dozen in all. It had never occurred to me that I might be robbed by a gang of young Gypsies.

Several months later, my travel companion and I were serenaded by Gypsy musicians in a candlelit restaurant in Budapest on my birthday. I loved the tempestuous energy of their music and was delighted to cross their palms with forints in return. Then, on a crude overnight ferry from Athens to Crete, I ran into a Roma man and woman in the bathroom in the middle of the night. I was wearing my first *gypsy* skirt and they pointed to its embroidery and smiled at me, speaking in a language I didn't understand. I was surprised to find a man in the women's bathroom and a little nervous, so I smiled back and left, without having used the bathroom.

Since then I have often seen Gypsies in the English countryside and panhandling in many European cities, but until more recently, these were my only direct encounters with them. Then, after I had been reading and writing about the archetypal *gypsy* for weeks, a Swiss Gypsy appeared at my door on a shimmering June morning in Zürich. It was so unexpected that I wondered if I'd conjured him up. There he stood facing me, tall, sturdy, rough-hewn, with a large gold hoop in his right ear, and there I stood, two large gold hoop earrings in both my ears. For a moment we just looked at each other, and the air between us crackled. In heavily accented Swiss German he asked whether our knives needed sharpening.

"The landlady isn't here right now," I said. "Can you come back later in the day?" It was clear he understood my High German.

"*Ja,*" he said, nodding emphatically. We stood there with broad smiles, sparkling at each other. Then I closed the door and burst out laughing. His merry brown face, stocky build, and single gold earring met something in me. For one magical moment, inner and outer Gypsy had come together and it was delicious.

While travelling in India later that year, I saw more Gypsies than I had ever seen before. They shared the Rajasthani love of vivid colours and patterns, and to my eyes, they were not always distinguishable from the other poor castes, but our driver Mukesh could identify them by subtle differences in their style of dress.

"There they are, that group over there," he pointed out excitedly as we drove down the endless dust-covered roads of Rajasthan. "Those are Gypsies."

Early one morning as we watched the sun rise over the Ganges in Varanasi, two little Gypsy girls ran up to us, demanding money. Tattered and dirty, with matted black hair, they seemed almost feral as they pushed and tugged in their attempt to get something from us as we climbed the steps of the ghat. We'd been warned that if we stopped to give them something we'd be swarmed by twenty more children, so we kept climbing and struggled to stay upright. We saw that wild look again in the desert fort of Jaiselmer, where an older girl of thirteen or fourteen approached us with a look of fearful suspicion in her eyes, demanding food but ready to run at the slightest whiff of danger.

Even so, I heard conflicting accounts of the Gypsies' role and status in India. While Mukesh claimed they work hard but are poorly treated in Indian society, Biji, our driver in the southern state of Kerala, dismissed them as the lowest caste in India.

"They're lazy and they don't want to work," he said, gesturing impatiently with his arms, as if to wave them away. "They just take what they want and don't pay for anything. They are not good people."

Since most of India's twenty million Roma live in the north, I wondered if Biji had ever met any Roma or was simply echoing India's own prejudice against them. But the Roma's ethnic origins were clear here. While their dark hair and countenance set them apart in other countries, in India they were mostly indistinguishable from everyone around them.

The largest gathering of Gypsies I have ever encountered was at the annual Roma pilgrimage to honour their patron Saint Sara in Les Saintes-Maries-de-la-Mer on the French Mediterranean. I drove there with a friend in 2009 and described the celebration in my journal, as I sat in the courtyard of our small hotel with my late-afternoon café au lait.

Saturday, May 23rd.
I am in Les Saintes-Maries-de-la-Mer with thousands of Gypsies. It's a sun-baked Mediterranean town and the sea is a brilliant turquoise. Hundreds of modern caravans sit in every parking lot and along the streets and hundreds more in trailer parks just outside the town. I even saw some traditional horse-drawn vardos, beautifully decorated with dark green paint and elaborate floral designs. As we drove into the town, we saw herds of magnificent

wild white horses and flocks of pink flamingos. There's a potent sense of untamed wildness here, and everything shimmers with heat.

And there are Roma everywhere. They seem uncannily familiar to me, especially the women. Like people in India, and yet different. Most of the local French people also have olive complexions and dark hair so I'm not always sure who is Roma and who isn't. But many are unmistakeable, with their prideful bearing, dark attractiveness, and an edge of roughness.

Most are short and stocky, and their behaviour is loud and boisterous and unrestrained. The atmosphere sizzles with excitement and anticipation. From photographs I saw on the internet, I expected to see women in traditional Gypsy dress, but instead, there's a sea of polyester dresses, shirts, and pants, mostly black, despite the relentless heat. It's obvious that they aren't wealthy. Earlier today I wandered through the market in the town square hoping to buy something, but nothing caught my eye. There's no gold jewelry or crafts, just heaped-up bed linens, costume jewelry, and more polyester.

This afternoon we heard wonderful music by *Urs Karpatz*, a band of eight skillful and charming musicians. The more spontaneous music-making and dancing seem to take place later at night, but by nine o'clock Yvonne and I were happy to be back at our hotel with a glass of wine. The hotel is on a street crowded with parked Gypsy vans and last night we both heard loud talking and music outside our windows for most of the night. Tonight it's much quieter; maybe they need to catch up on sleep too!

It doesn't feel strange at all to be surrounded by Roma. Their dark eyes and swarthy complexions are the faces of the Gypsies in my dreams over the years. My inner world has always been filled with dark-eyed men and women, urchins and infants, and now they are simply on the outside. Occasionally there's a face of great beauty in the crowd, and I can see that many of the women must have been lovely in their youth, but by middle age they look worn and weary. This morning as I walked through the town I felt and sensed their primal fierceness, something I recognize in myself as well. I am thrilled to be here and wonder what it's like for the Roma to be together with so many of their own. How I wish I could speak their language and ask about their lives!

THE GYPSY JIGSAW

There are no people in the Western world as mysterious and elusive as the Roma. We may feel an affinity with them that we don't quite understand, and yet what do we really know of their lives? The Roma themselves have often been secretive in their attempt to protect themselves from the *gadje* who have threatened their existence throughout a thousand years of hardship and persecution.

"You will never learn our language," a Romanian Gypsy activist told Isabel Fonseca. "For every word you record in your little notebook, we have another one—a synonym, which we use and which you can never know.... We don't *want* you to know."

It's not always easy to sort out the relationship between these gypsy stereotypes and the realities of Roma life. The popular image of the gypsy musician with a violin tucked under his chin and his beautiful partner dancing flamenco beside him surely reflects the crucial importance of music and dance in Roma culture itself. And the common depiction of dark-haired Bohemian women in flowered skirts and gold bangles bears a striking similarity to photographs of Roma women in central and eastern European towns and villages whose olive skin and dark features herald their Indian ancestry amid populations that are mostly blonde and fair-skinned.

Yet even though they make up Europe's largest minority, the Roma remain a largely invisible and unknown people. And while the stereotype of carefree wanderers forever on the move is a false representation, they may indeed be the only people in the world without a homeland. I was fascinated to discover that throughout their history, the Roma have never fought a war or attempted to establish their own state. Peaceful and non-aggressive, they have wanted simply to follow their beliefs and traditions without persecution. What does it mean, then, for a people who have never aspired to have a homeland, to call themselves Roma, or Gypsy?

In an early account of Gypsy lore I read, "Until the ethnologists began, in the late nineteenth century, to piece together the gypsy jigsaw from
the evidence of physical characteristics, tribal myths and, most significantly,
the study of language roots, nothing was known, least of all by the gypsies
themselves, of Romany origin." The jigsaw metaphor is very striking. In
trying to discover something of Roma origins, I've often had the sense of
taking intriguing bits and pieces of information from here and there, and
trying to fit them together in order to see what kind of colourful picture
might emerge.

However, while delving into Roma history and culture has been an
endlessly fascinating journey, as I've said already, this is not a book about
the Roma. My sincere hope is that this brief introduction might be read as
a respectful acknowledgement of the distinction between a vibrant people
whose lives have been obscured by prejudice and endless misrepresentation and who continue to suffer discrimination—and an inner soul image.
The last thing I want to do is contribute to a further misrepresentation of
the Roma people. Through the often contradictory information available, I
have trodden as carefully as I could, both here and in subsequent chapters
where I take the liberty of weaving compelling glimpses of Roma culture
into my own *gypsy* memoir. I freely acknowledge that from all I have read
about them I've selected the bits and pieces that hit home most strongly
with me. And I have tried to distinguish as clearly as possible among the
actual conditions of Roma life, the prevailing gypsy stereotypes, and what
I am referring to as the archetypal *gypsy*, whose story I will take up in the
chapters that follow.

ORIGINS OF THE ROMA

You are Mother India's forgotten child
Ramni, now called Romni.
In fact, you are the flowing Ganges water
mixed with the waters of the river Nile, Euphrates and Danube.

Long before I knew that the Roma came from India I dreamed I was standing by the Ganges River, a sea of turquoise, green, and purple saris spread out along its banks. The vivid colours and mystical atmosphere stayed with me over the years and when I finally travelled to India it too seemed familiar, as if that outer landscape mirrored the one I had seen in my dream.

Perhaps each of us is drawn to other countries and cultures for reasons we don't understand. For me it has always been India. I shouldn't have been surprised, then, to discover that the Roma people originally came from the northwest regions of India or that the Romany language derives from Punjabi and Hindi, with their ancient Sanskrit roots.

Nevertheless I've found it quite a challenge to piece together their story. For the most part the Roma have been an oral, non-literate culture with a nomadic strain and frequent forced displacements, and this has meant there is relatively little historical information available. Donald Kenrick, one of the first scholars to write a comprehensive history of the Roma, similarly described his work as "putting together a jigsaw puzzle, when some of the pieces are missing and parts of another puzzle have been put into the same box." In *Gypsies: From the Ganges to the Thames*, he explores many different accounts of the Roma's origins, including Old Testament references to the Roma as offspring of Abraham and his second wife, Hagar. English Sanskrit scholar Sir Ralph L. Turner felt there was linguistic evidence that Gypsies had moved from central to northwest India as far back as 300 BC and lived there for a thousand years before beginning their westward migration. However, it seems that the most widely accepted version dates their original involuntary exodus out of India at approximately AD 900–1000, and tracks their migration northwest toward eastern Europe and westward through Egypt, where they stayed for some time. Along the way, the Roma picked up new words from other languages—Arabic, Persian, and Armenian—so that the Romany language provides a map of the route they travelled.

Some sources claim the Roma were a warrior caste in eleventh-century Rajasthan. Others say they were a caste of musicians, twelve thousand of whom were sent by the king of India to Persia at the shah's request during the fifth century in order to provide musical entertainment for Persian courts—they were noted to be excellent musicians, particularly on the flute and lute—and, from there, dispersed throughout Persia. With time they travelled farther west along the old Silk Road trade routes, picking up the customs, music, and vocabulary of the countries they moved through.

Yet another account suggests that they were a population of captives seized during the Muslim invasions of India in the seventh and eight centuries and deported to the Middle East, where they were forced to work the fields along the banks of the Tigris River. In the ninth century, they were moved again to Greece and eventually brought to the Balkan countries as an unpaid labour force. As slaves, in other words. Early in the fifteenth century, they began to appear in western Europe, where they worked as craftsmen, shoemakers, blacksmiths, and acrobats. Wherever they appeared, they were known for their music.

These differing myths of origin only deepen the mystery surrounding them. So much is uncertain, including their exact numbers today, estimated to be between twelve million and fifteen million Roma spread throughout almost all the countries of the world, including over a million in North America and another twenty million in India.

Resilience and defiance, adaptability and perseverance all characterize the Roma's thousand-year migration. And despite the endless versions of how they came to leave their home in northern India, there is little dispute about the relentless persecution they've endured throughout the centuries. Reviled and enslaved, rounded up and driven out of many lands and across many borders, the Roma have survived, proud bearers of a common identity forged by the Romany language and by *Romanes*, the Romany way of life. Ian Hancock, a prominent Romany scholar and activist and the founder of RADOC (Romani Archives and Documentation Centre at the University of Texas at Austin), offers many examples of the simultaneous fascination and revulsion that have characterized outsiders' attitudes toward the Roma over the centuries. In *The Pariah Syndrome* he tells the story of their gradual movement out of India and subsequent five-hundred-year enslavement in the Balkans from 1350 to 1850.

And what a horrifying story it is. I was well aware that hundreds of thousands of Gypsies were murdered by the Nazis—the only people arguably more despised by Hitler than Jews. But for most of my life I had no inkling of five centuries of Gypsy enslavement in central Europe that equalled the worst horrors of black slavery in the Americas. In 1837, a Romanian journalist observed, "The Europeans are organizing philanthropical societies for the abolition of slavery in America, yet in the bosom of their own continent of Europe, there are 400,000 Gypsies who are slaves, and 200,000 more equally victim to barbarousness." In fact, Gypsy slavery in the Balkans lasted until 1864, one year before the legal emancipation of African-Americans in the United States. What a terrible irony there is in the common stereotype of gypsy freedom, given the fact that Roma were being bought and sold like cattle for five hundred years. Isabel Fonseca suggests, "Had this ignominious episode in Gypsy history become better known, then perhaps that pervasive free-spirit fantasy might have failed to establish itself in the first place."

But the Roma's suffering didn't end with the abolition of slavery in the Balkans. The worst was yet to come. It's estimated that half a million Gypsies perished in the concentration camps during World War II, approximately the same proportion of their entire population as the number of Jews who were murdered. And while having one Jewish grandparent was enough to establish Jewish identity in Nazi Germany, for Roma the regulations were more virulent. If a person had either one great-grandparent or two great-great-grandparents who were Gypsies, that person could be sent to Auschwitz. In *Gypsies Under the Swastika* I read, "One-eighth 'gypsy blood' was considered strong enough to outweigh seven-eighths of German blood—so dangerous were the Gypsies considered."

The *Porraimos*, or "Devouring," is not nearly as well known as the Jewish Holocaust; it was unknown even to many Roma over the intervening years. Unlike Jews throughout the world, the Roma have not emphasized the importance of keeping this historical event alive in memory but many songs tell the story of their suffering, with lyrics such as those sung by an elderly Czech Gypsy in *Latcho Drom*. In a haunting scene, she sings a mournful melody with her tremulous and ravaged voice, gazing into the distance with weary eyes that have seen too much.

> At Auschwitz, we die of hunger
> In huge sheds they imprison us
> At Auschwitz the kapo is cruel
> We can't find bread anywhere
> Life is so far off and death so close
> The black bird wants to tear out my heart.

As she sings, she clutches a photograph of Václav Havel in her right hand, the tattooed numbers on her left forearm a stark reminder of her time in the concentration camp. A Romany proverb about the *Porraimos* says, "They led us in through the gates; they led us out through the chimney." In the 2011 documentary *A People Uncounted*, Roma concentration camp survivors offer harrowing personal testimony of their experience. One elderly man describes how Jews and Gypsies tried to help each other during the war and quotes another Romany proverb that states, "Our ashes were mingled in the ovens." According to this film, more than ninety percent of Czech Roma perished in the *Porraimos*.

Following the collapse of Communism in the Eastern bloc countries, the Roma faced a new fever of discrimination. Even the late Václav Havel wasn't able to ensure their safety in the Czech Republic, where Gypsies can't count on police protection from vicious attacks by skinheads who carved swastikas on the body of a young woman, burned Roma homes to the ground, and committed other atrocities against the Roma. In Slovakia and Bulgaria, the segregation of Roma children in special schools for children with mental disabilities has been rampant; up to three-quarters of children in those schools are said to be Roma. In Germany, thousands of Roma and Sinti (German-speaking Roma) have faced deportation, while in Romania, more than eighty percent of infants and small children in orphanages are said to come from Roma parents unable to care for them. Their prospects for adoption are dismal. Romanians don't want to adopt them and won't allow international adoptions, so many of these children are doomed to miserable, premature deaths.

While women pay exorbitant prices for gypsy fashion in Milan's top boutiques, the Italian government declared a "nomad emergency" in 2008, with plans to fingerprint all 170,000 Italian Roma, remove children from their parents, and drive them all out of Italy. Many settlements were destroyed and several children murdered by angry mobs in a renewed wave of racist violence. While Armani and high fashion have capitalized on the gypsy image for decades, Italian Roma live in poverty and terror for their lives, facing forced expulsion from the only home they have ever known.

Amnesty International cites widespread atrocities against Roma all through central and western Europe in recent years. In 2012 a Roma report documented a long list of human rights violations throughout the European Union, including police brutality, forced sterilization and widespread trafficking of Roma women, and ongoing racial attacks and murder. Meanwhile in Canada and the United States many Roma disguise their identity in order to avoid prejudice. This pervasive fear and hatred toward the Roma has given rise to the word "Romaphobia," deplored as "the last acceptable form of racism." As newspaper headlines too frequently consistently attest, the precarious and marginalized lot of the Roma has continued.

A "MOVEABLE COUNTRY"
ROMANY AND *ROMANES*

Although the word "Gypsy" is derived from "Egyptian" and the erroneous belief that Gypsies originally came from Egypt, philological studies starting in the eighteenth century have established the Roma's roots in northern India. In 1760, Vályi Stefán, a young theologian studying in Holland, noticed striking similarities between the language of three visiting Indian students at the University of Leiden and that of the Roma population in his native Hungary. The Romany language, it appeared, had much in common with Punjabi and Hindi, with their roots in ancient Sanskrit, and the linguistic connection with India is considered the most significant development to date toward an understanding of Roma history and origins.

Charles Godfrey Leland, the renowned nineteenth-century Gypsiologist who lived with European Gypsies for many decades and observed their patterns of culture and language, hoped that the Roma's language could serve as a unifying factor throughout Europe if only the revilement of Gypsies could come to an end. Obviously that hasn't happened, but Romany crosses many national borders and serves to affirm bonds of solidarity among the Roma, while at the same time setting them apart from surrounding peoples. Most Roma are bilingual, in fact, speaking both Romany and the language of the country in which they live. Ian Hancock says there are up to eighty dialects of Romany currently spoken. Historically the Roma also used a "tree language" called Patrin, an elaborate system of carvings and symbols on tree trunks and fences that indicated whether or not the inhabitants of the next house or village were friendly.

In the absence of a homeland, Roma nationhood is defined by the use of Romany throughout the world. Since the first World Romani Congress in London in 1971, the Roma have also had their own flag and a national anthem, "Djelem Djelem," whose lyrics are a call to self-determination after the horrors of the *Porraimos*, as this excerpt shows.

> I once had a great family,
> The Black Legions murdered them
> Come with me Roma from all the world
> For the Romani roads have opened
> Now is the time, rise up Roma now
> We will rise high if we act
> O Roma, O fellow Roma.

"Gypsies use their language and core-culture as a kind of moveable country," Ian Hancock tell us. "Wherever they have gone, ethnic identity has usually been maintained." That core-culture is known as *Romanes*, or the Romany way of doing things.

"OUTRAGEOUS EXPRESSIVITY"
HOW THE ROMA MAKE THEIR MUSIC

"Stay where there are songs," says an old Gypsy proverb. Music is the heart and soul of Roma life and has sustained them since their earliest exodus out of India. Entire books have been written on the subject, among them David Malvinni's *The Gypsy Caravan: From Real Roma to Imaginary Gypsies in Western Music and Film,* and Garth Cartwright's *Princes Among Men: Journeys with Gypsy Musicians.*

What has defined Gypsy music over the years, and how do we recognize its sound? Like Indian and Middle Eastern music, the music of the Roma is based on the Phrygian scale, also known as the Spanish Gypsy scale. Its mournful, minor key sound reflects both its Asian roots and the sorrow underlying centuries of oppression. Throughout the years Roma musicians have employed a wide variety of musical instruments, and the first known instance of a Roma violinist dates to the middle of the fifteenth century. During the centuries that followed they gained widespread acclaim as musicians throughout Europe. In Hungary they were known for their instrumental music, especially violin. In Russia, where it was a mark of prestige for the wealthy to have their own resident musicians, Romany singers made up the great choruses that performed in royal courts and at large social functions in the homes of the nobility. In Spain the Roma created flamenco, which only later came to include dance as well as music.

It turns out that countless European composers were influenced by Gypsy music over the years, among them Bach and Brahms, Verdi and Dvorak, Janacek and Rachmaninov. Liszt even wrote a book titled *The Gypsy in Music,* published in 1859, in which he described Hungarian Gypsy music as possessed of great "passion and temperament and an undertone of India." And more recently, Yehudi Menuhin expressed great admiration for the musical improvisation of Gypsy violinists, and their ability to "imitate the sounds of nature, the singing of the birds, and even the sound of the human voice in sobs."

Reciprocal influences between Romany and local musical traditions have given rise to a rich variety of "interethnic" musical styles throughout the centuries. Music in the Balkans contains the oriental rhythms of Turkish music, for example, while Spanish flamenco carries an Arabic pulse. Klezmer and many Hasidic tunes from eastern Europe, along with some forms of European and American jazz, all have roots in Gypsy culture. In the 1930s, Django Reinhardt created gypsy jazz out of a blend of New Orleans jazz and blues and Sinti (German Gypsy) music. Along with Stéphane Grappelli and Eddie South, he recorded Bach's *Violin Concerto in D Minor* in a gypsy swing performance, demonstrating that the cross-fertilization of musical styles actually goes in both directions.

Garth Cartwright describes his experience of travelling with Gypsy musicians in eastern Europe in rousing terms. "Wobbly rhythms, creaking violins, exploding brass...here was music full of living colour, sounds conceived in a forgotten Asia, shaped by the bitter European experience and sung in a tongue few can translate." Jarko Jovanovic, a renowned Yugoslavian Gypsy musician, has described a unique Gypsy temperament or flavour in music as "fevered, soaring, tempestuous, extravagant, erotic, fragile, subtle, bitter and full of the sufferings of love." What matters isn't polished sound and performance but "outrageous expressivity...a heartrending cry that rips through the guts and immerses the listener in the sacred ecstasy of the *duende*."

Masters of innovation, the Roma often used non-musical objects to accompany song. Pans served as drums, and spoons, pots, glasses, and cans were all used to create sound. Scholars of Romany music have described how the Roma use their bodies as musical instruments. Flamenco, in fact, began as a vocal and rhythmic music. Because the Spanish Gypsies were poor, they clapped their hands and snapped their fingers, stamped their feet and sang, making music with their bodies, which is all they had. That tradition continues even today. In Les Saintes-Maries-de-la-Mer, I saw spontaneous dancing that was accompanied only by clapping hands, slapping knees, and mouth sounds, a kind of spontaneous body percussion by the audience. But this is the music the Roma make for themselves and each other. Their professional music making—the music they play for the *gadje*—is geared toward local audience tastes and often adapts a country's own musical traditions for performance, as is the case with Hungarian café or restaurant music.

On a practical level, music has always been one of the most popular trades among Roma because it brought a measure of recognition and respect, and allowed them to earn a living of sorts. But just as importantly, it has provided a means of preserving stories, memories, and cultural history, and of giving expression to the community's beliefs and concerns. Songs are handed down from one generation to the next, as we can see in this invitation of a Swedish Gypsy in the middle of the previous century: "Now listen, my children! I shall now sing a very old song, which was sung in my father's childhood, and his father's, and further back, in the childhood of many of his forefathers. Listen and learn, so that you can also sing it to your children." Improvised autobiographical ballads are sung spontaneously at Roma gatherings. Frequently a song might begin with a general theme like lost love or shared suffering, and then take a personal direction with specific names and circumstances, as these lines from the Swedish Gypsy's song demonstrate.

> There were Gruitsa and Novako.
> On the slope beneath the mountain,
> There lies Gruia's roadside inn,
> Yes, old man Gruia's.
> By God, they eat and they drink,
> And of nothing else they think.

The song lyrics in *Latcho Drom* tell notable stories of the Roma's suffering throughout hundreds of years. In the final dramatic scene a young woman stands on a hillside in Spain and sings a plaintive lament to the town below.

> The whole world hates us
> We're chased, we're cursed
> Condemned to wandering through life
> The mountain is green, the forest as well
> Fortune takes flight and then returns again
> The sword of anxiety cuts into our skin
>
> The world is hypocritical
> The whole world stands against us
> We survived as hounded thieves
> But barely a nail have we stolen
> At the foot of a bloodied Jesus
> God have mercy! Deliver us from our trials.

Other frequent themes in the long tradition of Roma song include their longing for a lost freedom, living as perpetual wanderers and outcasts; the world of nature; and descriptions of feasts, traditions, trades, poverty, impossible love, rootlessness, and *lungo drom*, or "the long road." "Nostalgia is the essence of Gypsy song," writes Isabel Fonseca.

But perhaps the most intriguing discovery I made was that the Roma haven't always distinguished between singing and speaking, or among poetry, storytelling, and song. A poet or storyteller might spontaneously break into song or a singer begin speaking in the midst of the song. The Irish scholar Walter Starkie travelled with Gypsies throughout Europe in the first half of the last century and observed that they frequently use music as an adjunct to storytelling. "Ask them to tell you a *paramish* [folk tale] and they will first of all clear their throats and hum a tune, and then fit the words of the story to the tune." The great Polish Roma singer and poet Bronislawa Wajs, known as Papusza, composed long autobiographical ballads—part poem, part song—drawing from Gypsy stories and folk songs, which she spontaneously performed. For example, one is titled "Bloody Tears: What We Went Through Under the Germans in Volhynia in the Years '43 and '44," and describes her experience of hiding in the forests during the war.

Singing also affirms group identity and community ties in the midst of hostile environments. During the eighteen months that anthropologist Michael Stewart lived with Hungarian Gypsies he was privileged to participate in the *mulatsago*, an important communal ritual celebration among the men that affirms brotherhood and solidarity and allows them to make *true speech* to each other. During the *mulatsago*, individual men spontaneously sing their life story to the group, beginning with, "I beg for your permission to make a true speech to you." Along the way other men join in, and each song ends with the refrain, "Be lucky and healthy!" One after another, the men sing *slow songs* that express the sorrows and hardships of their lives and strengthen the ties among them all. This continues long into the night, with abundant food and alcohol served by the women, who recognize the importance of the ritual for their men, Stewart tells us. Since it's widely agreed that women carry the heavier burden in Roma society, I can't help but wonder whether the women have rituals of their own to sustain and renew them, or whether it's simply the shared preparation of food for their men that creates solidarity.

Not surprisingly, singing is above all the foremost means of celebration among the Roma. As one musician said, "We don't live for tomorrow. We live for today. And it shows in our playing—we put everything in, the heart and the soul. To make music is our happiness and we love to share our happiness." Small wonder, then, that to be a Gypsy musician is both a trade and a calling that brings with it the highest regard. Music has held and shaped their experience, both individual and collective, joyful and sorrowful. And because this rich blend of cross-cultural influence, soulful expression, and spontaneous improvisation has roots in what Jung referred to as the collective unconscious, it has the power to move us all, Roma and *gadje* alike.

"PROTECTRESS OF THE ROMA" SAINT SARA AND ROMA RELIGION

I would like to end this brief overview of Roma life by considering their religious beliefs and practice. Although the Roma have incorporated religious elements of many countries they've lived in, the roots of their religion are to be found in Hinduism. This is evident in the emphasis on purity and pollution (*mahrime*) and the ever-shifting balance of good and evil in the world. However, there are Hindu, Muslim, and Christian Roma, and their common patron Saint Sara (also known as Sara-la-Kali, Mary the Gypsy, and Maria-Sara) is honoured in the annual pilgrimage to Les Saintes-Maries-de-la-Mer I described earlier. Her origins, too, are mysterious. For some, she represents Sarah, the Egyptian maid who accompanied the three Marys—Mary Jacobé, Mary Salomé, and Mary Magdalene—after the Crucifixion, and helped them spread word of Christianity. On the *Patrin Web Journal on Romani Culture and History* I read, "In truth, no one knows who Sara really was, or how the cult of Sara came to Saintes Maries de la Mer, where pilgrims came to pray well before the French Revolution. For Gitans (Gypsies), she is *Sara-la-Kali*, a Gypsy word that means both Sara the Gitane and Sara the Black."

The Roma practice *Shaktiism* or goddess worship, further evidence of their link with India. It seems clear that the Romany Goddess of Fate is a Black Madonna whose origin is the beloved Indian goddess Kali. The fact that Dark Goddesses are celebrated in other, similar rituals throughout eastern Europe points to their common origins in India, where a statue of Kali is bedecked with garlands and carried to the water every year in a ritual of loving homage. Each October a second, smaller Roma festival coincides with the annual celebration of Kali/Durga in India, and Roma writer and activist Ronald Lee concludes, "Kali Sara is now finally coming out of the closet and emerging as a Romani Goddess, the protectress of the Roma and our indisputable link with Mother India, the cradle of our emerging Romani Nation."

The first time I watched *Latcho Drom* I was moved by how the men played music to Saint Sara in the crypt below the church and spontaneously poured kisses on her neck. There was a sensuality one cannot imagine in the western adoration of the Virgin Mary. I witnessed this in person in 2009. The descent into Saint Sara's crypt on a hot May afternoon was other-worldly, the highlight of my pilgrimage to Les Saintes-Maries-de-la-Mer.

As I stepped carefully down the stone stairs of the narrow passageway into the subterranean chamber, it was as though I'd entered an overheated sauna. I could hardly breathe. With hundreds of candles lit throughout the confined space and no ventilation, the heat was so fierce that most of the tapers had softened and curved over on themselves, giving an arched look to the soft light in the cavelike chamber.

Tucked around the corner to the right of the stone staircase was the statue of Sara-la-Kali, with her beautiful chocolate-brown face, dark almond eyes, and many colourful Gypsy shawls draped around her shoulders. One after another, men, women, and children of all ages stepped closer, caressing and kissing her face, stroking her body, even reaching under her clothing. Sometimes they draped more shawls around the statue or tucked scraps of paper into her shawl or sleeve. Dozens of small, folded papers lay at her feet and on the shelf behind her, each one a scribbled plea for healing and blessing for themselves or a family member, I later learned. Behind her lay several pairs of crutches and I wondered whether they'd been placed there as requests for healing, or out of gratitude that they were no longer needed.

Their fierce intimacy with Saint Sara was palpable. In contrast to the boisterous enthusiasm of the crowds in the streets just above us, the conversation was muffled, but people greeted each other in animated fashion and there was no sense that talking was taboo. The flickering candlelight threw dark shadows on the ancient stone walls of the crypt, creating an eerie atmosphere, and I half expected Saint Sara to blink her eyes and start speaking to us.

I wanted to stay and absorb the smoky scene, but the vault was small and a constant stream of visitors were coming and going. With all the burning candles and warm bodies the heat was almost unbearable, and I knew I would soon begin to feel faint. After ten or fifteen minutes I climbed back up the narrow stone steps into the plaza, where the heat of the afternoon sun felt cool in comparison, and I had to close my eyes against the brilliant Mediterranean light.

That afternoon my friend Yvonne and I joined the great procession accompanying Saint Sara's annual passage into the Mediterranean. We managed to climb up onto several huge stones near the shore but even so, the crowd was so thick that it was difficult to see anything. Finally, after waiting in the sweltering midday sun for several hours during which nothing appeared to be happening, we began to hear faint music in the distance. Eventually four men on horseback came around the corner of the church and rode by, leading the procession, and two others followed, carrying a cross covered with flowers. The music had grown louder and then half a dozen musicians strolled by, playing trumpets and various percussion instruments.

At long last Saint Sara came into view, adorned in a white and peach-coloured cloak, and borne aloft on a stretcher by half a dozen men. They carried her to the edge of the sea, paused for some time and then proceeded in, until the water was halfway up their chests. I'd read that they would immerse her in the sea but they simply held the stretcher up at water level. A little while later everyone turned to leave, the crowd dispersed, and it seemed that the ceremony was over.

That night the streets were filled with music and dance. We were told that the festivities would continue the next day and there would be another procession, this one with statues of Mary Salomé and Mary Jacobé from the church, but we left in the morning, unable to face another day of extreme heat and crowded conditions.

Throughout the festival the feeling in the crowd was primal and intensely alive. The atmosphere was charged, extraverted, and unexpectedly raucous for a religious celebration. The communal ritual seemed to obviate the need for individual soul-searching or reflection, and it seemed to me that the Roma had projected their spiritual life onto Saint Sara, and that her ritual baptism served to purify everyone in attendance, perhaps even Roma all around the world. As I watched the Gypsies carry their beloved saint into the water like a large, brown-complexioned doll, I was caught up in the collective drama of the event, so alive to everyone there. Undaunted by their difficult lot in life, the indomitable vitality of the Roma was everywhere evident, and their interactions did not appear subtle or nuanced but larger than life and drawn with the stark colours of passion and survival.

The entire Languedoc region, with its rolling hills and fields, reminded me of a dream I'd had a few years earlier in which the undulating earth was also a woman's body. Mary Magdalene is believed to have stepped ashore in that vivid landscape of red poppy fields and pink flamingos, magnificent wild white horses, and everywhere the roundness of the earth, sheltering little villages in its countless curves and turns. An archetypal landscape harbouring the ritual celebration of a mythic people.

The Transparency of Stereotypes

We know that actual Roma lives are very different from the prevailing gypsy stereotypes and yet we continue to spin our fantasies. Could it be that we discern faint rumblings of a living archetypal energy still present in these stereotypes? Jung compares the archetype to "an old watercourse along which the water of life has flowed for centuries, digging a deep channel for itself." When the water of life dries up, the archetype loses its dynamism and only the outer shell remains; the life-bringing archetypal image devolves into a transparent stereotype. Even so, if we can see through the gypsy stereotype to its archetypal roots, we may catch glimmers of the longing for freedom, beauty, and *duende* in our daily lives. In the following chapter I want to explore the archetypal image of the *gypsy* and the living energies embodied there.

WANDERERS ON THIS EARTH

THE ARCHETYPAL GYPSY AND HER CLAN

We are all wanderers on this earth. Our hearts are full of wonder, and our
souls are deep with dreams.

Gypsy proverb

My heart has been cut open
My blood drained in the name of freedom
What remains?
Sweet music in my veins,
Ancient dance in my broken bones.

Happy and sad,
My spirit sails into the unknown
With no land, no home to call my own,
Hopelessly searching through the past
To find my people, who scattered
Like glass that shattered
Long ago.

Listen and you'll hear the song of longing
Look into the far distance beyond the horizon
And there you'll see dancing
My lonely Gypsy soul

—Nadia Hava-Robbins

We are always in one or another root-metaphor, archetypal fantasy, mythic
perspective. From the soul's point of view we can never get out of the vale
of our psychic reality.

—James Hillman

The *archetypal gypsy* is an image of passion and mystery, of yearning and exile, of recklessness and resilience. Her ground note is *nastos*, an endless longing for home, for an archetypal abode of comfort and belonging whose reality is palpable even while we know there is no such place on earth.

Evoking the red fire and black earth of alchemy, the *gypsy* is elemental. As a soul image, she belongs to the feminine realm and holds the fire of passion and creativity, the air of spiritual longing and buoyancy, the earth of flesh and bone, and the water of emotion and abundant life. But she also holds the dark side of these primal forces. The fire that consumes into ashes, and the air that wafts its poisonous gases. The water that drowns into unconsciousness, and the earth that swallows its dead. Love and hatred, ecstasy and anguish are writ large in the *gypsy* soul and the archetypal drama of *O lungo drom*, the long road.

More readily experienced in music and dance than in words, the *gypsy* is unbridled and edgy, mercurial and rife with contradictions. One moment she demands centre stage; the next, she disappears into the shadows. Shunning collective norms, she is bound by a strict inner code of personal ethics and integrity. Untroubled by the constraints of logic, time, or place and unconcerned with thoughts of past or future, the *gypsy* lives in the present moment, alert and alive to every moment's fullness; its taste and smell, its texture, touch, and sound. Sometimes I feel her dark gaze looking out from behind my eyes.

> The desire to sing, which would have put me centre stage—and the fear of being seen. Ambivalence about wearing my gypsy skirts, which always drew attention. Anything to be inconspicuous and safe. Sitting quietly in the back of class or near an exit, on the periphery, ready for a fast getaway, ready to escape. The inability to accept the prevailing values of the collective, and need to live according to my own uncompromising sense of integrity, a lifelong theme. Someone once told me, "You are capable of a great freedom if you can allow yourself to claim it." Have I claimed it? Yes. No. I don't know.

James Hillman says we're forever gripped by root metaphors and archetypal fantasies that shape our deepest sense of who we are. One morning in Zürich I awakened with the question, *How many times has the gypsy been born and reborn in my soul? Or is it she who gives birth to me?* In this chapter I want to wander into the mythic landscape of the *archetypal gypsy* and meet some of the *gypsy's* renegade relatives who dwell there.

The word *archetype* shows up often these days. Derived from the Greek *archein* (original or old) and *typos* (pattern, model, type), archetypes are original models or patterns—Jung called them "*a priori* inborn forms"—from which copies are made. These copies come to us as *archetypal images* that he described as "a set of variations on a ground theme." We can't see, or touch, or even clearly delineate archetypes but it's clear that we find ourselves forever in their magnetic field. There's no avoiding them, for, as Jung says, "archetypes are complexes of experience that come upon us like fate, and their effects are felt in our most personal life. [They are] living psychic forces that demand to be taken seriously."

Jung wrote at length about the archetypal currents that roil beneath our everyday experience. If we ignore them, we live our lives in thrall to unconscious forces infinitely larger and more powerful than our fragile egos can handle. If we identify with them, we fall prey to possession by all the gods and goddesses in the pantheon, and to endless illusions and projections. But if we approach them with curiosity and awe, they imbue our lives with mythic depth, and connect us with a vast ocean of meaning. When I feel a sudden attraction to a stranger across a crowded room, experience a surge of energy and hope on a crisp morning walk in spring, or find myself gripped by sorrow after losing someone I love, I am attuned to the archetypal energies of eros, rebirth, and loss. It seems that archetypes are at the heart of all meaningful experience. They function like psychic DNA, carrying the potentials of every conceivable expression of human life and making up the core of our personal complexes, the emotional motors that propel our lives.

We often think of complexes in negative terms because of their power to knock us sideways, and feel we should be able to conquer or dispel them with maturity. But without complexes we'd live flat and colourless lives devoid of emotion. Marie-Louise von Franz describes them as "nuclear centers which give the drive, the impulse, and the aliveness to the psyche" and claims, "If we had no complexes, we would be dead." When I feel the energy of the *Great Mother* archetype alive in me, I am nurturing, accepting, receptive toward others and myself, but, caught in a *negative mother* complex, I may torment myself over my own perceived imperfections, or wound someone else with a harsh word or glance.

Because they are invisible forms that manifest in an endless variety of images, archetypes are difficult to talk about; even Jung seemed to circumambulate their meaning through metaphor. Here are some quotes that I have found helpful in understanding their effects on our lives.

Jung says:
An archetype is like an old watercourse along which the water of life has flowed for centuries, digging a deep channel for itself. The longer it has flowed in this channel the more likely it is that sooner or later the water will return to its old bed.

According to Marion Woodman:
Archetypal patterns are like magnets in the unconscious that control what the ego does. These big archetypes—father, mother, divine child—these are the forces underlying our existence. They are energy centers that propel us beyond our transitory existence.

James Hillman suggests that we imagine archetypes as:
the *deepest patterns of psychic functioning*, the roots of the soul governing the perspectives we have of ourselves and the world….By setting up a universe which tends to hold everything we do, see, and say in the sway of its cosmos, an archetype is best comparable with a God.

From Christine Downing:
Archetypal images feel basic, necessary, and generative….They seem to give energy and direction. Archetypal images give rise to associations and lead us to other images; and we therefore experience them as having resonance, complexity, and depth….These images feel numinous, magic, fascinating, daemonic, or divine.

Murray Stein says:
The archetypes undergird the ego in all of its activities and functions. This is a key to perceiving sacredness in everyday life.

And from Marie-Louise von Franz, once again:
An archetypal image is not only a thought pattern [but] the emotional experience of an individual. Only if it has an emotional and
feeling value for an individual is it alive and meaningful.

In recent years many attempts have been made to delineate a set number of core archetypes but Jung said, "There are as many archetypes as there
are typical situations in life." Nor can we make tidy distinctions among
them because in the unconscious, the archetypes permeate each other in a
state of "complete mutual interpenetration and fusion." He concludes, "It
is a well-nigh impossible undertaking to tear a single archetype out of the
living tissue of the psyche."

Perhaps, then, we should speak rather of an *archetypal field* that contains not only the *gypsy* but a large extended family of related mythic figures. *Wanderer* and *exile*. *Rebel* and *trickster*. *Pilgrim* and *nomad*. *Orphan* and
victim. *Virgin* and *crone*, and their *dark sister*, the *witch*. *Dancer* and *musician*.
Magician, *shaman*, and *craftsman*. All are members of the *gypsy's* tribe. There
are related archetypal processes at play too, such as revolt and liminality,
homelessness and transformation, creation and destruction and the paradox
of their coexistence. Here I would like to introduce them briefly, and in
the next chapter I will explore their presence in my life, drawing also from
literature and film. Like dreams, movies mirror the unconscious, the realm
where the archetypes reside, and offer rich illustrations of the archetypal
energies at play in our culture.

My inner eye scans the archetypal field and alights on two of the *gypsy's* closest cousins, *wanderer* and *pilgrim*. Archetypally and stereotypically
the *gypsy* wanders, and wandering, by both choice and necessity, has been
part of the Roma's historical experience as well. English Roma sometimes
call themselves Travellers. Gypsies are often portrayed as happy wanderers who pick up and leave as their mood dictates, as if life were one endless camping trip. "The harsh conditions of life on the road are never dealt
with," notes Ian Hancock, "and the day-to-day responsibility of feeding a
family and keeping it clothed and warm is trivialized out of existence." By
all accounts it would seem the Roma's wandering—symbolized by the traditional horse-drawn caravan and, more recently, its motorized twin—has

been a double-edged sword. Too often they have been forced to leave their settlements, even countries, by hostile neighbours and governments, and yet many of their songs celebrate the *lungo drom*, the long road and never-ending journey of the Roma.

The archetypal *wanderer* answers the inner call to journey to foreign shores and encounter unknown people and experiences. Literature and film are full of wanderers, from Homer's *Odyssey* to James Joyce's *Ulysses*, where wandering is transposed into the inner realm as we traverse a day in the life of Leopold Bloom in the streets of Dublin, in June 1904. Resistant to dogma or orthodoxy, the *wanderer* refuses to be brought into the fold of obligatory routine, instead carrying all that is wild and free and instinctual within, out into the world. According to Jung, the figure of the wandering Jew "sprang from a component of the personality or a charge of libido that could find no outlet in the Christian attitude to life and the world [and represents] a part of ourselves that has contrived to escape the Christian process of domestication." So too the *gypsy*.

In our own time, the *gypsy* is a symbol for a powerful current of shifting populations, displacement and homelessness, and restless spiritual wandering in a technological global society. Beneath all of this lies the sense of "permanent provisionality" that Fernanda Eberstadt described in her work with Spanish Gypsies. Many of us feel cut off from the traditional affiliations and structures of meaning that provided stability for earlier generations; the old certainties no longer hold and often we feel ourselves betwixt and between, without solid ground to support us.

In the film *Chocolat*, free-spirited Vianne Rocher is carried by the north wind to a tranquil French village dominated by the local church and centuries of stultifying tradition. Her generous heart and sensual love of life bring new vitality and joy to the town, and there, too, she meets her soulmate in the River Gypsy Roux, a fellow wanderer and free spirit. Through her expansive humanity and innate joie de vivre the town is reborn. But the urge to wander can also have sobering consequences. In the movie *Into the Wild*, based on the life and death of Chris McCandless, the young protagonist ventures into the Alaskan wilderness without adequate preparation or supplies, loses his orientation, and gradually starves to death. An example also of the solitary *hero* archetype, McCandless has tempted the gods by refusing to acknowledge his human limitations in an epic landscape.

While the *wanderer* is attuned to the earth's gifts and wonders he or she encounters along the way, the *pilgrim* sets out on a quest for spiritual renewal in order to transcend everyday reality and step into ritual time and space. The Hindu's pilgrimage to the Ganges, the Buddhist's trip to Sarnath, the Muslim's odyssey to Mecca, the Jew's journey to the Wailing Wall in Jerusalem, and the Christian's trip to Bethlehem—all express the pilgrim's longing to experience the place where the sacred has appeared in the flesh and to re-establish contact with the Divine.

Exile, *refugee*, and *outcast* similarly belong to the *gypsy's* extended family. These are familiar to those of us raised in immigrant families whose roots are elsewhere and whose gaze is cast backward with yearning and sorrow on what was unwillingly left behind. In Eva Hoffman's memoir, *Lost in Translation*, we see these archetypal energies at play in the life of a young girl whose move from Krakow to Vancouver marks the decisive *before* and *after* of her life. The book's three sections—"Paradise," "Exile," and "The New World"—tell the tale. It is only at the end of the book and well into middle age that the author feels herself no longer an exile from her idyllic point of origin, but at home, and finally at peace, in her present life. "Time pulses through my blood like a river," she writes. "The language of this is sufficient. I am here now." But it has taken half her lifetime to arrive.

The *refugee*, too, has been forced to flee home and country in hopes of finding safe haven elsewhere. Under threat of war or persecution, the *refugee* is a vulnerable stranger in a strange land, at the mercy of the new dispensation while trying desperately to find a place within it. This has surely been the never-ending plight of the Roma, driven out of many countries and forced to flee for their own survival, throughout the ages.

My own parents spent part of their youth in a refugee camp in northern Germany after the war before emigrating to Canada in the late 1940s. Fleeing their respective homes in East and West Prussia as the Russians marched westward, they found themselves in refugee resettlement camps anxiously awaiting news of my grandfather and several uncles who were prisoners of war in Belgium and Denmark. When my father's family was finally reunited they made their way to Canada, shell-shocked immigrants to a country they knew little about and whose language they didn't speak, at a time when German nationals were anything but welcome. I was born during the following decade and became their interpreter in the large and small affairs of everyday life.

And what about the inner *outcast*, comprising all those parts of us that we refuse to acknowledge because they frighten or embarrass us and could alienate others, leaving us friendless and bereft? Jungian analyst and writer Ann Ulanov describes the importance of going down into the rejected parts of ourselves, "those parts that do not get housed in the civilized Inn." Bursting with repressed energy and unlived life, often that's where the seeds of new life are buried.

And then there's the *rebel* who defies accepted codes of belief and conduct. The focus of so much literature and film, the *rebel* is frequently shown as an unwitting agent of change who challenges the status quo, causes upheaval, and prompts society to take another look at itself. We see the *rebel* archetype in films as diverse as *Gandhi* and *Silkwood*, *Frida* and *The Matrix*.

The Roma themselves embody this archetype. After encountering a Gypsy woman in a Paris bookstore, Anaïs Nin wrote in her diary, "In spite of being considered thieves, of being humiliated, of resorting to begging, gypsies' pride is not broken or corroded. It remains smoldering and strong. It is as though our morals were not acceptable to them, as if they lived by other values, and did not feel ashamed of their activities." Sometimes, too, the *rebel* may simply steal quietly away in order to follow a different path from the one offered by the collective, transmuting into the archetypal *individualist* or *Einzelgänger*.

As the "cousin" who carries the sins of the tribe, the *scapegoat* was originally a human or animal sacrificed to appease the gods, but has long since lost religious significance and taken on the meaning of group "whipping boy." Throughout history there have been individuals and groups of people onto whom great ill has been projected and who have suffered greatly as a result. Jews and many other groups under Hitler; artists and intellectuals under Stalin in Russia, Mao Zedong in China, and Pol Pot in Cambodia; women burned as witches during the Middle Ages; and indigenous peoples all over the world—history is shamefully replete with examples. It's clear that the Roma have been among them, "carriers of our collective shadow who represent denied polarities within the scapegoaters—the settled people of Western Europe for example—that are being split and projected." Among these polarities are freedom and security, discipline and disorder, spontaneity and control.

The *victim* is equally powerless to turn the tide of suffering and hardship. Whether the source of affliction is war or natural disaster, physical or mental illness, domestic or cultural violence, the *victim* is helpless in the face of calamitous circumstances and, to top it off, is often blamed for the injury. But we also carry the *victim* inside, betraying ourselves through thoughtlessness, poor judgment, and self-deception. Those of us with a harsh inner critic know all too well the dynamic of *persecutor* and *victim*, at times feeling ourselves caught in the cruelty of the inner *tyrant*.

How often while writing I have felt assaulted by the Serbian bully who appeared in a dream some years ago, taunting me for not working hard enough and for daring to think I have anything worthwhile to say. I can only be grateful for another dream that followed in which a rough-hewn Slavic man leapt fearlessly into deep waters in order to save an egret, the Bird of Spirit, from drowning. What a relief to know that alongside the bullying *tyrant* in my psyche there exists a rugged defender of my spiritual values.

While I would never want to trivialize the Roma's suffering during the war, I do wonder if the *Devouring* itself is an archetypal process. During our lifetimes most of us undergo some experience of persecution where we feel ourselves assaulted by powerful outer forces or tormented by inner demons, and which may cause us to fear for our physical or psychic lives. I recall how often Marion Woodman reminded her audience of the inevitability of great suffering in our lives. "You can't get to the Resurrection without going through the Crucifixion," she'd say, and on whatever level it occurs, crucifixion is torment indeed. When lifelong dreams are shattered and we collapse in despair, something in us has died and the anguish may be fierce.

The *gypsy* also belongs to the archetypal *dark feminine*, the realm of repressed, earthy, sensual energies embodied by the Indian goddess Kali and the Black Madonna. Kali is dark and marginalized, and lives on the outskirts of town like the Roma, and the Black Madonna is known to the Roma as "Mary the Gypsy." Irving Brown tells us that Kali is the secret name for "Gypsy girl" among the Roma.

For men the *gypsy* is often an alluring *anima* or soul figure, an image of feminine essence and mystery. While the Virgin Mary represents all that is noble and pure in woman, the dark side of the feminine is "a gypsy, illicit, wildly sensuous, chaotic." In Robertson Davies' *The Rebel Angels*, Maria Theotoky, the brilliant and alluring daughter of a Hungarian Gypsy mother, brings eros and beauty to the dry academic dons of the College of St. John and the Holy Ghost. For women, too, the *gypsy* may conjure a darkly romantic masculine figure or *animus*. Yvette, the young English girl in D.H. Lawrence's *The Virgin and the Gipsy*, doesn't even learn the name of her Gypsy lover until after they part and he sends her a letter. The last line of the novel—"and only then she realized that he had a name"—reveals the symbolic nature of his role in her life. At the other end of the *dark feminine* is the *witch*, whose power to curse and destroy is the stuff of many fairy tales and legends, including those of the Roma.

But for women as for men, the *gypsy* is above all a feminine soul image related to the *virgin* archetype. In *Woman's Mysteries*, Esther Harding writes, "The woman who is virgin, one-in-herself, does what she does—not because of any desire to please, not to be liked, or to be approved, even by herself; not because of any desire to gain control over another, to catch his interest or love, but because what she does is true." While the archetypal *father's daughter* seeks masculine approval and excels in the public realm, the *virgin* lives according to her authentic soul values, even when they run counter to those of the collective. The cost of living her own truth may be her outcast state, and Marion Woodman writes eloquently of "the fierce and poignant energy the outcast embodies." For Woodman the *gypsy* is a *shadow sister* carrying the instinctual life force that allows us to experience our own passion in body and soul. In her modern fairy tale about the Kingdom of Suburbia, the princess cannot wed her shining prince until she learns to love her dark gypsy sister, "her own rejected self."

And it's the *gypsy's* energy that saves Woodman's life on more than one occasion. In her harrowing account of surviving cancer, she describes her dream of a barefoot, young Gypsy woman with long flowing hair on board a ship coming to shore. A month later she reflects, "Now it is time for me to reconnect with my Virgin self—the *I am* within that is one in herself—the Gypsy in my November initiation dream....She is my survivor."

During one of her darkest times as she lay in the hospital on life support, her doctor came to her and said, "I am doing everything I can to keep you alive. But you are not doing the same. Do you want me to pull out the life support or not? I can do it right now." Woodman was shocked. "Death? I hadn't even realized I was that close to dying."

"I could be out of here in one minute," she thought. "I could just leave." Suddenly she was horrified by the thought and heard herself saying, "I'm in no hurry," in a sweet, singing Gypsy voice that sounded strong but utterly relaxed. Everyone, the doctor, his residents, and Woodman herself, burst out laughing. "There she is again," Woodman thought. "There's the Gypsy."

The process of reconnecting with that primal life force is at the heart of *Bone*, which ends when "Gypsy" suddenly ignites and thrusts her onto the dance floor at a friend's fiftieth birthday party. Woodman writes:

> I feel the archetypal energy lifting me off the couch, propelling me across the room—I feel it pushing through my benumbed feet, legs, thighs, torso, arms, hands, through every cell into my head. It is TOTAL. I feel myself Gypsy—a twenty-four-year-old glowing woman. I am being danced. People are gazing at me aghast, probably thinking, "This old lady sat on the couch all evening; suddenly she's transformed into a hands-in-the-air gypsy. What's she up to?" Do I care?

The *puer aeternus*, or "eternal youth," shares the high spirits and spontaneity of the *gypsy*, along with her creative spark. We see this in the Indian god Krishna, who wanders through the world with his flute, bringing joy and laughter wherever he goes. "He runs, jumps, scampers, and bounds through the forest in a constant display of irrepressible vitality and enthusiasm," David Kinsley writes in *The Sword and the Flute*. Krishna's life is not constricted by duty but one great celebration of rambunctious revelry and freedom. After years of living with Gypsies, Irving Brown wrote, "If there is something of the rogue in the Gypsy, there is also something of the child in him, and something of the artist. His life, his work, and his play are one. Like the artist, his chief aim in life is to *live*."

The shadow sides of the *puer* and *puella* are the temptation to run away when things lose their novelty and excitement, and difficulty alighting in one place long enough to form bonds of connection and commitment. The movies are full of charming *puer* men unable or unwilling to grow up, perpetual Peter Pans who flit from one woman to the next. While writing *Gypsy Fugue*, I often felt the *puella's* shadow in my unwillingness to settle down and focus and my impatient turning away to more immediate rewards and gratifications. For *puella* and *puer*, sustained focus and commitment are quite a challenge.

Musician and *dancer* share the *gypsy's* immersion in the eternal present where time is not a series of measurable, chronological increments, but a ceaseless unfolding of present moments. Music and dance exist only in the moment—there is no tangible artifact as there is in art or sculpture. At the annual Roma festival in Les Saintes-Maries-de-la-Mer, musicians wandered freely through the town streets with their instruments under their arms, ready to make music at a moment's notice. Suddenly they began playing and out of nowhere a dancer appeared, and people gathered close to clap time and cheer on the spontaneous performance. After living with Gypsies over several decades Jan Yoors observed, "They lived the moment, oblivious to all else, with a single-mindedness and intensity that disturbed the western mind." Every time I see Roma music and dance I'm struck by that edgy vitality.

Don't we all yearn for a passionate channel of self-expression, a Dionysian release in which we hold nothing back but just let loose and give it everything we've got? A release from the cramped rationality that rules our everyday lives? Ann Ulanov writes of a feminine mode of perception whose secrets "are imparted in mysterious ways reaching back to ancient mythological rites and ecstasies associated with music and the dance, such as the Orphic and Eleusinian mysteries. Thus it is the feminine muses who preside over rhythm, over soothsaying and artistic creativity." This sounds like the world of the archetypal *gypsy* to me.

Union of body and soul, masculine and feminine, heaven and earth. The archetype of the *hieros gamos*, or "divine marriage" (also known as *coniunctio*), brings the opposites together in a transcendent experience of unity and wholeness. Wim Wenders' film *Wings of Desire* (1987) is an archetypal love story of heaven and earth; of angels who yearn to have bodies, and mortals who long for weightlessness and ascent. The angels Damiel and

Cassiel move through the world invisible to everyone but children. They know what mortals think and feel, witness their suffering, and gently touch them as they pass by. But they hunger to experience what it's like to walk on the earth or bite into an apple. Meanwhile, in the realm of mortals, Marion, the beautiful trapeze artist, aches for a soulmate. When she and Damiel finally meet she tells him, "We two are more than just we two. We personify something. Everyone wishes for what we wish for. The whole place is full of those who are dreaming the same dream. There is no greater story than ours, the story of man and woman." When Damiel steps down into the human dimension at last he says, "I learned amazement last night. She took me home, and I found my home. The amazement about man and woman made a human being out of me. I know now what no angel knows."

"The differences between the sexes offer the most striking instances of the dark mystery of otherness," Ulanov writes. In Sally Potter's movie *Yes* (2004), a woman and a man from very different worlds are drawn to the dark mystery of each other, and then encounter the huge gulf of their differences. She is an Irish American scientist trapped in a deadened marriage. He is a disillusioned Lebanese surgeon working as a cook in Ireland. His sensuous gaze opens her tightly petalled self like an exotic warm breeze and she comes to life in his embrace. Until their differences threaten to rupture their love. Here it's the man who awakens the woman. We never learn their names, and in the film credits they are listed simply as *He* and *She*, the archetypal man and woman. In the end, they are united in an archetypal third space (Cuba) that is neither Hers (Ireland) nor His (Lebanon), but new, yet to be explored, and Theirs.

I think we all long for the inner *coniunctio*. For union with the dark stranger within whom we don't know but who we somehow feel may be our missing half. The unknown other in ourselves whom we adore and shun, fear and long for; who carries our unclaimed vitality and creative passion, our mischief and deviousness. What else is the projection of erotic appeal onto outer figures, whether movie stars, singers, or Gypsies, but an external manifestation of that longing to unite with our own inner mystery and dark otherness?

The archetypal *gypsy* contains all these opposites in spades. Exuberant joy alongside profound suffering. Ecstasy and anguish expressed in music and dance, often at one and the same time. I feel both poles of the *gypsy's* energy in me—yin and yang, creative and destructive, soaring and leaden, radiant and dull. Perhaps the very intensity of these opposites balances out the measured, responsible, perfectionist side of me.

And then there's the *gypsy's colour*. The striking red and black of flamenco evoke extremes of passion and death. But for me, the *gypsy's* colour has always been fuchsia, the intensely saturated blend of red and purple, colours of the Whore of Babylon, another cast-out rule breaker within patriarchy. Picture a sensuous oil stain in every shade of crimson and purple, fuchsia and mauve, magenta and red. An organic shape that spreads and slowly encroaches on a dark green background of field and forest. A fluid, shape-shifting stain permeated with old blood and the deep crimson of *duende*. An archetypal *gypsy* stain that seeps and creeps into the surrounding territory and soaks it with rich, dark hues.

And since archetypes are dynamic patterns in motion, imagine too an impulse toward movement, an arc or gesture that expresses the *gypsy's* essence. Flamboyant sweep of the arms and proud tilt of the head. So much of the *gypsy's* energy—perhaps even the greater part—resists being captured in words. It pounds in the blood and courses through the veins, enlivening tissue and bone and shaping the body's gestures. As if the cells of the body were charged with extra oxygen and the blood just got a little redder.

There are many other members of the *gypsy's* tribe. The *trickster*, who often appears as the fool or *dummling* in fairy tales and dreams, is a mischievous and not always benign free spirit that delights in upsetting the status quo and turning everything upside down. "There is something of the trickster in the character of the shaman and medicine-man," Jung says of these three archetypes that move freely among animal, human, and supernatural realms. *Shaman* and *medicine man* move between the upper and lower worlds in a state of altered consciousness in order to bring healing and restore meaning through an expanded experience of life.

The *magician* belongs here too, for there is surely an aura of magic surrounding the *gypsy*. Given his great interest in other cultures and peoples, it's puzzling that Jung's only reference to Gypsies in the *Collected Works* occurs in a footnote to his discussion of the *magician* archetype, where he observed, "Very often it is the older folk-elements that possess magical powers. In India it is the Nepalese, in Europe the gypsies." Long associated with tarot and the telling of fortunes, Gypsies have had a close connection with plant and herbal remedies. And the figure of the medieval magician is an echo of Hermes, trickster god of the crossroads where, according to folklore, Gypsies were traditionally buried. The *nomad*, close friend of the *wanderer*, travels from place to place in search of green pasture for livestock, and the *craftsperson* creates useful and beautiful one-of-a-kind objects for everyday use, even in this age of mass production. All are cousins of the *gypsy* and all are subversive energies in our times.

The final archetype I want to mention is the *mandala*, ancient Hindu and Buddhist symbol of cosmic wholeness. In 1971, the international Roma community adopted a mandala as its flag at the first World Romani Congress in London. The sixteen-spoked red chakra in the flag's centre is based on the ancient Indian wheel of fate, and suggests the wheels of Roma caravans. It derives from the flag of India and represents continual movement and "the burst of fire from which all creation emerged at the beginning of time." The blue band at the top evokes the sky and the Roma's connection to spirit, while the green band below symbolizes their relationship with nature and the earth. Sixteen is the number of wholeness and mystical transformation for Jung, and the imagery of the Roma flag illustrates his claim that "psyche and matter exist in one and the same world, and each partakes of the other." I picture that fiery red wheel of life turning its spokes through heaven and earth, uniting spirit and matter, consciousness and the unconscious, in the never-ending circle of life.

❧

In this chapter I have tried to sketch in broad strokes the territory inhabited by the archetypal *gypsy* and her clan, and to begin weaving a web of imaginative associations. When imagination is free to wander and follow dreams, desire, and delight, our souls are fed and life has meaning. Our images reveal our souls and the *anima mundi*, the ensouled world in which we live. They also nourish it, evoking mythic depth and resonance in the simplest of everyday tasks and connecting us to the timeless, spaceless world of the eternal. Feeling the presence of these energies flowing through us connects us to the mystery of our own being. That is my hope for the next chapter, where some of the *gypsy*'s clan appear in a series of autobiographical vignettes that are windows into my soul. In the Fugue I want to explore and celebrate the presence of the archetypal *gypsy* in the tapestry of my life.

Fugue

On foot
I had to walk through the solar systems,
before I found the first thread of my red dress.
Already, I sense myself.
Somewhere in space hangs my heart,
Sparks fly from it, shaking the air,
to other reckless hearts.

—Edith Södergran

There is a *gypsy* queendom in my soul. It is dark but luminous, vibrant and aglow. In the background, jewel colours shimmer darkly. There is always music, except when stillness reigns. Tapestries, embroideries, and exotic beads abound. I love its rough edges and hidden corners, its throbbing pulse and sudden grace, its quicksilver movements and radiant mysteries. Everything is possible here, and nothing is out-landish.

There is a *gypsy* queendom in my soul. It is full of prickly inklings and whiffs of knowing, dancing gestures and drifting melodies. For years it has been a subterranean territory whose reality I sensed but did not know. Wanting never to exploit its mystery or expose its deepest secrets, I invite in all who want to enter now, to join me in my vagabond wanderings.

There is a *gypsy* queendom in my soul, a vast and open field of possibility. There are no fences, walls, or gates here, no restricted areas or exclusive properties. Certainly no border patrol or customs office; no guards in uniform posted at the window. No roadblocks, Do Not Enter signs, or ticket takers here. No passport required. Anyone can come and go—no one is outlawed. This is where the *gypsy* lives, and it's from this space that I want to write.

Writing is the passageway, the entrance, the exit, the dwelling place of the other in me—the other that I am and am not, that I don't know how to be, but that I feel passing, that makes me live—that tears me apart, disturbs me, changes me.

I am the *gypsy*. She is the other who makes her dwelling place in me. May she live her life in these pages, and may all travellers freely come and go.

ON MEANDERING

And now I want to meander. Derived from the Phrygian Meander River, *to flow in a winding course, a circuitous journey or movement, as in the dance.* Not linearly then, but, following desire and the *gypsy*, step further into this numinous archetypal landscape, explore its treasures, and circumambulate the dark and shimmering mystery at its core. *Circle it on foot, ritualistically.*

Feminine process is characterized by encirclement and circumambulation, writes Jungian analyst Ann Ulanov. "The feminine quality of understanding conceives a content, walks around it, participates affectively in it, and then brings it forth into the world." It's not only women she is talking about, but a way of moving through the world that artists and creative individuals of both sexes know very well.

Fugue derives from *fuga*, Latin for "flight," implying a flight of fancy, possibly the flight of the theme from one voice to another. A contrapuntal composition in three or four voices, in which a theme or subject of strongly marked character pervades the entire fabric, entering now in one voice, now in another.

I want to sing a flight of fancy, in all my many voices. The personal voice of my autobiographical stories. The scholarly voice of my intellectual passions, and the Jungian voice of symbolic association. The vulnerable, self-questioning voice of my journal, and the many voices in my dreams. The voice of the singer in me, and the edgy and lyrical voice of the *gypsy* herself. Invoke them all, invite them all, and love them all—not exclude even one of them. Weave them all together in this *gypsy fugue.*

Other voices are welcome too. Roma voices. Poets and songwriters, novelists and filmmakers, and other *gypsy* voices. Quotes and melodies from far-flung sources. And the voice of you, the reader, as you meander through these pages with me. An open invitation to this *gypsy* chorus.

Can these words convey the simmering, shimmering, singing, sorrowing energy of the *gypsy* in my soul? *Open up the space where woman is wandering, roaming (a rogue wave), flying (thieving)?* More than anything, that's what I want. To open up a *gypsy* space.

✺

I love the word *gypsy*, the way it looks and sounds. It delights me that four of its letters have tails reaching underground. The other one is humble, no letters reaching to the heavens unless we make the *g* upper case. Upper caste. *G* says, "I am important, with my round containing curve." I picture those long tails—*g*, *y*, *p*, *y*—hiding underground and biding their time before sprouting up again into upper case importance. The closed circle of the little *g* and the luscious double roundness of the *s*—I like them too. Word as visual image, as pictorial character, as hieroglyph.

I love the sound of *gypsy*—its daring lilt and edgy energy catapult me into dance. The open vowel at the end that wants to burst into song. The mysteriousness of the final *y* rather than the insignificance of *i* or explicitness of *ee*. Word as acoustic image. As kinesthetic image.

I love the etymology of Gypsy, derived from the erroneous belief that the Roma come from Egypt. The mystery of Roma origins, reflected in their names. One theory says that *Roma* derives from *ramante*, the Sanskrit word for "roaming." Another says it comes from *Dom*, the Sanskrit word for "man." Roma is an anagram of roam, but also of amor. Word as cultural marker.

I love the dance and flow of words, their dark roots and mysterious origins. Many years ago in Germany I once spent an entire day exploring the etymology of *Sehnsucht*, or "yearning." Literally, "the longing to see." I fell in love with its roots. Word roots.

Through fleshing out the bones of words and making our way back to their origins, we discover hidden worlds within them. We feel the secret resonance they carry, the power of all that is evoked without our even knowing it. Staking their claim in the realm of the unsayable, words divert attention from everything that cannot be said and tempt us into certainty. Yet all the while, their roots are quietly pulsing underground, bursting with significance, with the vitality of the etymological unconscious.

James Hillman writes of the *etymon* or hidden truth of a name. "The search for the roots of words, the etymological fantasy, is one of the basic rituals of the imaginative tradition because it seeks to recover an image within a word," he says. Through etymological excavation and fantasy, we arrive at word roots, word bones, word origins. This is how the Roma's beginnings were traced back to India in the middle of the eighteenth century, when Vályi Stefán recognized that the language spoken by his Indian colleagues in the Netherlands was strikingly akin to that of the Hungarian Roma at home.

It's appropriate, then, that the love of language and hidden depths of meaning lies in the realm of Hermes, the *gypsy's trickster* cousin. But that's another story.

A Story of Red

When I was a young girl, my favourite colour was red. I loved all vivid colours but given a choice of sapphire, emerald, or ruby, my preference was clear. As a teenager I had three red dresses: a long-sleeved cherry-red wool knit dress with covered cloth buttons, purchased during the January sales at Auld Phillips Ladies Clothing Store; a bright red Fortrel dress with short sleeves that my grandmother sewed according to my design; and a simple sleeveless crimson dress she and I made together from a textured polyester remnant that cost almost nothing. It was the passion and energy of red I loved, its brazen, unabashed enthusiasm. Most of all, I loved wearing red with black.

One evening during my early twenties, my friend Kate and I went to a lounge to have a drink with Martin, her accountant friend from work. I wore a black peasant blouse and my first *gypsy* skirt with its rows of red and green embroideries, gold braid, ivory lace roses, and hand-sewn pearls from a broken necklace. Although I felt shy wearing it, I thought it was beautiful. As we sat down with our drinks, Martin scanned me up and down and then looked me boldly in the eye. "You shouldn't wear red and black together like that," he said. "It looks like you're asking for trouble." He seemed serious.

What strikes me now is that I didn't laugh or ask Martin what he meant. I just absorbed his words silently and felt humiliated to discover that something that came from a deep part of me was giving off signals I'd never intended to send. When he sent me a dozen red roses a week later, I threw them out and wrote Martin a short note explaining that his attentions were not welcome. And I stopped wearing red. I didn't make another *gypsy* skirt for close to two decades. There is more to the story of my lost fire and passion, but I still remember the shock of discovering that my *gypsy* skirt had been perceived as blatant sexual invitation.

It wasn't that I stopped loving red. When a friend in London offered to knit me a sweater a few years later, I chose a brilliant red wool yarn, but I never wore the sweater. It glowed with such vitality and desire that I feared the consequences. Another friend brought me a piece of flowered red silk from China. I loved its soft, sensuous sheen, but I never sewed anything with it. Eventually I passed both sweater and silk on to friends who had no trouble wearing red.

Many years later during a Body Soul Rhythms Intensive I dreamed of three sheer lace blouses in ivory, sage green, and red. All three were glorious, but the red one set my body ablaze and that was the one I wanted. In the dream everyone agreed it was the right one for me and I bought it, but it was so beautiful that I was afraid to wear it in public. As I shared the dream with the group the next day, I realized it was about my red-hot youthful passion. The primal life force held in the red dresses made for me by my beloved grandmother (symbolically the *Great Mother*) during my young womanhood, and subsequently suppressed out of shame, was returning to me in that semi-sheer, flame-red lace blouse.

That night I had another dream. I was sorting through a stack of colourful blouses I'd planned to give away, but I suddenly decided to keep the red one after all. I just knew I hadn't worn it enough. All that week I lived in red. I breathed red, dreamed red, and danced red until it filled every cell in me. Even afterward as I sat in the airport awaiting my flight home, exhausted by what I'd experienced during the week's work, it seemed that every man who passed by stared hard at me, and I felt it pulsing in me still.

According to Ian Hancock, the Red Dress Gypsies' Association was the name of the earliest Romany benevolent organization in the United States, founded in 1927 in hopes of improving education and housing for American Gypsies. Try as I might, I have not been able to find out anything more about this group, and I'm curious to know where their name came from, and what that red dress symbolized for them. For the Roma, red carries paradoxical connotations of contamination, protection, and joy. Bright colours are believed to attract good luck and blood is the source of vitality and life, but the primary shade of red is considered unclean and tainted, as if tempting the gods. Which gods, I wonder? Strict taboos govern the expression of sexuality within Roma culture. Is that what I was afraid of when

I swore off red for all those years? That I might tempt the gods or transgress taboos with my too-passionate response to life?

In the summer of 2003 I went to Switzerland in hopes of enrolling at the C.G. Jung Institute in Küsnacht. One day I was walking down the Seestrasse in the midday heat, back to my room at the Hotel Sonne, site of revered Jungian memories over the years. Suddenly a tall, husky man walking in the opposite direction on the sidewalk stepped abruptly in front of me and grabbed my breasts, then continued down the street as if nothing had happened. After the first moment of shock I turned around and cursed him in German, then ran away lest he come back and throw me into the oncoming traffic. I was wearing a red vest and black capri pants, and for a moment my mind flashed back to Martin's warning so many years earlier. Did the stocky stranger, clearly deranged, imagine he saw an invitation in red and black?

Not long ago I came upon these lines in a Roma poem: "i found / my body / on red velvet / For a long time / i'd roamed / toward this mountain / toward the black / pain at / the body's core." Don't these lines suggest the intensity and anguish of our blocked lust for life? For the medieval alchemists, the *rubedo*, or "reddening," was the stage in the never-ending flow of psychic life that marked "the reanimation of fresh spirit by the red blood of experience, in the living of human life." The *rubedo* takes us into the earthy, ensouled world. Isn't this exactly where we want to be? Isn't that what Joseph Campbell meant when he claimed what we seek is not the meaning of life but the rapture of being alive?

A few years later I arrived in Zürich to begin my Jungian study. On one of my frequent pilgrimages to the Black Madonna of Einsiedeln, I stopped in at Daimon Press, the venerable Jungian publishing house. As I browsed through the shelves, my eyes fell on a book titled *Dreaming in Red*. I opened the book and read the first lines of the preface. *The red of Dionysus belongs to women. So dark it is almost black, it calls up old wine, deep wounds, and the marbled walls of the womb itself heavy with twisted veins reaching inevitably toward the heart.* The images reverberated through my body and soul. From the intoxication of old spirits and the deep wounds left by centuries-long humiliation and abuse of the feminine to that interior sanctuary, the hidden place of our primal origins and fierce longing for love—the dark red of Dionysus is my home territory.

I wear red now. A sleeveless lace blouse that makes me glow. A soft knit top with a band of embroidered silk around the middle. A floral skirt that swings around my legs and red sandals that make my feet feel sassy. It still feels like a bold act.

EMBROIDERIES

Even when I joined Steve in New York after completing my doctoral work in London, the *gypsy* energy remained underground. But I remember well the golden October Sunday afternoon when I began to sew my first *gypsy* skirt in two decades, and how that process nourished me. It felt like part of me had been hibernating for a very long time and was slowly waking up again. Perhaps it was no accident that it was my birthday, because that day marked the rebirth of the *gypsy* in me.

I sewed for hours in trance, and time melted away as I created a design from antique ivory lace I'd brought back from Naples, shiny red and green satin ribbons from England, and burnished gold braid I'd found in the Hasidic district of Brooklyn. Later I embroidered and stitched pearls into the centre of the lace flowers. On smooth black crepe with a hint of sheen, it was a thing of beauty and when I wore it for the first time, it was as if I'd found a part of myself that had gone missing for a long time. I affectionately referred to it as my ur-*gypsy* skirt because it looked like the first one I'd sewn, twenty years earlier, just before embarking on my six-month journey through Europe and the Middle East in 1979. I'd worn that one until it fell apart and I patched it up and it fell apart a second time. Wherever I wore it, people made comments. A man in an Athens market told me it looked like a Greek folk costume and a Roma couple on a ferry to Crete pointed to it with delighted smiles. Once, on a busy street in downtown Vancouver, a woman had offered me two hundred dollars for it and I briefly considered designing and selling my *gypsy* skirts.

In the months following that Sunday in early October I sewed two more skirts, one with antique gold trim and sparkling mauve, green, and blue sequins, whose colours reminded me of India; the other one with heavy red, black, and gold braid in a more classical pattern that looked Persian to me. I'd discovered a store in lower Manhattan where I could purchase fabric in just the right weight very inexpensively, and my imagination went wild creating patterns and designs for closets full of *gypsy* skirts. I was completing work on a book at that time and wrote:

> Draped over the back of the blue couch at the far end of the living room are various lengths of jewel-toned fabrics—midnight blue, forest green, plum wine, deep burgundy—and an array of burnished gold braids, creamy laces, glittering sequins, satin ribbons, and brilliantly hued crystal and cloisonné beads. My gypsy skirts, so long deferred, are in full swing, and provide such pleasure in the making that for the life of me, I can't remember why I stopped sewing them twenty years ago. Did my gypsy self really go underground for all those years?
>
> As friends and strangers ask about the origins of my skirts, I have been prompted to think about the meaning of gypsy for me. The outcast, the one not welcome, the one outside the collective who refuses to abide by society's dictates, the perpetual wanderer with no permanent home, the wild one, free spirited and uncontainable. The archetypal resonance of the gypsy has been so powerful for me, surfacing vividly in my dreams and now, once again, finding tangible expression in my colourful skirts. My imagination, my creativity, my fantasy of all the exotic lives I might have led in other times and places—all are reflected in my darkly shimmering skirts.
>
> They also carry the energy of my shadow, the reckless, flamboyant underside of my serenely responsible and balanced Libra temperament, unashamedly lusty and in love with colour and music and dance. I've been dipping into Thomas Moore's *The Soul of Sex: Cultivating Life as an Act of Love*. He surely would say that my skirts are a manifestation of my desire to eroticize the world and immerse myself in beauty. And he would be right.
>
> That's a lot of meaning for my gypsy skirts to carry. But it's all there, in those richly-hued fabrics and luxurious trims. Other people respond to them too, as if they recognize something familiar. And my affinity to gypsies is not altered in the least by the fact that historically, the Roma themselves have been as obsessed

with purity as any fundamentalist religion and harsh toward perceived violators to their rigid moral codes. Both *Latcho Drom* and Isabel Fonseca's *Bury Me Standing* held me in thrall, as if the Roma's story were also my own.

I still remember the excitement I felt after coming across a review of *Bury Me Standing: The Gypsies and Their Journey* in the *New York Times Book Review* in December 1995. I bought the book the very next day and read into the wee hours of morning, unable to put it down. Through the years, one photograph has remained vivid in my memory. A Roma woman who appears to be in her fifties sits with her hands clasped around folded legs under a bordered skirt, dark hair tucked under a scarf, small gold hoops in her ears, and a look of quiet self-containment on her face, turned slightly away from the camera. The black-and-white photo conveys the sharp contrasts of light and dark in her clothing, of attentive watchfulness and inner liveliness in her bearing, and of a long-suffering dignity and humour laced with acceptance and resignation in her expression. She seemed oddly familiar and I recognized her expression. I'd seen it often on my mother's face and could imagine it on my own. *That's what I will look like in twenty years,* I thought. Beneath the photograph I'd pencilled in, "Myself, in another life."

Tucked away in a corner on the top shelf of my closet is a large, clear Rubbermaid storage box filled with embroideries, laces, and beads I have collected from far corners of the world for more than thirty years. During my last year in New York I realized that Manhattan's famous garment district consists of endless rows of stores selling nothing but fabrics, laces, and every kind of decorative trim imaginable. On occasional shopping excursions I'd wander up and down those streets for hours and bring home bags filled with colourful ribbons, sequins, and lace.

When I travelled to India I resisted the temptation to buy more embroideries. Despite the abundance of homespun textiles, I didn't see many decorative trims and felt relieved that I wouldn't have to choose. Then, wandering through Delhi's Janpath Market on my last day before returning to Vancouver, I came to a dusty road crowded with women selling nothing but fabrics, tapestries, and embroideries recycled from old saris. I can still see the sea of eager dark eyes and great heaps of colourful cloth piled high. Still I resisted, but as I turned to leave, my eye caught the glint of a wide band of magenta sari trim studded with opalescent beads and gold embroidery. Its saturated hues and intricate pattern seemed to capture the essence of my time in India, and I brought it back to Vancouver where it frames the little altar on my desk, an extravagant reminder of India and her Gypsy connections.

I have always loved embroidery and lace. I think it's their impracticality and excessiveness I love. Most often they don't serve any functional purpose but bear exuberant witness to our desire for embellishment and superfluous loveliness. *Superfluous* derives from the Latin for "flowing over." An overflow of beauty spilling into our lives and clothing.

Embroideries betray an unrestrained profusion of feeling so contrary to the cool and streamlined sophistication of high fashion. One dictionary defines embroidery as "elaboration by use of decorative and often fictitious detail, something pleasing or desirable but unimportant." Unimportant to whom, and by what standards? I wonder. I prefer the *Oxford English Dictionary*, where to *embroider* is "to make splendid, dignify." Who wouldn't want to be made splendid?

In *The Story of Craft* I read that during the Middle Ages embroidery was used to identify rank and vocation of the wearer through an elaborate system of patterns and symbols. Even today folk embroideries often use motifs and colours that are significant within the culture, including spirals and mandalas, meanders, triangles, and geometric patterns. These archetypal patterns hint at timeless themes far more interesting than current fashion trends contrived to supersede the previous year's designs. Sometimes I suspect that contemporary fashion—with its rejection of the curves and roundness of womanhood, its anorexic ideal of feminine beauty, and its fleshless and emaciated adolescent models—simply mirrors the starving soul of our youth-obsessed culture.

Years ago I dreamed of a larger-than-life black woman who appeared after a devastating earthquake carrying an exquisite black velvet handbag covered with embroidered trees and flowers, birds and butterflies. Her ample presence comforted me and pulled me back into life, and I was overcome with gratitude when she offered me her handbag as a gesture of love. Embroidery's patterns writ large as a sculptural frieze don't move me; it's the everydayness of wearing them and the way they envelop me in feminine care and love of beauty that count. Embroidery holds time. Subjective time, feminine time, the precious moments of our lives. It's counter-efficient to create those elaborate designs. They take us out of the prosaic realm of mere usefulness into a lyrical experience of time as process. According to Rumi, "The beauty of careful sewing in a shirt is the patience it contains," and, I would add, the loving attention to small detail it reflects.

Marie-Louise von Franz writes, "Everyone who has knitted or done weaving or embroidery knows what an agreeable effect this can have, for you can be quiet and lazy without feeling guilty and also can spin your own thoughts while working. You can relax and follow your fantasy and then get up and say you have done something!" And you *have* done something, of course. Following your fantasy while your hands create something useful and beautiful—what could be better? When I'm sewing I feel quiet and peaceful, as if sewing and knitting and embroidery had their inner correlates, and something were being woven together inside me as well.

Embroidery itself is an archetypal process. To spin a yarn or embroider a tale is to relish detail and add nuance and richness in the telling. The Roma tell their stories with great flourish for the sake of dramatic effect, but also to show off their individual skill. With each telling the story is made new. In the Gordon Boswell Romany Museum in Lincolnshire, embroidery abounds, as if there can never be enough colour and exuberant decoration. The same love of flourish abounds in their music. Irving Brown says Gypsy musicians excel at the art of musical embellishment and "the arabesques and virtuosities, characteristic of much of Gypsy song, provide an outlet for the overflow of feeling." Musical embellishment as an expression of extravagant emotion and vitality.

Doesn't all art adorn and embroider, take an often simple theme and lavish detail and flounce and superfluous beauty on it? What else is the first movement of Mozart's *Piano Sonata in A Major* but an intricate musical embroidery where each variation embellishes the lilting opening theme? Indeed, the musical *arabesque* is a passage or composition with fanciful ornamentation of the melody. Embroidered music.

Is the love of adornment and beauty itself, then, a *gypsy* trait? A wandering off the beaten path of usefulness in favour of a high-spirited romp through what is extravagant and fanciful, and filled with delight?

Musical Body

Once during those years when the *gypsy* went underground, she appeared unexpectedly in the course of a writing workshop. In a voice I barely recognized, she poured herself onto the page.

The frame of her life contains all that is ordered and predictable, tidy and articulate. It is everything else that she yearns for, that fills her imagination and spills through her dreams. Wildness, dark, rich, jeweled gypsy colours and melodies, shameless with urgency and desire, dance beyond the bounds of decency and decorum, so free in range and uninhibited in intensity. Why not fill these days and years with glorious motion?

The living room is unlived in—the thread in her dreams that puzzles and disturbs her. Where is the living being done? Can she continue in measured and graceful strides, kindly attending to all around her and on every side? What is the price being paid? What is the life being missed?

Are there two lives in one here? Perhaps as she moves through serene rooms and days with solicitous attention, her other self is reveling in some dark tavern or thrashing her arms and body in wild ecstasy under stars that illuminate her skin and pierce her flesh.

Who can determine the facts of her life? Is she the careful one, or the volcano of passionate immersion? The facts can't even begin to tell the truth about this woman. It's everything else that creates the full-hearted sound of her story. And maybe she'd rather sing it anyway, liltingly and with great affection, sing the yearning, the secrets, the exultation and the sorrow of her full, full life.

Word and story, speech and sound, music and movement, rhythm and resonance—these have been the pulse of my existence. "You sang before you talked," my parents told me. "You danced before you walked." I don't remember, but I believe it. Those early ecstasies of sound and movement and exuberant galumphing are lodged in my body's memory, and it doesn't take much, even today, to get me going. But even though I studied classical piano for many years and then went on to teach, it's singing that has filled me with ecstasy, as though my body and soul were echoing the harmony of the spheres and I were being sung.

For too many years I have not made music and it calls to me now in my waking life through yearning, and in dreams filled with singing and dancing, mandolins and flutes. My musical body wants to be re-membered, and the more deeply I enter the feminine mysteries of embodiment, the more I recover of that singing, dancing infant. But there is still much more to be reclaimed. Ann Ulanov writes:

> The accented rhythms of music and dance often play an important part in activating the feminine style of consciousness and establishing a consonance between it and the unconscious. We read, for example, of the intoxicating power of music in ancient mystery rites and orgiastic rituals associated with feminine deities. We know that music puts us in touch with our own body rhythms.

Her words ring true and familiar. Though rhythm and resonance are part of our instinctual nature and carry our life force itself, there is so much we don't know about their role in our own bodies, and in the larger social body. In the course of many Body Soul Rhythms Intensives my voice gradually opened up as I began to trust my body's experience. With more breath and spaciousness inside, my voice found its natural vibrato and timbre, and I became conscious of the unique pulse of my energy in the world. Sometimes my body felt frozen in one spot until I was able to connect to a thread of melody, whether inner or outer, that allowed me to move safely and freely through the workshop space.

I think we all carry traces of that first rapturous response to music throughout our lives. Almost every woman I know yearns to sing and dance, whether folk music or opera, belly dance or ballet, and I'm pretty sure this is true of many men too. Most of us long, at times, to escape the prison of our minds and the relentless need to figure things out, and surrender to the sweet, unencumbered rhythms of our bodies.

✐

Curious to discover what Jung said about music, I found fewer than twenty references in the Index to the entire *Collected Works*. Yet in a letter to a friend in 1950, he wrote, "Music expresses in sounds what fantasies and visions express in visual images. [It] represents the movement, development, and transformation of motifs of the collective unconscious." Elsewhere he noted, "Bach talks to God. I am gripped by Bach. But I could slay a man who plays Bach in banal surroundings." Strong words indeed, and certainly not those of a man indifferent to music!

There are apocryphal stories about Jung's relationship with music, but the only published account I've come across was written by Margaret Tilly, a concert pianist Jung invited to his home in Küsnacht in 1956 to demonstrate her work with music therapy. What she showed Jung must have affected him deeply, for she quotes him as saying:

> This opens up whole new avenues of research I'd never even dreamed of. Because of what you've shown me this afternoon— not just what you've said, but what I have actually felt and experienced—I feel that from now on music should be an essential part of every analysis. This reaches the deep archetypal material that we can only sometimes reach in our analytical work with patients. This is most remarkable.

I've often wondered what Margaret Tilly did that impressed Jung so greatly that he wanted to include music in his own work with patients. Did she invite him to sing along with the music and feel how it resonated in his body? Ask him to track his inner images and responses as he listened? What could have prompted Jung to make such a dramatic statement?

But I'm not surprised by his response. During my Authentic Movement sessions in Zürich, there came a time when I needed music, and the work became something else. Moving to music gave me a richer experience of the images in my dreams than talking about them. Particular music allowed me to explore emotions and archetypal currents alive in me and those in turn gave new shapes and colours to my movement explorations.

One afternoon just before the end of term and my return to Vancouver, I moved to a song from Loreena McKennitt's *An Ancient Muse* album. I danced my experience of liminality, of leaving Zürich and walking down the long hallway in Vancouver International Airport toward the beautiful waiting body of my husband. While dancing I was aware of overlapping images and experiences, as if I'd stepped into mythic time. As the music began, quietly and slowly at first and then picking up increasing energy and rhythm, my body unfurled and shaped itself in response. With half-closed eyes I moved through the room, feeling an ancient and timeless tide of yearning, joy, and sorrow pass through me. Following the session I wrote in my journal:

> The haunting sonorities come into me, fluid and plaintive plunking of strings, I am drifting and lost. Suddenly her gorgeous voice comes in and I am at home in the music. I twirl and sway through the room and my body expands—there is so much space—feel myself scoop up round energy of the earth, sense my arms curving, giving shape to my longing. I feel ecstatic and filled with grief. I want to weep. I lose track of time, feel myself voluptuous and whole.
>
> Then the music ends and my body slowly comes to rest on the sofa at the far end of the room. Eileen is quiet and when I open my eyes, she comes and sits down beside me. There is something mysterious about the dance, she says, a "beautiful roundness" in my gestures. She senses there's a story and wonders what it might be. I feel myself moving between two countries and lives, I tell her.

"Let your body become the music," Marion Woodman writes. "Let her sing." And in that safe space and mythic time, my body becomes the music, and I dance the yearning and the secrets, the exultation and the sorrow of my full, full life.

WINTER MUSIC

Years ago I was listening to a Yiddish melody with my stepson's family in Geneva, when four-year-old Hannah commented mournfully, "That sounds like winter music." Klezmer shares common roots and influences with Roma music and frequently also its plaintive minor key sound. Given the centuries of persecution and suffering endured by the Roma, their music is surely a kind of "winter music," with the comfortless cold and dark this suggests. In Gypsy music—which encompasses an enormous variety of music made by Roma throughout the world—ecstasy and agony are never far apart. Often they're almost indistinguishable.

Music has saved my life. Symbolically, to be sure, but perhaps literally as well. In the emotional turbulence of my childhood, playing our old upright Bell piano gave me a sense of order and stability, and a way to ground myself. When the barely suppressed sorrow I sometimes felt at home threatened to overwhelm me, I found solace in the serene flow of Bach's *Two- and Three-Part Piano Inventions* and my LP recordings of the *Brandenburg Concertos* and the *Christmas Oratorio*. Music was my refuge.

I am in the eighth grade at A.D. Rundle Junior Secondary High School. As I wander down the main hall from my homeroom to my locker, those three boys are standing together at my left, talking. I hope desperately that they will let me pass by without comment but as I walk past them, they look at me and smirk. One of them, probably Jim Snyder, pasty-faced and full of nasty bravado, makes some snide remark about my weight. I pretend I don't hear him and keep walking but it cuts me to the quick. I know Gary Braun hates me because I am smart and the teachers like me, and because I am friends with his younger sister, Karen, a budding piano prodigy and local star. I also know that his parents won't leave the two of them alone at home together because they fear he might hurt her. Gary is a good-looking boy and the girls would like him if he weren't so self-conscious and downright mean. He and his two buddies are the bane of my existence. I never know when I will run into them in the hall and feel their scornful derision heaped upon my unhappily bespectacled thirteen-year-old self. Just seeing them makes me want to erase myself. It isn't very Christian of me but I would like to kill all three of them with one poisonous glance, knock them full onto the floor so they can never again torment me in the hallways of my school or the streets of downtown Chilliwack.

At my full height of five feet four inches and weighing 135 pounds I am slightly round in the hips and certainly not fat, but in the mirror of their contempt I feel disgusting to myself. I resolve to shed twenty pounds so that I will never again be vulnerable to their cutting comments. I can't even imagine wanting to date a boy although I am in love with any number of my teachers, men and women alike. I just want to walk down the hallway without the threat of humiliation and exposure. Instead of losing weight, I put on twenty pounds that year and then I really do look plump.

The Gary Braun trio continues to haunt my junior high school existence, but a part of me remains inviolate and knows this too will pass. My life at home is rocky but my love of music and choir teacher, Mr. Vincent from Australia, and a fragile but stubborn sense that despite all outer evidence I am worth something, carry me through those years. I feel myself reviled, outcast, even abused at times. Secretly I hope that there is also something special about me that I can't see yet, although I am not convinced of this and have no idea of what it might possibly be. Is this when the *gypsy* energy really blossoms in me?

And always, I make music. Even as a babe, my parents tell me, I pulled myself up on the old hi-fi system and threw my arms around it in ecstasy at the sounds of the music pouring out of that sturdy rectangular box.

When I begin school I beg for piano lessons like my older cousin Annette, and when my parents finally buy a used Bell piano in the third grade and I start taking lessons with Miss Regehr, I am in heaven. The finger exercises she wants me to do are boring and I am too impatient to practise my scales, but I save up my weekly allowance and birthday money and buy piano music, and, later, LP records, like someone starved for refuge and beauty.

Week after week I resist the practice routines Miss Regehr neatly records in the small lined notebook I bring to my lesson every Saturday morning. Instead, I roam through all the extra music I've purchased at MacAlpine's Music Store on Yale Street with my savings. I spend hours after school and on Saturday afternoons browsing through their collection and voraciously sight-read my way through the music I buy until a particular theme or bit of melody catches my fancy. Sometimes I play for hours, and Miss Regehr finds it mysterious that the exercises and pieces of music she assigns to me don't improve from one week to the next. Not given to praise, she tells me during my final lesson ten years later, "You are very musical, you know. If only you'd worked a little harder, you could have been one of my best students, even better than your cousin Annette. But she worked harder."

I am genuinely shocked. Miss Regehr is also Karen Braun's teacher so I know this means a lot. Every week she holds Karen up as an example of brilliant talent and informs me of her latest musical conquests. I've always felt I was in the hoi polloi of her students, among the humdrum plodding middle class; I had no idea she thought I had real talent. I haven't even told her I've been composing my own music for years or that a song of mine won first place in the *Back to the Bible* radio contest and was performed by their resident choir for many Sunday mornings running. I'm not sure why not. Maybe I fear she'll top it by telling me Karen Braun has composed a symphony, just as she topped the Amway fine English soaps I bought her for Christmas with my babysitting money the year before by showing me the stunning amethyst ring Karen's parents had just given her. Or maybe I just want it to be my private domain, unsullied by comparison with Karen's achievements, and not subject to Miss Regehr's approval. (I continued improvising at the piano for years, and realized only recently that all those plaintive melodies follow the Phrygian Gypsy scale I would learn of decades later. At the time, their haunting strains were simply the music I carried inside me. My own "winter music.")

After Annette moves to another town with her parents I become the default church pianist, choir accompanist, and occasional organist, although I am never very good with the foot pedals. I also play my father's accordion. By ninth grade I'm singing in the school choir along with Karen Braun, who has perfect pitch and a ringing soprano voice, stronger and surer than my own. Despite her stunning talent it's me Mr. Vincent seems to favour, and I feel seen at last. Singing my heart out, my eyes glued to his lean, expressive face, I have found a refuge. With my friends Doris on my right and Grace on my left, and a room full of singing girls around me, I am safe from that unmusical male trio's nasty attentions, free to bask in the approval of Mr. Vincent, who regards Karen, Doris, and me as the most gifted of the bunch and as leaders of the choir.

Then I move on to senior high school and Mr. Vincent moves back to Melbourne. The new choir teacher doesn't even come close in terms of musicality or charisma. The summer before we graduate, Doris and I join the other local high school's choir and band on a summer tour through Europe. Doris has moved on to play clarinet in the band but her prickly younger sister, Monica, and I are stuck in the alto section of the choir. The conductor, Mr. Bryant, is short of second altos and knows we read music well enough to fill the gap.

We travel through eight countries in a month, and despite the fact that I cannot ride ten miles on a straight highway at home without getting carsick, I am one of the few to sail over the Swiss Alps in our chartered bus with nary a problem but for the pimples that plague us all from drinking too much Coke. Given that my family has never travelled farther from home than a three-day train trip to Cleveland, Ohio, when I was five years old (I was excused from a second trip two years later because I'd been so violently ill on the train), this is no small thing. And perhaps this is the real start of my love of travel, and of my connection of travel with music. World music. Roaming music. Roma music.

Music is my spiritual home wherever I go, the sound of Bach, my soul's sanctuary. In the endless church services I sit through as chief church musician, with their congregational singing of "Onward, Christian Soldiers" and "The Old Rugged Cross," it's the serene grace of the occasional Bach chorale that awakens in me a sure sense of transcendence, of something beautiful beyond the narrow constrictions of my present circumstances. Wherever there is music I am no stranger, but part of a greater whole whose shared centre is the heart of the Mystery into which the music has led us all.

✆

"There is no gypsy existence without music," a Gypsy musician tells Garth Cartwright. "We have such a heavy life and if we didn't have the music we would kill ourselves. The music is our medicine." Another one adds, "Music is the only and cheapest entertainment of poor people. You can turn on the radio and forget hunger."

For the Roma, music has served as a survival strategy. Many songs tell stories of the persecution and endless hardships they have endured. In the concentration camps of World War II where they were forced to provide music to entertain the guards but forbidden to sing for themselves, they hummed quietly and changed the song lyrics to reflect their resistance to their desperate situation.

Winter music, indeed.

In centuries past, I read, Gypsies used music in their traditional folk medicine and healing spells, where soothing songs were believed to be part of the cure. Charles Godfrey Leland tells us the Roma believed music had the power to distract witches from their evil deeds because of their attraction to the melody. In our own time clinical studies show that listening to certain kinds of music—classical, Celtic, and Indian ragas—alleviates suffering, eases pain and anxiety, and lowers blood pressure. Music therapy has proven to have dramatic results in the treatment of illness and disease, such as epilepsy and cancer, high blood pressure and heart disease, autism and mood disorders. As Jung discovered, music has the potential to affect our emotions in a profound and immediate way and to put us in touch with the deep currents of our psychic lives. It's no surprise, then, that it can help heal both physical and psychological distress. "Sing! You'll see Sorrow flee," says an old Spanish proverb.

But it's always the darker music—*winter music*—that evokes the *gypsy* in my soul. The life of the great Russian poet Anna Akhmatova, tormented witness to the long Stalinist reign of terror, was surely one long winter. She captures its dark radiance in "Listening to Singing," and I end this vignette with her words.

A woman's voice, like the wind, rushes—
Nocturnal it seems, moist and black,
And as it flies, whatever it brushes
Changes and will not change back.

Its diamond-shine comes to bathe and bless,
Things are draped in a silver light,
It rustles its suggestive dress,
Woven of fantasy, silken and bright.
And the power that propels the enchanted
Voice displays such hidden might,
It's as if the grave were not ahead,
But mysterious stairs beginning their flight.

Five Singing Lessons

While writing an essay on Kali and the Black Madonna during my studies in Zürich I became aware of an old and painfully familiar emotional complex that pushed me to read more, research more, and prove that I really did know something about the topic. All the while, another part of me just wanted to "sing" the essay, just as I had "danced" my earlier essay on the *gypsy*. The need to "know something" took the pleasure out of this process, which otherwise felt like a treasure hunt, each insight and intuition taking me deeper into a numinous mystery alive in my depths. When I could relax and allow myself to follow those vibrant clues, I felt engaged in *lila*, in divine and spontaneous play. But when I reminded myself that I was preparing for an exam, my delight dissipated and my heart felt heavy. Following a day of inner turmoil, I had a dream.

May 9, 2007.

Last night I asked for a dream with some insight into this sense of dread, and this morning I woke up with the Phrygian scale, mournful and exotic, echoing in my inner ear. As the dream ends, I am singing softly and I can hear my own voice, deep and rich and full of resonance, begin to emerge. Here is the dream.

I am in conductor Bruce Pullan's study for a voice lesson. He is youthful and radiant, and I wonder if he remembers me. He says I will need five singing lessons and I wonder how he can be so precise without having heard me sing. I think I might need more than that.

The room is narrow and cluttered, filled with books and music scores. Two long desks that look like pianos are heaped high with printed materials in opposite corners of the room. Bruce plays a scale on one of them and tells me to sing it to "la la la." It sounds foreign to my ear and I ask him if it is the Phrygian scale. He says he doesn't know, but I seem to recognize it.

Then he takes me into an adjacent room that is large and square, with much more space. We circle slowly around the room together and I'm supposed to sing the scale. I begin hesitantly and want to tell him that I need a few minutes to relax so that the complex in my throat can subside. I begin to sing the scale again and this time it's a little louder and surer. As I come down the scale I can hear the resonance and vibrato in my voice. I want Bruce to hear my authentic voice so he knows what he is working with. I feel that I am on my way now.

I wept as I recorded the dream in my journal because it mirrored my emotional state at the time but also my lifelong passions. The desk that is also a piano, suggesting that writing and music are one (just as storytelling and song are, for the Roma). Piano *key*board. Computer *key*board. In both, the musical key is *gypsy*, and *gypsy* is key to my soul. The need for a larger space in order to move freely, and the slow, counter-clockwise, mandalic circling (into the unconscious) around a square room, accompanied by an experienced singing teacher. The encouragement to *sing* my essay and five exams according to the Gypsy scale.

And the figure of Bruce Pullan, the most brilliant choral conductor and voice teacher I have worked with, as vital in the dream as he was when I sang in the Vancouver Bach Choir years ago and he urged me to pursue a career as a singer. Appearing here as a supportive masculine presence who invites me to move freely and take all the space I need, and who knows the scale best suited to my voice, even without being able to name it.

Five singing lessons to strengthen my voice in the midst of taking five exams, with no clear idea of whether I will continue in this Jungian training program. The archetypal significance of five as quintessence, from *quinta essentia*. According to Marie-Louise von Franz, the number five is related to the philosopher's stone of medieval alchemy, which symbolizes the wholeness within us and represents "the centered four, the most refined, spiritually imaginable unity of the four elements." In China, the number five stands for the element of the earth that carries and grounds us in life and "the principle of k'un, the expanding feminine, which brings the spirit into material and spatial manifestation." This seemed especially relevant given my desire to bring what I was learning in my Jungian studies into my own life and teaching as fully as possible.

The Phrygian scale, which consists of the piano's white notes from E to E, has an exotic and slightly mournful sound to Western ears, more readily attuned to the upbeat resilience of the major modes. I've always loved the key of E major for its joyful hot-pink exuberance but realized recently that much of my favourite music is actually based on the more melancholy Phrygian scale. Even my youthful attempts at composing music had followed suit; the melodies were always plaintive.

This dream released me from the grip of the exam complex. It restored the joy of exploration and discovery and gave me confidence that I could "sing" the exams in the *gypsy* register authentic to my voice. When I walked into the exam room a few weeks later, I brought all of me—intellect, imagination, emotion—to bear in answering the examiners' questions, and when it was over, I knew I had *sung* my exams.

I've always loved Marie-Louise von Franz's description of how Jung worked with his own dreams. "Jung did not interpret his dreams by immediately forming a clear idea of what they meant," she writes. "Instead, he carried them around within himself, lived with them inwardly, as it were, and asked questions of them. If he came across something in a book or in an outer experience which reminded him of a dream image, he would add it to that image, so to speak, so that a fabric of ideas developed, with a constantly increasing richness."

I picture Jung going about his daily work alert to associations and when he happens across one, tucking it quietly into his elegant Swiss trouser pockets until they are stuffed full with meaning. That's how I carry this dream with me, its images alive in me as I write. I find myself asking: How can I make music as I sit at my desk? How can I sing this book?

Song is the essential feminine mode of communication, writes Hélène Cixous. "In feminine speech, as in writing, there never stops reverberating something that, having once passed through us, having imperceptibly and deeply touched us, still has the power to affect us—song, the first music of the voice of love, which every woman keeps alive....Within each woman the first, nameless love is singing." Words arise out of bodies and resonate between bodies, and that resonance is as important a connector as their content. Visceral impact precedes abstract signification. When did *singing* become *signing*? Here again, the memory of speech as song, and the invitation to allow our spoken and written words to summon feeling and magic into the space between us. To be incantatory. *Incantation* comes from "to sing into, or upon." What would it be like to *sing into* each other?

For the Roma, the most intimate form of song is the *lovara*, a passionate heart-and-soul song that reveals the raw essence of their lives. Perhaps it's what those five singing lessons are teaching me—to sing my own essence, my own *lovara*, into the world.

When, if not now?

You Are Flamenco

O body swayed to music, O brightening glance,
How can we know the dancer from the dance?

—W.B. Yeats

Flamboyant and decisive gestures, the ardent stance and proud turn of the head, tempestuous footwork that roots the moving body firmly on the ground—none of it tentative or moderate. The dance of flamenco is fiery, full-bodied, and impetuous. But flamenco is not just dance. It's an all-encompassing philosophy and way of life involving emotional extremes that seem larger than life to our more sedate cultural temperament. Characterized by forceful, often improvised rhythm and movement, flamenco is life lived on the edge between ecstasy and anguish, with little in between. As one Roma musician explains, "You don't do flamenco. You don't play flamenco. You don't sing flamenco. You *are* flamenco."

It all began in the rich melting pot of Jewish, Islamic, and Gypsy cultures in Spain, during the Inquisition. "From the common life of these persecuted peoples appeared the first semblances of flamenco, as we know it," I read in the classic *The Art of Flamenco*, currently in its forty-third edition. "Muslim, Jewish, Indian and Christian religious and folk music blended, developing over the years into a musical form clearly sophisticated in many ways, yet developed at a primitive level by an outcast society." And so it has continued, for flamenco has always been the music and dance of outcasts. The origin of the word *flamenco* has been debated but the most convincing explanation suggests it derives from the Arabic *felag/mengu*, or "fugitive peasant," the term used to describe those persecuted peoples who fled to the mountains during the Inquisition. Eventually the term became identified with their music as well.

In flamenco—whether song, dance, or guitar music—the artist's capacity to convey intense emotion is far more important than technical brilliance. Most important of all is the elusive presence of *duende*, the electrifying experience of divine or demonic inspiration. The values of flamenco—impassioned expression, heat, instinct, creative improvisation, and contempt for materialism—couldn't be more at odds with those of modern civilization, with its emphasis on cool, sleek sophistication. In Carlos Saura's film *Flamenco* (1995), bodies and voices are charged with fierce and focussed energy. Passion and pride, and plenty of attitude. The audacious sounds and proud gestures proclaim, "This is who I am—take it or leave it." And who wouldn't take it? Flamenco is *duende* embodied. Not surprising, given that it began among people too poor to buy musical instruments, people who snapped their fingers, clapped their hands, stamped their feet, and sang and danced the rhythms of their marginal lives. Their passion for flamenco was surely a survival strategy for *Gitanos*, or Spanish Gypsies. The persecution endured by Roma over a thousand years was not widely documented but their music carried the knowledge, and their bodies must have remembered it.

For me, too, dance enabled life. There was a time during my adolescence when I often stayed home to dance on Friday nights while everyone else in my family was out grocery shopping. I must have been thirteen or fourteen years old. As soon as our trusty black-and-white Ford disappeared down the road, I changed into the sleeveless cherry-red dress that my grandmother and I had sewn together. It was simply cut, and allowed me to move without constraint. I drew the curtains so no one would see me and I wouldn't have to look at my own reflection in the window glass. Then I stacked my favourite LP records on the hi-fi record player and danced to Mozart and Bach, Beethoven and Chopin.

My body yearned to be graceful and free and loved. I danced until grief overcame me, a bottomless sadness that I didn't understand. Then I collapsed on the sofa and sobbed my heart out, and got up and danced some more. I made-believe I was a ballerina, that my dancing was real and beautiful, that what I was doing somehow mattered. Keeping one eye on the clock, I made sure to splash cold water on my face before my family returned, wondering if anyone would notice I'd been crying. No one ever did.

It had the quality of a ritual. I know now that I was releasing powerful emotions through my dancing, but at the time I had no idea what was happening. Self-conscious and fearful of ridicule, I never told anyone about those Friday nights, and I never understood why my secret dancing had such a powerful hold on me. Until I read Marion Woodman's books. Then I realized that, without even knowing it, I had been countering the unhappiness I sensed within my family and my own terrible self-loathing. Dancing was seen as sinful in the German Baptist Church, but my body knew better. I danced my anguish and longing for freedom and beauty, and expressed emotion that might otherwise have destroyed me.

"Dance is archetypal imagery," Woodman writes. "The steady beat activates the central nervous system that in turn releases the healing power of the instinctual unconscious, often accompanied by a healing image or voice."

"You are a dancer," said a voice deep inside me. "You will survive."

"Few modern women know anything about 'becoming the dance,'" Woodman continues. "To give themselves up to their emotions and the music and thus experience their own corresponding depths terrifies them. That leap into the unconscious, however, is the very link that could connect them to the life force." Looking back now, I love that young girl for dancing her own survival. Her body, my body, expressed its truth, and somehow she knew enough to listen. Even in the midst of anguish, my young soul found a way to claim her own life.

I was in my early twenties when I danced in public for the first time. The man I was dating had invited me to the Psychology Department's graduation banquet to celebrate his newly acquired bachelor's degree. When the band began to play after dinner I longed to get up and dance but it felt like an enormous risk. As the adrenalin raced through my body I told myself I would watch from the sidelines. Perhaps next time I would get up and dance. Then Carl took my hand and led me to a far corner of the dance floor where we were hidden from onlookers. We started to dance and I was in ecstasy. Not an ounce of fear as I dipped and swayed, twirled and spun. I had found my element, and we danced the whole evening, until suddenly I saw we were the last ones left on the dance floor.

"You've come a long way tonight," Carl laughed, as I reluctantly sat down when the music stopped. In my altered state I half expected the German Baptist police to arrest me, but there was no going back. I was a woman who danced. In public. I was a dancer. I *was* flamenco.

DEEP SONG

In 1929, the Spanish poet Federico García Lorca delivered a passionate lecture on a group of Andalusian folk songs with roots in the ancient musical traditions of India. *Cante jondo*, or "deep song," began among persecuted peoples who fled into the mountains during the Spanish Inquisition in the fifteenth century, blending elements of Arabic, Sephardic, Byzantine, and Gypsy music with the native folk songs of the region. The heart and soul of flamenco, *deep song* is "imbued with the mysterious color of primordial ages," and Lorca described it as "a stammer, a wavering emission of the voice that makes the tightly closed flowers of the semi-tones blossom into a thousand petals." He credited Spanish Gypsies for *deep song*, for "the building of these lyrical channels through which all the pain, all the ritual gestures of the race can escape."

Like various forms of Indian *raga* (from the Sanskrit *Raag*, meaning "red," "colour," "beauty," and "melody"), each linked with a particular emotion and time of day, there are countless styles of *deep song*, each with its own mood, theme, and verse form. During the 1920s, an early student and scholar of the art observed that the *soleá* or *soleares* expresses passionate love and conveys sadness but not resignation, while the *martinete* deals with the sorrows of prisoners, and the *siguiriya gitana* has the greatest depth of expression and conveys "the essence of human feeling purified by suffering." All styles of *deep song* share a primal power and emotiveness that evoke both the personal dimension of existence and our collective human condition. Lorca writes, "The true poems of deep song belong to no one—they float in the wind like golden thistledown, and each generation dresses them in a different color and passes them on to the next."

The tradition of deep song has also had a far-reaching influence on composers such as Glinka, Rimsky-Korsakov, and Debussy, along with Albéniz and Manuel de Falla in Spain and many others as well. "It comes from remote races and crosses the graveyard of the years and the frond of parched winds. It comes from the first sob and the first kiss," says Lorca. From his description it's clear that deep song is archetypal music, a timeless, lyrical channel for the experience of sorrow, loss, and love. That his own poetry carries this yearning quality in spades is evident in these lines from his "Ballad of the Spanish Civil Guard."

> Oh city of the gypsies!
> Corners hung with banners.
> The moon and the pumpkins,
> and cherries in preserve.
> Oh city of the gypsies!
> Who could see and not remember you?
> City of musk and sorrow.

The poem's haunting imagery resonates in our souls even if we have never been anywhere near Seville or the other Gypsy cities of southern Spain.

Every era has its own *cantaores* or singers of *deep song* who express the blood truths of that time and place. For the children of the sixties there are many, among them Joan Baez, Bob Dylan, Joni Mitchell, Simon and Garfunkel, and above all Leonard Cohen, whose poetry and song over half a century carried the idealistic passion and world-weariness of an entire generation, and who rose like a phoenix from the ashes of his embezzled fortunes to create himself anew just about the time we feared we'd seen the last of him. His most loved songs like "Hallelujah" and "Dance Me to the End of Love" have become the *deep song* of our time, reflecting the yearning hopes and self-ironizing melancholy of millions. Like Joan Baez, Leonard Cohen adapted Lorca's poems into his music, even naming his daughter after the great Spanish poet.

In his acceptance speech for the 2011 Prince of Asturias Award for Literature in Spain, Leonard Cohen told the story of how an unknown Spanish guitar player he encountered in a park near his childhood home in Montreal taught him the basic flamenco chord progression. "It was those six chords, it was that guitar pattern that has been the basis of all my songs and all my music," he told the clearly enthralled Spanish audience. "Now you will begin to understand the dimensions of the gratitude I have for this country."

The Spanish Gypsy influence was palpable in Leonard Cohen's concert performance, as I saw for myself in 2013. From his characteristic easy lope onto the stage to the last of his half-dozen encores, the Gypsy tonalities were unmistakable. It seems to me that we love Leonard Cohen because he never feared the sombre notes of *deep song*; his music mirrors the soul's dark ground to us and we hear our deepest longings echoed there. Even to the title track of his final album, *You Want It Darker*, with its sombre foreshadowing of his own death a few weeks after its release, and the eerie premonition of what was to be unleashed on the world just a few days after that during the fateful US presidential election.

The first time I came across a reference to *deep song* I was riveted, as if it had come to me in a dream. For weeks I spun fantasies of a mysterious unknown music that encompassed all the dimensions of human experience and invoked the souls of the ancestors. What gave it its depth? I wondered. Was it the subject matter? Its emotional intensity? Layers of ancestral experience? A mystery at the heart and soul of a culture? What was the "song beneath the song" suggested by *deep song*?

And what would the *deep song* of my own life be? I wondered. Would it echo the dark suffering of past generations? Of ancestors forced to flee across the ever-shifting borders of central Europe in search of menial work and food? Of families ravaged by endless wars, and parents who had lost one child after another to starvation and disease? Would its cadence and melody carry the stifled weeping of my grandparents, and theirs?

Deep Song in Three Stanzas

I.

Persephone, dark sister of my soul. You, whom I love and fear, who come to me as wise woman and witch, and show me my own endarkenment more clearly than I dare to know it. Are you the beginning, or the end? The end, or the beginning?

Gladly would I roam and dance with Kore all my days, blessed sunlight on my animal body, merry laughter of my maiden companions ringing through the air as we run through fields filled with flowers, never doubting that spring is everlasting.

But the narcissus calls me to another realm. A nether realm.

What is this fall from Motherlove into dark depths of unknown, alien Otherness? All lightness fled from my limbs, I sink into the Underworld. Gravity pulls me, compels me down into my own dark weight, where I find—not sunlight—but the merest glimpse of lunar rays reflecting off the face of water I have never seen before. The deepest, stillest pool of water I have ever known. What is this water? How deep is it, and what is hidden there? Will I drown in its fearsome depths, or be baptized into new life?

A never-ending span of timeless time flows through me.

Who am I here? A daughter lost to earth above, but perhaps not only that. The Otherness so strange at first comes into me, and I am shocked to find that Here is also Home.

II.

I was born in Hades. The earth cracked open under my mother's feet and she plunged into bottomless despair when she lost her own mother, Pauline, unexpectedly and far too soon. Not yet forty-four, and never to be my grandmother.

From 1950 to 1952, Pauline wrote letters full of love and longing to her eldest daughter, Lilli, my mother, who had been sent against her will at age nineteen to far-off Canada to earn money so that her mother, father, two younger sisters, and brother could join her there. My mother, sick with yearning for Pauline, worked as a chambermaid in a language she did not know and saved every penny for her family's passage, living only for their joyful reunion.

There would be no joyful reunion.

Pauline died in the spring of 1952, on the train carrying the family and their meagre possessions to Hamburg, Germany, to board the ship that was to bring them to Canada and into my mother's aching arms. They turned back to bury her instead, and it was seven more years before Lilli saw her father and younger siblings again. Seven endless years.

I was conceived not long after Pauline's death and drank my mother's bitter tears and bottomless grief with her milk. An infant Persephone, Hades was my native land; a raging, sorrowful Demeter my mother. Ungrandmothered, I carried my mother's unanswerable loss in blood and bone, felt her terrible yearning permeate my cells and reach into my soul.

III.

Persephone, I never wore pastels. As your handmaiden, it was richer stains of colour that I sought. The mystery of indigo, purple passion and the fiery heat of red, the emerald of green and obsidian depths of black. Magenta, burgundy, vermilion. Sienna, amber, saffron. Cerulean, lavender, scarlet. Words as sumptuous as their colours.

Your colours, Persephone. Vibrant with longing and radiant with depth, I carried You inside me all along. I know that now.

Life goes on. We dance the Dance of Ages, ceaseless flow of heartbreak and desire, abandonment and joy.

Persephone. I meet you once again—so new, and so familiar.

You, my darker, wiser Sister.

Keeper of the Mysteries. Taproot of my life.

All my life I have loved Pauline. In the handful of black-and-white photographs that survived she looks much older than her years, worn out by the endless demands of caring for four children in a two-room shed with dirt floors, by illness and the grief of two stillborn baby boys, and by a difficult and abusive marriage. Years ago she came to me at night. In the dream I lay my head in her lap, threw my arms around her, and told her how sorry I was for all the suffering she'd endured during her brief lifetime. She didn't speak, but seemed serene and pleased. When I told my mother about the dream we both wept.

Not long after that, my other grandmother, Olga, also came to me in a dream. "I don't know why, but every time I'm with you, I can cry," she said in German, looking relieved, even happy. Oma had lost five of her eight children, including four little girls. I'd always known about Johann, Lydia, and Emma, but when I learned about the two stillborn baby girls, I wept for my grandmother's broken heart, and for the depth and breadth of sorrow in my motherline.

There was little time for grief in the lives of my parents and grandparents. Over the years I have felt the dark weight of their stifled rage and anguish, accepted during their lifetimes as the inscrutable will of God, and carried in their bodies as illness, depression, and killer disease. "No one is ever lost without consequence to others," writes Susan Griffin. "Loss and longing move from body to body, expressed in one place as sorrow, in another as illness, then as destruction, and everywhere as desire."

I want to sing the lost lives of mothers and daughters and cherished grandmothers known only in dreams. Give voice to those precious children whose early deaths were lodged as unrelenting longing in their parents' grieving hearts and bodies. As I sing, may the eros and creativity held captive by sorrow's leaden thrall through generations blossom into a thousand fragrant petals. Move from body to body, and be expressed in one place as healing, in another as laughter, then as creation, and everywhere as joy.

✑

We all have *deep songs* of ancestral loss. I know that mine belongs to a larger chorus of sorrow and resilience throughout generations and centuries. In 2012 my mother died unexpectedly, following what was to have been a routine biopsy. Sixty years after Pauline's death, we buried Lilli on her mother's birthday, June 16.

✑

My mother never kept a journal. She did not understand my compulsion to fill notebook after notebook with my own thoughts and feelings from the time I was eleven years old and read *The Diary of Anne Frank* in school. All these years later I'm still writing and my journal now spans close to two hundred volumes. Whose story am I trying to capture on those thousands and thousands of pages? Whose voice am I hoping to hear?

Perhaps my mother's journals were her fabrics, carefully selected through the years and stacked neatly in her chest of drawers and in the cedar chest my father had built for her shortly after they were married. Cottons and linens, polyesters and silks, rayons and velvets. The inside of the chest smelled of mothballs she'd tucked into thick bolts of wool her father brought from a textile factory in Cleveland many years earlier. I imagine every piece of fabric as a journal entry and wonder what story it wants to tell.

For all her German Baptist loyalties, my mother had a rebellious streak and her hungry eyes, like mine, were drawn to anything bright and floral. Between us we amassed mountains of fabric, a disproportionate amount of it with red, mauve, and purple flowers against a black background. She was partial to green and blue too, but in the end, purple and mauve usually won out. I think she had a *gypsy* streak in her.

Neither of us was an enthusiastic seamstress but for years it seemed we couldn't stop buying textiles, as though their vibrant beauty could redeem the drab poverty of my mother's childhood in wartime Germany and the many sorrowful losses that followed. As though those bright, rich colours and textures might restore her to a future with a happier trajectory, a future in which her own mother lived long enough to taste the comfort and abundance she'd never known during her brief lifetime, and which we now enjoyed. As though we could create an alternate version of the story wherein Pauline survives the fateful train journey that plunged my mother into a black hole of grief and despair from which she never really recovered.

❧

When my mother died she left behind a slender packet of faded green airmail letters that Pauline had sent her following her reluctant immigration to Canada after the war. They're all I have of Pauline—those parchment-thin, fragile letters, the handwriting stark and angular like their lives in postwar Germany, no time or space for flourish or the gentle mercy of curves. They are written in the old Gothic German script and the few phrases that I can decipher consist mostly of godly encouragement and support. "My dear Lilli, we pray for you every day, and long to see you soon," and "Have faith that our loving heavenly Father will watch over us until we are together again."

But Pauline's longing for her daughter is thinly veiled. I imagine I can feel her love and tenderness saturating the space between the narrow lines and upright words, welling out among her frequent appeals to God's goodness and mercy. Did she kiss the letters before entrusting them to the postman in the little village in central Germany where they ended up after the war? Did she weep and marvel to think that in a week or two the flimsy sheet of paper would arrive into the eager hands of her beloved oldest daughter, an inconceivable half world away? Did my mother stroke those precious letters and press them gently against her cheek like a caress spanning the thousands of miles between them? Trace the outline of her name on the envelope with her fingertips, overwhelmed with longing for her *Muttchen*? "I was always Mama's girl," she told me. "Ella was Papa's girl."

There are letters from her sister too. Ella describes learning to type and her letters are easier to read. On February 10, 1950, she writes, "Dearest Lilli, after much longing we finally received your dear letter with great joy. Everyone in our youth group asks about you and wants to know how you are doing. Please write to me soon because I miss you terribly and I live in hopes that we will be together again before long. Please, try to make it as soon as possible. Your loving sister, Ella."

Pauline and Ella both express gratitude for the letters my mother sent them, so I know there was a time when she did write, and I am envious. What became of those letters—the only evidence that my mother ever wrote about her life?

Once, she showed me a slightly beaten, dog-eared black notebook her parents had given her decades earlier. It was empty except for her name, *Lilli Fender*, in the top right corner of the first page, and I wondered what they'd imagined she might write in it, but she didn't know. When I asked if I could have it she said yes, and seemed surprised that I would want it. I carried that notebook with me for years but I couldn't write in it. Although it was empty it seemed to hold the unwritten story of my mother's broken heart, the weight of which forbade any lesser concerns I might have recorded there. Some years ago I gave it back to her but now that she too is gone, I would like to have it back.

✐

"Every mother contains her daughter in herself and every daughter her mother, and every woman extends backwards into her mother and forward into her daughter," Jung wrote.

The conscious experience of these ties produces the feeling that her life is spread out over generations [and] this leads to a restoration or *apocatastasis* of the lives of her ancestors, who now, through the bridge of the momentary individual, pass down into the generations of the future. An experience of this kind gives the individual a place and a meaning in the life of the generations, so that all unnecessary obstacles are cleared out of the way of the life-stream that is to flow through her.

I was already present in my mother's unborn body inside Pauline's womb. Do men feel this passionate bodily link, this cellular connection with their mothers? Or is it passed down through the motherline in the way our bodies hold eggs within eggs, like Russian matryoshka dolls nestled inside each other, each generation of women holding the next tightly enclosed within itself like a secret still to be disclosed?

Among the prayers for God's guidance and protection in the aching uncertainties of their lives, it's everything I can't read and everything that Pauline didn't say in her letters to my mother that haunts me. I know so little of her life beyond the fact that she was always sickly and sustained six pregnancies that resulted in four living children. I am the eldest daughter of the eldest daughter of an eldest daughter, and beyond that, little is known to me about my motherline.

I was born the year after Pauline died. Deep in shock and grief, my mother spent her twenty-third birthday in terrified and lonely labour, trying to push out a reluctant earthling.

"You didn't want to be born," she told me. "They put me in a small room on my own and I pushed and pushed, but you didn't want to move down the birth canal."

"I knew where I had it good," I teased her. "Why would I want to leave?"

What remains of Pauline are the letters. About forty of them. A tablecloth that she sent my mother as an engagement present, and a few surviving pieces of a simple Bohemian coffee service that my mother's parents gave her as a wedding gift. That was what my mother had of Pauline in the New World.

❧

Yearning encroaches. When I give it space, it spreads and expands, grows larger and wider, and I feel the true dimensions of my longing.

Yearning seduces. Pulls me out of the sunlit present and plunges me into memories of untold suffering and loss, and I don't know if those memories are mine or my mother's or grandmothers' or beyond, or where they belong, or where I begin and end.

Yearning is dangerous. For my mother, torn from everything she knew and loved so soon after fleeing the Red Army's revenge, and for my grandmothers, worn out by poverty and ill health through two world wars, endless pregnancies, and the care of small children, the expression of yearning was a luxury they could not allow themselves. Once acknowledged, it could swallow them whole, paralyze and leave them unfit for the demands of daily life.

Unspoken and unwritten, their yearning imprinted itself on their bodies, inscribed itself on their flesh in symptoms like heart murmurs, irregular heartbeats, high blood pressure, heart attacks, and congestive heart failure.

I felt their yearning. In my mother's underlying sadness that nothing could touch and in my grandmother Olga's gentle hand on my cheek and distant gaze that seemed to look through and beyond me. Not that their lives were without happiness, celebration, or joy, but it always seemed as though a part of them were somewhere else. As if their attention was split between the living and the dead, and their imagination had taken refuge somewhere safe and whole in a time before their worlds were shattered by loss.

And so it falls to me, third-generation eldest daughter, to voice their yearning. I will say that throughout the horror of endless wars they persevered, did their best to care for their families in the ways they understood, often went hungry so that their children would have food in their stomachs, and rejoiced in every tender green shoot that broke through the hard earth surrounding them. Their lives were stalwart and heartbreaking, I will say. Common and beautiful. They were not notable women or feminist role models, I will say, but they endured the hell of war and starvation and survived with their courage and patience and kindness intact.

I will sing the sorrow and the yearning of my ancestors. Sing my own longing to remember them and honour their humble and shining lives, to write them into their own story and sing them into their own song. I will love the mystery of their being and their presence that dwells inside me. I will hear the lament of my beloved dead and say who they were.

Not everything is lost.

BEAUTY, UGLINESS, AND THE LADY FROM PAPUA, NEW GUINEA

"The ground of the soul is dark," Meister Eckhart said. Darkness evokes many things, but above all else, the unknown. Depths we can't measure, and mystery we can't fathom. Ann Ulanov writes that darkness holds "the mysterious processes of the unconscious where creative activity starts, and the soul's wounds begin to heal themselves."

The soul's dark ground holds the promise of both beauty and ugliness in its depths. Luscious crimson and purple rhododendrons in May, the scent and softness of a baby's skin, familiar strains of beloved music—who doesn't adore all the manifestations of beauty in the world around us? Our imagination and senses are eager to experience it, whether as fragrance or taste, visual image or tactile delight. Our bodies respond to beauty with heightened attention, a sense of being opened up and expanded, and a feeling of profound peace that suffuses our being and affirms the world's goodness. When we feel beautiful in our own skins and others mirror our loveliness back to us we glow, for beauty embodied is a kind of radiance, a manifestation of spirit shining through matter.

Ugliness is something else. An aberration to be rectified, covered up, hidden away with all haste. When we inadvertently glimpse it in ourselves, we turn away in embarrassment and smooth it over with rationalization or denial. "That isn't really me," we tell ourselves. "I don't know what happened there." Never mind that the existence of beauty implies its opposite and the law of enantiodromia ensures the pendulum will always swing with equal energy in both directions. Even Aphrodite, goddess of beauty, revealed an ugly underside in her jealous rage and brutality toward Psyche, when her son refused to destroy the radiant mortal woman who threatened to outshine her. In *The Soul of Beauty* Ronald Schenk reminds us that "Aphrodite was born from a monstrous element, the severed genitals of Uranus and the chaos of the primeval waters." Aphrodite, he says, "both radiant and associated with death, gives form to the totality of soul."

As a young girl I was sure that if only I were beautiful, both inside and out, everything in my life would fall into place and I would finally be happy. Convinced I was plain if not downright ugly, I yearned to look in the mirror and see a slender body and perfect features, long dark hair and glowing eyes. After I shed a significant amount of weight during my early twenties, my outer world changed dramatically, but inwardly I suffered imposter syndrome. For years I heard the words *I pretended I was beautiful and they believed me* like a relentless mantra I could not get out of my head.

And yet it dawned on me over time that for the most part I liked the way I looked. At times this seemed almost shameful as if it reflected an unbecoming vanity but I loved feeling myself part of the world's beauty. I even loved the words *a beautiful woman*, which evoked for me a radiant body and soul, and a tenderness and vitality that had nothing to do with any classical or cultural norms. But I never spoke about this except with one or two close friends. It seemed too frivolous, too narcissistic, somehow.

"The soul shrivels without images and sensations of beauty," writes James Hillman. Including the perception and experience of our own, I would add. The yearning for lustre and loveliness reflects our longing for the soul of things, for an innermost essence that shines through and offers itself to the world. Beauty nourishes me more than anything else and Hillman's insistence upon its importance is one of the things I love most about his work. "The soul is born in beauty and feeds on beauty, requires beauty for its life," he writes.

Its utter disregard of beauty is a large part of why I decided not to study academic psychology. Music and literature, my two other loves, practised beauty and displayed beauty, but psychology, it seemed to me, valued statistics, behavioural norms, and reductionist explanations. It was more keenly attuned to the deviant than to the marvellous. From what I could see, there was no reverence for the mystery of life, no eros or love for the psyche, and surely no celebration of beauty. And in my own psychological work with three different Jungian analysts it was not therapeutic intervention or the naming of deep-seated emotional wounds but the contemplation of beauty—in my dreams and fantasies, in myth and the outer world—that nourished and expanded my soul, and brought a sense of wholeness and belonging. If beauty is itself a cure for psychological malaise, as Hillman claims, why wouldn't we hope to find beauty, to create beauty, and to embody it ourselves?

Curious about how the Roma regard beauty, I came across the following passage.

> Sociability is expressed as beauty of demeanor, but physical beauty is also valued by the Roma and the Roma experience it as an act of sociability and sharing. To put effort into one's appearance, to wear bright colours, have properly plaited hair and other traits that the Roma consider beautiful are a way of showing respect and generosity towards one another. A beautiful appearance may be seen as a gift that is offered the community as an adornment.

The love of beauty is part of my Libran personality, under the rule of Aphrodite and always seeking harmony and balance. In the past I have tried to shove ugliness into the shadows, but throughout the last decade I've found myself having to come to terms with its reality in the world around me and also in myself. I have often explored this theme in my journal, and on one occasion it led to a written dialogue with a harsh inner figure whom I referred to as the "Dark Voice."

Marlene: Dark Voice, who are you, and where do you come from? Why do you take pleasure in tormenting me and robbing me of joy? How can I begin to know you, so that one day I can make peace with you and not feel so tortured? I don't want you to rule my life as you do.

Dark Voice: I am the part of you that you hate and don't want to see. The destructive part. I am nasty and cruel. That's how I have power over you and don't let you get too cocky or feel too good. I'm the ugliness that you hate. You're always talking about beauty and gracefulness. You love it when people say you are beautiful.

Marlene: That's true. What's wrong with that? I was called ugly as a child, and it made me feel terrible. Now I just want to feel beautiful. Why do you try to destroy that and tell me it's all phony and untrue?

Dark Voice: I want you to see me, too. You keep pushing me away and refusing to have anything to do with me as if I am not a part of you. If I have to scream and shout and create havoc just to get your attention, that's not my fault. I want you to acknowledge that I am a part of you.

Marlene: That's really tough. I can't find anything good about you, and you're right—I'd rather not have anything to do with you. I want to believe I can become more compassionate and generous, loving and understanding. I don't want to be reminded of the meanness and envy and pettiness in me.

Dark Voice: In that case I will have to go on clobbering you just to get your attention. You're no better than anyone else. You're just as weak and fragile and self-centered. You can be selfish, you know.

Marlene: Yes, I know. I try not to be and I don't like it, but it's true. I guess I should be less selfish.

Dark Voice: Why? Can't you just accept the selfish part of yourself without always trying to make yourself better? Everyone is selfish at times, it's just part of being human. Stop trying to push it away. I'm here to stay!

Marlene: Really? But selfishness is an ugly quality, and people won't like that part of me. I've tried so hard to be unselfish—to think of others and their needs.

Dark Voice: Blah Blah Blah! Boring! I know all that crap. But sometimes you are just plain selfish because you want what you want at that moment. You can't deny it. And as long as you keep trying to be perfect, I do what I have to do to get your attention.

Marlene: Please don't clobber me anymore. I promise I will look at my own imperfection and ugliness, but please don't keep trying to convince me that I'm terrible and ugly and phony. I want to have a dialogue with you, but I'm asking you to step back and put your bat down instead of always being ready to beat me up with it.

Dark Voice: I'll think about it. And I'll try to keep control of the bat. But I'll be watching you.

Marlene: I know that. Let's talk again soon.

That was the beginning of an ongoing conversation with an inner critic who both taunted me with my imperfections and seemed to want me to accept them as a permanent part of myself. Over time the Dark Voice transmuted into the "Inner Depotentiator," whose relentless criticism appeared in a series of dreams. I did my best to hold my ground in the dialogues that followed.

Marlene: For a long time I have wanted to ask you why your attacks on me are so virulent and nasty. Sometimes I could howl with anguish and frustration at the way you talk to me and undermine me. You're like a virus that feeds off my energy and turns it against me. How can we begin to communicate with each other so those attacks can stop? There's nothing I want more than to claim my creativity without your constant stream of negation inside me. But how? And what do I even call you? Do you have a name?

Inner Depotentiator: I want your attention. I want you to pay heed to me and not reject me so ragingly. I have something valuable to tell you.

Marlene: Really? What is it? Mostly I feel flattened and wiped out, as if you are out to destroy me. What is it you want me to know?

Inner Depotentiator: That you are flawed and imperfect, and always will be. You cannot ever achieve perfection and you are no better than anyone else, just as you are no worse. You are who you are. Stop expecting the world to take notice and support and encourage you. You know what your own desires and passions are. Just get on with things. If you are wandering with gypsies, you have to be prepared for some difficult and lonely times. Why be surprised—that's just the way it is.

Marlene: It's not like I *chose* the lonely path! Those gypsies keep coming up in my dreams and magnetizing me—something in me knows them so well.

Inner Depotentiator: Then you should be prepared for their shadow side too. Those dark beggars on the bridge in your dream, they can be nasty. Don't expect to live with only their passion and joyful energy. Get real here!

Marlene: You're right. I did feel that dream was showing me the gypsy part of me can also get in my way at times. I just do the best I can to follow my unconscious and make good decisions.

Inner Depotentiator: Let me be the reminder of your own dark energies in a fuller way.

Marlene: Yes, but will you please find a kinder way and not be so destructive? I know you are a part of me that wants attention but is there a more constructive way for us to dialogue?

Inner Depotentiator: Let's try. I will modify my attacks. If you see them coming, stand aside a little and let them fly by—don't take them on. It might take me some time to get used to softer ways. You aren't the only one learning here.

Marlene: That sounds good. I don't know if you have a name, though. I don't even know if you are male or female or both. Are you "nasty animus," "negative mother," or both, or neither? How shall I address you in the future?

Inner Depotentiator: I'm neither and both—male and female. I have all your critical voices in me—the Serbian bully from your dream and the nasty witch who wants to kill everyone. I do what I must, to get your attention. Do I have a name? It doesn't matter, you can call me whatever you like. Inner Depotentiator is fine.

Marlene: Let's see where we go from here. I sure hope your attacks will be less vicious from now on, and won't strike at the very core of me. Could you just give me a good push instead of knocking me flat? I will pay attention to you, and let's be in touch again.

From time to time the Inner Depotentiator still appears in my dreams. Much as I might like to think otherwise, it seems he is here to stay, and the conversation continues.

Then I encountered in a dream the "Lady from Papua, New Guinea," an older Crone figure who is better able to hold the opposites of beauty and ugliness in me. She has brown skin and calm eyes that see things as they are, and her grounded presence has the power to turn down the volume on the Inner Depotentiator. Her dark gaze serves as a still point when I'm caught up in an emotional vortex or fall into despair, and she has gradually allowed me to recognize beauty and ugliness as aspects of one and the same reality, because her presence holds acceptance of both. By conventional standards her countenance is homely, but she is suffused with quiet nobility and her steady gaze is unflinching. She is wiser and kinder than I am, and I call on her when I need deep counsel. Here is an early excerpt from a dialogue that began shortly after she first appeared in my dream.

Marlene: Lady from Papua, New Guinea, I really need to speak with you. I feel my critical voices have become a little more subtle but they so often undermine my joy and optimism and creativity. It makes my heart heavy and it affects my relationships. I so much want to let go, to "live and let live." Can you help me?

Lady from Papua, New Guinea: Don't give in to those voices. You know them too well. Don't bother trying to fight them. You have been saying that you don't want to waste your energy but you have a hard time letting go of resentments and grievances. What about your own beautiful creative work? Can you take that as encouragement and focus on all that is good and constructive?

Marlene: I sure want to. I know my time and energy are limited and I don't want to squander them with resentment or unwillingness to forgive real and imagined hurts, or invidious comparisons, or envy, or other negative emotions. I just want to channel my energy into creative work and nourish myself and others with it. And not expect or need their love and praise and admiration in return. I'm not singing or dancing very much these days, and sometimes I feel out of touch with my soul. I'm not remembering many dreams either. Is there anything I can do to welcome my unconscious to show me something from my depths?

LPNG: You've been busy with many external tasks and that has called for extraversion. But you haven't left your soul behind. I am with you and you can always feel my dark gaze looking out through your eyes. Just continue being aware and attentive. In recent years you have been reminded of your inner and outer beauty, and now you are becoming aware of your darker energies and nastier aspects. We're doing the work together and you are taking it seriously. Stay open to whatever appears and humble about everything that is in you. It's all part of being human. I'm always present inside you, but you need to relax and slow down enough to drop more deeply into my presence. Your usual energy is like quicksilver, and my way is slow and deep. Like the voice that began to come out of you during those singing lessons. No rush, and no urgency to be heard—just your authentic voice rising out of your own body. That's my voice, beginning to emerge in you. So when you hear the inner criticism, allow your voice to drop a register or two, and slow down. Breathe, wait, and see what comes.

Marlene: Thank you for reminding me that the low and resonant voice in the dreams is the voice of my authentic self and the voice of my crone. Maybe I also need to bring that low, deep voice to my gypsy book, in counterpoint to the sparkling gypsy exuberance. Both are real. Both are in "her," in me.

LPNG: That's true. You contain both. Why not live the full range of them and celebrate that richness and diversity? We are all inside you, and you can call on any of us for your creative work and for your life in general. You know that I am your deep self, and you can count on me and know that I also support your upper registers. Can you accept that?

Marlene: I think so. I hope so. I want to feel and live from those depths, for my soul's sake, for my clients' sake, for the sake of my relationships and my creative work. Please step forward as you feel it's necessary and make yourself present to me. I love you.

LPNG: I will. And you must release your grudges against those you feel have injured you in the past. Forgive them and put it all behind you. They are working out their own wounds and you can't afford to waste time—there's too much to create and too much joy to claim. Just keep moving ahead on your own path.

Marlene: I'm so grateful to have you inside me. And one more thing—please help me discriminate those attacks of self-negation from genuine shadow material that needs attention. I can't always tell the difference. I want to grow into your crone wisdom and not depend on outer praise or validation, to know my own value and worth.

My conversation with the Lady from Papua, New Guinea, has continued, sometimes in writing and at other times in my imagination. She is a touchstone and tuning fork in my life and her calm presence and steady gaze have become part of me, slowing down my innate quicksilver tempo and reminding me to breathe through the ups and downs and minor storms of life.

As Marion Woodman says, "Through the symbolic image the opposites are brought together, consciousness receives new life from the unconscious and we contact our essential being—our own wholeness, ourselves as both human and divine."

Bodies of Imagination

"The image by which the flesh lives is the ultimate ruling necessity," writes James Hillman. "We are in service to the body of imagination, the bodies of our images." The imagination is my homeland and much of my life has been lived in its spacious dimensions; when the outer world encroaches it has been my sanctuary.

As a teenager, I filled scrapbooks with bohemian themes and images of long-haired, dark-eyed women in embroidered peasant dresses and velvet skirts. I was writing journals too but these were books without words. Many years ago I threw them out during a purge of my parents' basement storage room with only a whisper of regret over lost youthful fantasies, but some of those images are indelibly etched in my memory.

In one, a young woman with curly black tresses sits in the back of an open caravan on a winding country path lined with tall trees and lush foliage. Her legs swing out the back of the caravan and the dreamy, open expression on her face tells of her eagerness for life yet to be lived, of passion still to be discovered, and sorrow not yet sustained. Aglow with promise, she is a few years older than I was at the time, and I wanted to be her. Or perhaps I felt that on the inside, this is who I really was—a young *gypsy* on the open road, with all of life's endless possibilities still ahead. I don't recall the details of the story I told myself about the picture I had clipped out of a magazine, but I do remember how that picture made me feel.

Through the years my flesh has lived by many images. While studying in Zürich I did so much active imagination with my inner images that I joked about rarely needing to leave my room because of the lively cast of characters who kept me company there. *To be in touch with soul means to live in sensuous connection with fantasy.* The *gypsy* energy has often been a double-edged sword for me, providing an inner realm of freedom and sensuous connection with fantasy while heightening my awareness of the many intrusions from outside.

I was born into a family of German Baptist immigrants to Canada. After their experience as young refugees of war, my mother and father wanted nothing more than to settle down and work hard, be active in their immigrant church community, and live quietly in our mid-sized town in the Pacific Northwest. My grandparents and great-grandparents in Europe and Russia had been farmers and skilled labourers, tradespeople and Baptist ministers. My parents' education during the war had been limited to elementary school, but they worked hard to make a good life for themselves and their young family in the new land. Ingenuity, frugality, and practical skills were highly valued, but the imagination was a foreign country and not one that they felt they could afford to visit very often.

I was their first-born, and, by all accounts, a lively child. In a formal portrait taken when I was perhaps one and a half years old, I look enormously pleased with myself. The tip of my tongue is tucked stubbornly into the corner of my mouth, and the mischief in my face is unmistakable. And this after a rocky start that left my poor young parents wondering who would collapse sooner, they themselves or their infant daughter who hardly slept, day or night.

Unlike my practical, earthbound mother and father, I was a fanciful child who loved to sing and dance, read and write, and later wanted nothing more than to travel the world. For most of my first twenty years, I felt like a tarnished copper penny in a bowl of shiny nickels. From one year to the next it seemed everything that felt most intense and urgent to me on the inside had to be suppressed if I wanted to survive and belong. My memory of those years is of the liveliness and creativity and everything spontaneous in me forever being slapped down in the effort to render me a good Christian girl. In the process of stuffing down my imagination, passion, and hunger for love, I became overweight, which only increased my sense of being an outsider as I approached adolescence.

On the inside, however, things were very much alive. The characters in the books I devoured—sometimes four or five a day—were as real to me as the people around me, and much more sympathetic. I was feisty Jo in *Little Women* who wanted to write, the most spirited and outspoken of her sisters.

I was George Eliot's Maggie Tulliver, running away to join the Gypsies. Later I was Anaïs Nin, who wrote about her lovers in her diary, propped up on pillows in her bed every night. The stories I wrote and the music I created expressed who I was on the inside, someone quite different from the person I was expected to be at home, school, and church.

In my darkest moments, books and music allowed me to imagine myself differently. Reading other lives brought a flicker of hope that somehow, sometime, things might change, and I would feel less torn and sorrowful. If I was Simone de Beauvoir, emerging from her restrictive Roman Catholic upbringing to reinvent herself with Sartre, I was also Mozart and Joan Baez, living in a realm of music so glorious that it soaked into the very roots of me. Michael Stewart writes of the Gypsies' ability to construct a fragile and temporary sense of coherence through art and symbols in order to create identity and affirm the value of their suffering. Writing stories and creating music gave me a sense of my own identity too, fragile and tenuous though it was.

When I look back now it seems that the endless outer constraints during my early years and my anguished sense of not fitting in anywhere only strengthened my resolve to find out who I really was. I remember a recurring inner refrain of "they can take everything else away from me, but they can't take my integrity," though I'd be hard pressed now to say who "they" were, or what it was I felt they were trying to take away from me. At times I was filled with despair that I would never feel at peace nor reconcile my desperate love for my family with the equally urgent need to live my own life.

During those years I often felt as though I were caught up in a life-and-death struggle. Sometimes I felt I had no skin and my nerves were raw and exposed, without protection. It seemed I could either chop off the parts of myself that meant the most to me or take the terrifying step of leaving the Church and community into which I had been born, and strike out on my own without knowing whether I would ever belong anywhere again. I was twenty-two when I left the Church and it's still one of the most terrifying things I have ever done.

When I finally admitted to myself that I was no longer an evangelical Christian, I hardly slept at all for three nights, and by the third night I was hallucinating. The following morning as we made our coffee, I asked my roommate, "Why did you come into my bedroom last night?"

Lisa looked shocked. "I wasn't in your room, Marlene. I slept through the night and didn't even get out of my bed."

I could see she was concerned about me. So was I. Lisa was my best friend and a devout Christian herself, and I had never felt so alone in my life. No longer bound or sustained by the certainties of the evangelical Christianity I had grown up with, who was I? What was my reality now, and how would I live a life that was authentically my own? At times it felt like everything was up for grabs, from my relationship with my parents and church friends to my much-guarded virginity.

When I read *The Pregnant Virgin* many years later, I felt Marion Woodman had described perfectly my impossible situation. Her wrenching account of the agony accompanying transformation, symbolized in the drop of blood spilled during the butterfly's first flight, comforted me no end. For Woodman the pregnant virgin is "the part of us who is outcast, the part who comes to consciousness through going into darkness, mining our leaden darkness, until we bring her silver out." This happens over a lifetime as we dare to go more deeply into our unknown depths and find buried there the energies of the *dark feminine*. "The Black Madonna is the patron saint of abandoned daughters who rejoice in their outcast state and can use it to renew the world," Woodman writes, and I clung to this sentence with everything in me. I recopied it by hand from one journal to another, read it out loud and taped it on my computer monitor, wondering what it would mean to rejoice in my outcast state and use it to renew the world. But perhaps only those who live outside the collective, whether by choice or necessity, can bring new life and eros to its entrenched orthodoxies. And the anguish of the abandoned daughter can be redeemed if she is able to claim the freedom and vast possibilities now open to her, and live her own life with joyous abandon. The alchemists claimed that the gold is in the dung, after all.

But it's not easy. After emerging from the chrysalis there is no going back, and as Woodman reminds us, one lives by a very different set of laws than a caterpillar does. Yet unexpectedly, Christianity's symbols too have been redeemed for me along the way: the birth of the divine child in the lowliest of circumstances; the Communion service that celebrates the common body of the community; and the Cross that symbolizes the agony involved in consciously holding the tension of the opposites. Freed from the prison of literalism, they offer another door into what Jung referred to as the symbolic life.

❧

For many women, as for me, the *gypsy* is also a kinesthetic image experienced in our bodies as a greater spaciousness, energy, and range of movement—even as I write this, my breath slows down, drops more deeply into my body, and I want to dance. In place of the constriction and shame we may carry, it brings greater enjoyment of our own beauty and sensuality, and increased lust for life in all its manifestations.

I had a dramatic experience of this during a Body Soul Rhythms Intensive many years ago. In the course of the week we made masks inviting new energies to emerge from deep within, masks that reveal aspects of ourselves we might have suppressed throughout our entire lives. I found myself creating an ancient feminine earth spirit, a dark rose and brown-tinted *gypsy*, her forehead studded with jewels, her face outlined with gold beads and shining with glitter, her wild hair woven of many strands of multi-coloured wool. Throughout the week's activities, *she* moved and danced as I'd never danced before, pouring new life into my body and soul. My next mask carried the energy of Medusa, another of the *gypsy's dark sisters*. As I worked with these masks and did my best to bring blood and warmth to Medusa's frozen face, I felt primal energies I hadn't known were hidden in me. Not the least bit inhibited by notions of polite femininity, they were raw and crude, passionate in their loves and hatreds. As I followed them into the fields and forest surrounding the workshop room, I longed to climb into the trees and merge with them. At one moment I was almost inverted, as if my head wanted to disappear into the earth next to the tree trunk. I clung to the trunk with my face pressed against the base, and every inch of my body straining for closer contact; the urge for that cool, moist darkness was overwhelming.

At another Intensive I dreamed of a young guitar-playing hippie who wanted me to run away with him. As I allowed his edgy vitality to dance me through the room, I felt enormous energy in my body, as if something that had been held in check was finally free to have its wild and exultant life.

More than a decade later, my partner in the exercise told me she could still feel the *gypsy* energy alive in her body.

"The symbols of the self arise in the depths of the body," Jung said. "The symbol is thus a living body, *corpus et anima*." There are so many bodies of imagination in our lives. While writing my essays in Zürich I had to sing and dance, I had no choice; it was the most embodied experience of writing I've ever had. Not long ago I performed Brahms' *German Requiem* with the Vancouver Bach Choir and Symphony Orchestra in one huge and glorious body of musical imagination. And there's the sand tray I created following my dance of liminality to Loreena McKennitt's music. In sand tray work, the client chooses spontaneously from a vast assortment of small figures and creates a scene in a large sand tray, complete with landscape and characters that express the essence of an experience, emotional state, or dream. After we talked quietly for a few minutes, Eileen asked me to create a scene of what I had just experienced during the dance. I made a sandy path that curved from one side of the tray to the other. Starting in the bottom left corner, I'd placed a miniature caravan with tiny purple and white amethysts in a little black bag inside it. Just around the first bend was a flamboyant turquoise peacock and, next to it, a large brown rhinoceros with huge, fierce horns. An evergreen tree towered behind them both, and farther along the sandy path stood a tiny statue of Saraswati, Hindu goddess of knowledge and the arts. To the right of the path I'd placed a monkey, and at the end of the road in the top right corner of the sand tray, a Ukrainian painted egg decorated in rich colours. As is customary in sand tray work, Eileen took a photograph of the scene and gave it to me. As I looked at it, it didn't take me long to see the story.

I imagined that the Gypsy travelling in the caravan with her treasure in tow cannot see around the curves on the path ahead of her. Along the way she encounters a peacock, showy and unafraid to flaunt its splendour, then a rhinoceros with enormous horns for protection. Evergreen trees are the landscape of my soul, and I discovered afterward that Saraswati's herald is the peacock. The monkey brings playfulness and mischief, and the painted Ukrainian egg suggests the treasure at the end of the journey. The Ukrainian word *pysanka* is derived from the word for "writing," because the eggs are decorated with elaborate designs in symbolic colours, patterns, and mythic motifs. Originally the *pysankas* symbolized the universe and were believed to have magical qualities; today they represent friendship and love in the world. But I didn't know any of this when I placed the egg at the end of the road. Looking back now, it seems that sand tray was an early image of this book, another body of imagination filled with caravans that meander along curving paths, moments of beauty and ferocity, and snippets of esoteric knowledge and trickster energy along the way.

So—what does it mean to serve the body of imagination? Attending the dark realm of soul with its many shades of yearning and nostalgia leads us into *gypsy* territory, an unboundaried realm of spontaneous movement and meandering. Soul territory. Virgin territory. Not trying to please anyone, but loving what presents itself, fleeting dream images and fantasies, irrational longings and passions. Free to follow the red thread of desire and feel the yearning for what we haven't lived yet, for what reaches out to us, craving our attention. And always, the invitation to enter more deeply into the bodies of our images.

Not All Who Wander
Are Lost

While visiting an elderly friend in her nursing home some years ago I parked behind a car whose bumper sticker proclaimed in bold letters, Not All Who Wander Are Lost. I have thought of that bumper sticker so often. It states an obvious but subversive truth in an era that prefers direct routes and shortcuts to wandering. *Wander* comes from the Latin *vagari*, the root of *vagabond*, and brings to mind the role of the Muse in creative activity. "Essentially the Muses' inspiration comes feet first," writes Jungian writer Nor Hall. "The word that best describes their hymns translates as *(feminine) wandering-journey-song*." The Muses themselves are *gypsies*, it seems, and so are all who join their wandering and await their inspiration.

Wandering-journey-song suggests movement, intention, and music. Along with open-hearted trust that something is happening, even when I'm not sitting at my computer, and even when there's little to show at the end of a day's work. But wandering requires time, eyes to see, and a receptiveness to everything around us. To sing as we wander demands space and fresh air to fill our lungs so that our song can resound. Inspiration comes from *inspirare*—"to breathe or blow into." Is that why the most fertile ideas and images so often arrive while I am walking or running? Does the Muse breathe inspiration into me with the deep breath moving through my body? Is the creative process itself a *wandering-journey-song*, a soul melody that accompanies us through life?

Nor Hall has more to say about this kind of journeying. "Women wander, in themselves and in the world, to locate the places where they feel at home." Not to carve out territory or stake our claim in foreign lands, but in order to discover who we are and where we belong. Like the Roma who don't want their own country, the feminine is inherently a *gypsy*, and feminine wandering is a rhythm of travelling and settling through darkness and light. *Women's very bodies are nomadic in their courses as we are always in flow; a woman's body is a Gypsy, ever moving on, in a state of flux.*

⚜

Many years ago I woke up one morning with the words *The Journey of the Roma, with its Passion, Reality, and Essence.* That was all I remembered of the dream but I knew those words were messengers from the depths, faint echoes of a larger story that was clearly my own. Wandering, journeying, singing—these have been my preferred modes of movement through life.

Travelling through the world has always been my fantasy. A longing to escape entrenched routine and a hunger for new landscapes and rhythms of life have left my heart restless to set out in search of inspiration and discovery. Each time I've returned from travel abroad, the experience has lodged itself in my body and heart and soul, enlarged through encounter with the new territory. The brilliant turquoise of Yugoslavia's Dalmatian coast during my twenties, the shy warmth of Egyptian women in the streets of Cairo and the exuberance of Mexico in my thirties, the teeming colours and smells and sounds of India in more recent years; they all live on as inner spaces I can enter whenever I want. Every weekend I dive into the newspaper's travel section as if its pages could transport me like a flying carpet to some unknown corner of the world—Johannesburg, Buenos Aires, St. Petersburg—a vagabond of word and image, vicarious traveller of the printed page.

⚜

However much I have loved travelling to distant shores, most of my wandering has been in the inner realm, among imaginal places and stories, characters and landscapes. In that realm I have never been lost. To keep a journal is to embark on another kind of journey. Both words have their roots in the French *jour* (day). *Journey* originally referred to the distance one could travel in a day and symbolically that is the journal's territory as well. My journal—approaching two hundred volumes now—bears witness to the peaks and valleys of my life, and everything between. For almost half a century I have wandered from one volume to the next, sorting the seeds of my dearest values and attempting to discriminate what is my ego and what is my soul.

In its pages I have questioned and raged, reflected and rejoiced, hoped and dreamed, and done my best to come to terms with myself and the world around me. Unable and unwilling to cast my lot with any particular "doxy" or "ism," I have meandered among endless perspectives and possibilities of living a meaningful life.

Beloved quotations and poems pepper the page in red and green ink, while dreams, sober in black, beckon like signposts of another world, surrounded by a sea of blue. Over the years, my journal, singular, despite multiple volumes, has come to include occasional doodles and dashes of colour, and dialogues with dream figures. Into its pages I pour the good, the bad, and the shameful. Primal shrieks of narcissistic wounding, and dark rants of self-laceration. But also whispered prayers, exclamations of joy, and flashes of inspiration. Enough creative seeds and sparks for the rest of my life, and, not least, the red sulphur energy of the *gypsy*. In the ongoing struggle to wrest truth from self-deception, the journal has been an unfailing mirror of my soul's journey. I feel myself loved and accepted in its pages. Here is an excerpt:

> My attraction to wandering, being unterwegs (on the way), and the world of the Gypsy converge in the inner journey. I am always on the way to somewhere and the Gypsy always wants to sing and dance her way there. She is high-spirited and explosive, "in the moment" and "in your face." I love her for all of that but she also gets me into trouble. Like her I often hide on the outskirts, in the shadows, where I feel safe.
>
> I don't want to be hounded or wounded or pounded. I don't want to be bound and sometimes not even found. I imagine being trapped in the "o" of these words and rolling up, then plunging down to the bottom of the "u," carried up over the top of the "n" and coming to rest and hiding in the bottom of the final "d." The only "ound" word I like is sound, where the slippery curves and defiant hiss of the "s" elude capture. Word-fantasy.

The *gypsy* wanders through the pages of my journal, delights in the play of tempo and rhythm, chooses colours at whim, chants the lament of the dispossessed and exults in her freedom. At home, like the Roma, in the wandering. Surely and decidedly, not lost. *Thus it is of the nomads that I sing…*

Pilgrimage and Lamentation

Of course I am a wanderer, a pilgrim on this earth.
But can you say that you are anything more?
—Goethe

All journeys have secret destinations of which the traveler is unaware.
—Martin Buber

Every year, thousands of people walk the ancient Camino de Santiago de Compostela in northern Spain, one of the most important medieval religious pilgrimage routes. For Christians the pilgrimage culminates at the cathedral in Santiago de Compostela in the northwest corner of Spain, where the body of the apostle Saint James was reportedly brought by ship from Jerusalem and buried. For some people, this is a way to honour crucial passages and milestones: a divorce or loss of someone dear to them, a major life transition such as career change or retirement, or simply an opportunity to contemplate their lives anew with hopes of finding a broader vision. For others, it's an initiation rite that tests their commitment and endurance, their willingness and capacity to relinquish the usual comforts of life and open themselves to a wider reality.

There are easier ways of arriving at Santiago than walking eight hundred kilometres through often taxing terrain and uncertain weather, but walking the Way of Saint James brings transformation for many. Absolved from their usual responsibilities and disconnected from technology's addictive grip, they may discover a new connection to the earth beneath their feet, to the ever-changing landscape and weather surrounding them, to their fellow pilgrims, and, not least, to themselves.

Having lost the old certainties and feeling rootless and adrift, we move out into the world, a community of pilgrims and wanderers on an ancient road, searching for the ground of our own being. The long days and weeks of walking ground the pilgrim's quest for spiritual enlightenment through constant contact with the earth and attention to the body's needs. When feet are blistered, throats parched, bladders bursting, and joints aching, the body is speaking loudly. It is demanding to be heard.

But pilgrimage is both an outer and an inner process. As the Greek poet Cavafy reminds us, by the time the weary traveller finally arrives at Ithaka or Santiago, he or she has long since realized that arrival was never the goal. Is there in everyone an archetypal attraction to travelling the world on foot and finding an intimate connection to the earth and her creatures? Are we all on pilgrimage, hoping to make our way back to the body of the Great Mother?

❧

In the spring of 2012 I walked the Camino with my twenty-four-year-old niece. I had planned to go alone but Chelsea was struggling to find her way and it seemed like a good time to invite her on a new adventure. I was keenly aware that this would be a very different Camino from the one I'd envisioned, but I hoped the dramatic break from her usual routine might bring a fresh sense of possibility and a wider vision for my niece's life.

Contemplating the long days and weeks of walking ahead, I tucked several beloved poems and quotes into the flap of my Moleskine notebook for inspiration, among them the following three:

> It is part of the business of growing up to listen to the fearful discords which real life grinds out and to include them among the images of reality.
> —C.G. Jung

> A free woman has a strong neck—an open connection between heart and head, a balance between reality and ideals.
> —Marion Woodman

> The creative is an achievement of love. It is marked by imagination and beauty, and by connection to tradition as a living force and to nature as a living body....Nothing can create without love.
> —James Hillman

I made a detailed packing list and gradually filled my backpack over several weeks. With the knowledge that I would be carrying it on my back for hundreds of kilometres, I weighed everything and took only the essentials, including miniature shampoo and toothpaste, and just enough blister cream and Tylenol to get us to the nearest pharmacy. Along with my little journal, I wanted to take a single paperback book. Not something to read and leave behind but one I could dip into during the evenings and reflect on as I walked. I decided on James Hillman's *The Force of Character and the Lasting Life*. On the eve of setting out for Spain I wrote in my journal:

> What is it I'm really hoping for in the course of this Camino adventure? A deeper understanding of my own aging process? Time to reflect—in solitude and away from my usual routine—on my remaining time on earth, whatever that might be? Some kind of loving transformation? Rejuvenation of my writing process? Perhaps something else that I can't even imagine now? I do know that I want to welcome each day and, as May Swenson puts it, "take earth for my own large room / and the floor of earth / carpeted with sunlight / and hung round with silver wind / for my dancing place."

I also wrote the names of the people I love in the notebook along with their most pressing concerns. Every morning I would dedicate the day's pilgrimage to one of them and hold them close in my heart. *Keep it simple*, I concluded the journal entry. *Give thanks for each new day, and be present in everything I do. Be patient with Chelsea and myself. Open my heart to those I meet along the way. Write down my thoughts and insights. Drink plenty of water!*

It was drinking enough water that proved to be the biggest challenge. Toilets were few and far between and I couldn't bring myself to squat in the often exposed fields along the way, which made the strategic intake of liquids a priority. With time we worked out a system of drinking very little until we were certain there were toilets ahead, then downing as much as we could (I would not recommend this system to aspiring pilgrims).

Chelsea turned out to be a hardy and hilarious travel companion and our conversation roamed in many directions as we walked together day after day. We listened to music on her headphones and sang along with Alanis Morissette's "Wunderkind," whose lyrics about attracting wonder and magic on the path of one's roaming destiny seemed to mirror our quest as we continued, mile after mile. We spoke often of Gavin, her baby boy who had been stillborn in the summer of 2008 and whose perfect little face was engraved in my memory, as it surely was in hers. Day after day I could not help but notice the constant attention her nubile blonde beauty attracted from men of all ages and how invisible, in contrast, I had become.

We fell into a rhythm of walking for six or seven hours with only a few brief stops along the way, finding a room and showering, then going out for the pilgrim's meal. During the evenings we lay side by side on our beds, relaxing and sharing our impressions of the day's experiences and the people we had met, or listening to music (Chelsea), and reading and writing in the journal (me). One evening Chelsea asked me to read out loud to her. *She really wants to hear James Hillman's thoughts on aging?* I thought. I read, and we had a lively discussion of "Gravity's Sag," "Erotics," and "The Force of the Face."

We laughed and called ourselves "the whiny pilgrims" for complaining when things went wrong. One night halfway through the Camino we both wept with exhaustion, stretching arms out across our beds to hold hands as we fell asleep. While drinking our morning *café con leche* we talked about our dreams and what they might be telling us, even noting similar themes at times.

Then I was laid low with tendonitis and Chelsea caught a stomach bug. We were forced to stop walking for five days and to rethink our itinerary. Due to Chelsea's time constraints we decided to take a train to Sarria so that she could walk the final hundred kilometres required for the official Compostela certificate. As we trekked into Santiago she protested, "But I'm not ready to go home, Aunt Marlene. I haven't learned all my Camino lessons yet." She said it half in jest, but it was the other half that interested me. We both knew the Camino had reached deep into her heart and soul in some way she didn't have words for.

After we'd said our farewells and Chelsea boarded the train to Madrid, I considered my options. Our change in plans had brought me into Santiago a week earlier than expected and I felt restless and dissatisfied with my truncated walk. The tendonitis had calmed down and my body wanted to keep moving so I decided to carry on walking to Finesterre, where land meets water at the legendary ends of the earth. I was anxious, knowing there would be far fewer pilgrims or signposts along the way, but seized all my courage and hoped for the best.

Sure enough, within half an hour of setting out the next morning, I was lost. As I stopped in the middle of a shady park on the outskirts of town to speak with a young Korean pilgrim who was equally disoriented, three German pilgrims walked toward us with confident strides, and the five of us eventually found our way out of Santiago.

And so it was that I walked the Camino Finesterre in the company of Klaus, a gentle woodsman from Hamburg who had worked as an agricultural expert in many developing countries but felt most at home walking in nature. Klaus told me he was walking the Camino in hopes of coming to terms with the sudden death of his little granddaughter the previous year. Occasionally he pointed out something in the surrounding landscape— an unusual tree or species of wildflower—or we stopped for something to drink, but most of the time we walked in companionable silence and I found his quiet, unruffled presence and unfailing sense of direction soothing and restful following the boisterous weeks with Chelsea. The Camino Francés had been *our* Camino, but the Camino Finesterre was *mine*. I even found myself being noticed by men, and realized I wasn't quite as invisible as I'd felt beside my lovely, statuesque niece.

I continued my morning ritual of holding someone I love in my heart each day as I walked. It was easy to do in the fresh, green stillness and my thoughts went often to my aging parents, especially my mother, who I knew was counting the days until my return. My sister, Nellie, Chelsea's mother, was planning to join me for a long visit at our parents' home a few weeks later and I wondered what we would cook and bake together this time.

On arriving in Finesterre, Klaus and I joined several other pilgrims in a trek up to the Cape, where I made a ritual sacrifice, burning what no longer served me in the small fire just above the rocky shore. Then we all drank a joyous toast to the Camino before heading back down for a celebratory dinner in town. After a day's rest, Klaus and I continued up the coast to Muxía, where we discovered a charming *casa rural* run by a young couple with loving care and delectable regional cooking. On May 23 I wrote in my journal:

What a glorious end to my Camino journey. We walked up to the Virgin of the Rocks and lay on enormous warm grey stones that look like the bodies of whales. The scenery was stunning and it felt like a wonderful culmination of everything I have experienced. Then we wandered back to the Casa de Trillo and I washed the Camino dust off my feet for the last time before heading down for another delicious dinner. My Camino is over. I walked 22 of the 30 days I'd hoped for, and completed 550 kilometres. It's not what I expected, but this was MY Camino, and I am grateful. Now it's time to relax, celebrate, and go home. A seven-year dream has been fulfilled, and soon it will be time to move on to other dreams.

I had no idea what would come crashing down on us all just two weeks later.

✑

C.G. Jung described archetypal wandering as "a symbol of longing, of the restless urge which never finds its object, of nostalgia for the lost mother." During my Jungian studies in Zürich I dreamed of the earth as a woman's body. Before me lay a lush and fertile landscape. As I gazed at it in wonder, I saw that the rounded hills were her breasts and belly, the soft green foliage her pubic hair. *All wandering is from the Mother, to the Mother, in the Mother.*

All of this took on new dimensions of meaning when, one week after I returned from the Camino, my mother died unexpectedly, following what was to have been a routine medical procedure. Although I had forced myself to imagine what it might be like to lose her—she'd had several close calls in the past—the shock and timing of her accidental death shifted the ground under my feet in a way I could not have prepared for.

"How long will you be gone?" she'd asked, shortly before I left.

"Six weeks," I told her. She looked sad.

"That's such a long time," she said quietly. Did she have any inkling that it was most of her remaining lifetime?

"I'll be back before you know it, Mum," I tried to comfort her. "And I'll come out and spend a lot of time with you in June."

I knew my mother didn't understand my desire to travel any more than she had when I was a child and couldn't comprehend why I would fly overseas at considerable cost just to walk for many hours every day for an entire month. Both she and my father were penniless immigrants to Canada after the war and by the time they could afford to travel, her health was unstable and any significant journey was out of the question. I remember her saying once, with a rueful shake of her head, "All those years and where have I been? Nowhere." Her voice was edged with regret.

"Where would you have wanted to go, Mum?" I asked her, surprised. She had never mentioned wanting to travel, although perhaps I should have known.

"Hawaii," she said. "Or California. Somewhere warm."

I had wanted to walk the Camino for many years and early in 2012 I'd felt that this would be the year. It seemed a cruel twist of fate that as I was walking toward Santiago at long last, my mother was living her final weeks on earth. Without a cellphone, I hadn't even called home often. There were few public telephones along the way, and I wanted to sink into the shared experience with my niece and immerse myself in our surroundings. I called my parents once at the beginning of the trip and tried again toward the end, but my mother had gone next door with some baking for her sick neighbour. A few days before she died she said, "I'm always at home and in those few minutes I was out, you called. I was so sad when I heard your voice on the answering machine and knew I missed your call."

In the weeks following her death, I was inconsolable. In my sorrow it seemed that just when she'd needed me most, I was absent from her life. I wanted those six weeks back. If I'd had any inkling of what was to come, the Camino could have waited another ten years. Or forever. In the face of losing my mother, it seemed like nothing. For many months I could not talk about my pilgrimage except to say, "I walked the Camino and a week after I got back, my mother died." The Camino felt like a miserable prequel to the biggest loss of my life. It didn't matter one ounce that we'd had her for longer than we ever expected to, or that my parents had celebrated their sixtieth wedding anniversary the previous September, or that there wasn't much left unspoken between us. I was flesh of her flesh, and she was dead. My mother-ground. The earth of my being.

For decades my mother had kept herself alive by means of her spartan diet and heroic efforts to exercise despite chronic pain and depression.

And, my sister and I were convinced, through the knowledge of our fierce love for her. She'd survived kidney cancer, congestive heart failure, several bouts of life-threatening pancreatitis, quintuple bypass and aortic valve surgery followed by a bad case of *Clostridium difficile* that put her back into the hospital for ten days, and in recent years, even a car accident. Every time her future looked bleak, she'd look at me and say, "Don't worry, Marlene. *Es wird schon irgendwie werden.*" Somehow it will all work out. And somehow, it always did. She'd redouble her naturopathic explorations, find new supplements, push herself a little harder on the treadmill. In the end, ironically, it wasn't even illness that took her life but a routine biopsy gone wrong, which, in the face of what looked like a possible return of the cancer she'd survived thirty years earlier, the doctors did not monitor with due diligence. Nine days later, she was gone. Inexplicably, unacceptably, irrevocably gone.

Our bond had been visceral. Often when she was unwell, we'd lie on her bed together, snuggling close and holding hands. "Do you think Chelsea will be all right?" she'd ask me after a long silence, or "Do you think Stefan will get married soon?" about my nephew. Whenever I hugged my mother, I buried my nose in her neck and inhaled her scent with deep gratitude. *Remember this*, I told myself. *One day she'll be gone.* And then one day she was.

Several weeks after she died, my mother came to me in a dream. "I can still smell you," I told her with quiet satisfaction. "I still remember your scent."

"I can still remember your scent too," she said. I was comforted by the dream but I never had it again.

⁓

There is more to this story, and I have been reluctant to tell it.

During the last decades of her life, my mother often ended up in the local hospital emergency ward because of pain and frightening palpitations related to her poor beleaguered heart. Once when I was visiting from New York, we were strolling hand in hand up Wellington Avenue, and I stopped and said, "Mum, promise me that if you ever have the sense that you're going to die soon, you'll let me know. I'll drop everything and come home right away." She had just been in Emergency with another scare. For years the doctors had been telling us they had no idea how she'd kept herself alive so long, or how long she could continue.

My mother looked at me with a quizzical smile. "What if I don't know?" she said. "Maybe I won't know ahead of time."

"I know, Mum. But if you do have that feeling, promise you'll call me." She seemed a bit puzzled by my request but agreed and we continued our stroll.

Two nights after Chelsea and I arrived in France my mother came to me in a dream. "I'm ready to leave now," she told me, and I knew that by "leave" she meant "die."

I put my arms around her and held on to her tightly. "But please not now, Mum," I said. "Can you wait until I get back?"

"I'll try," she said. "I'll do my best."

I woke up feeling uneasy, and told my husband about the dream on the telephone later that morning.

"You've had so many dreams over the years that she's dying or dead," he tried to reassure me. "This isn't the first time." It was true. Often when I returned to New York after visiting my parents I dreamed my mother had just died and I woke up in tears. I'd thought of those as anxiety dreams caused by the thousands of miles between us, and by knowing my mother longed for the day when Steve and I would move to Vancouver. But this dream was different. It wasn't emotional. The tone was matter-of-fact.

Throughout the day I wondered whether I should fly home. I thought of Chelsea and our hope that walking the Camino would give her a broader perspective on her life. What to do? I called my mother later that day and she sounded fine. I didn't mention the dream to her and tried to push it to the back of my mind. Another anxiety dream, I told myself. The next morning we began our pilgrimage. Six weeks later my mother was gone. She had almost died during the botched biopsy the day before I got back from Spain but hung on to life, then could not recover. She died a week after I got back.

I wanted to leave out this part of the story, ashamed that I hadn't said in the dream, "Hang in there, Mum, I'm coming home right away." I feared that in writing it down, I might conclude that I had broken my earlier promise to her. Should I have taken the dream as her way of calling me home? Abandoned plans for the Camino and gone to her side? The thought haunted me. After her death, the dream continued to replay in my mind. As she promised in the dream, my mother had done her best not to leave until I got back, and she'd succeeded. Although she had thought she was dying when the biopsy needle punctured her artery and the blood covered everything in sight including the doctors, she managed to live long enough that I could spend the last night of her life at her side.

It has taken a long time to separate my Camino experience from its shocking sequel. See it for itself, rather than as the ominous prelude to my mother's death. When I open my Camino journal now, I recall the freshness of each day's experience, the exhilaration of the adventure, the joy of meeting other pilgrims and sharing stories, the unexpected twists and detours along the way. The satisfaction at finally fulfilling my dream. What the sombre shadow of grief has dulled in my memory, my journal restores to its original vivid hues.

Another new landscape lies before me now—the country of my own rapidly approaching old age. Another kind of pilgrimage and another kind of adventure. And in that new country, my own mortality is no longer inconceivable. I think it's time to fulfil another dream.

✎

A friend hoping to help me come to terms with my anguish over my mother's wrongful death asked me, "Do you ever think that walking the Camino strengthened you and in some way prepared you to cope with losing your mother?" I appreciated her loving intention but said no, as far as I could tell, my Camino experience had not left me with any deeper insight into life and death. What it did offer, along with a colourful kaleidoscope of memories and the concrete, embodied experience of being on pilgrimage, was a few simple and lasting truths.

- Walk your own Camino, not someone else's. I might have avoided the tendonitis and foot injury, had we stopped more often for short breaks instead of following the lead of Giulia, a gregarious Italian woman determined to push ahead. Her facility in speaking Spanish and my own insecurity made it tempting to follow close behind her.

- Take it one day at a time, and be prepared to change course, if necessary. I'd hoped to walk for thirty continuous days with perhaps a day off in the middle to rest, but had to surrender to the reality of my injury. In the end, mine was not the perfect thirty-three-day Camino outlined in John Brierley's excellent guidebook. I walked my own idiosyncratic Camino.

- Carry only what is essential. I'd packed as selectively as I could but within days I left behind a small hot water bottle and several other items. It was the coldest, wettest spring in a hundred years and I was grateful for the old cashmere scarf and gloves I'd tucked into my backpack at the last minute, but once the weather warmed up I left them behind too. My Hillman book, on the other hand, was essential, along with the poems and quotes I'd copied into my journal, and a single tube of lipstick.

- Share what you have, whether it is fruit or chocolate, a rain poncho or an extra pair of socks, a Band-Aid or an inspiring quote. We're all in this together.

- Welcome the kindness of strangers. After arriving in Pamplona in the middle of a heavy downpour late on a Friday night, we couldn't find a room. Out of nowhere an older Spanish gentleman appeared and asked us in German if we needed help, then showed us to a new hotel not yet in the guidebook and spoke to the manager on our behalf. "He's our first Camino angel," Chelsea said as he drove off in the rain. There were others. It seemed that whenever we needed help most it was provided, and we did our best to pass on the kindness we received.

- Remember that every pilgrim is carrying a secret burden of longing, heartache, and hope. In the end, what calls each of us to the Camino remains a mystery. Be gentle with everyone you meet, and especially with yourself.

Not everyone can walk the Camino or even aspires to. But in some sense we are on pilgrimage throughout our lives. Nor Hall writes, "If people do not gather anymore on a sacred road to search for their lost souls, the gathering together and the search will be translated into the movement and language of our interiors. Rites of passage have turned inward where they can be lived out as stages of psychic transformation."

I have been a persistent *peregrina* of the inner world for almost half a century, as my many journal volumes attest. Several years ago I created *Body Soul Sundays*, a nine-month Jungian program that provides a structure and community for women's inner pilgrimage. One Sunday each month we come together as a *thiasos*, "a congregation of women attentive to the mystery in things." From September through May, we follow the rhythms of harvest, wintering, and rebirth, and as the months go by this inner journey has its own seasons of harsh weather and difficult terrain. Beginning with one of the great myths of the archetypal feminine—the story of Demeter and Persephone or Amor and Psyche—we read and write, dance and draw, create sound and ritual, and support each other's soul journeys. When women began to return year after year, it became clear we were creating a community of courageous and adventuresome *peregrinas* committed to a nine-month psychic pregnancy without knowing what wanted to be born. The length and archetypal arc of the program allow time for the myth to take root in our psyches and enter our daily lives. Each woman's pilgrimage is unique.

I would like to close this vignette with one final Camino lesson. On the Camino and on the journey of life itself, it's so important to find the poems and quotes that ignite our spirits and nourish our souls. Carry them in our journals and in our hearts, wherever we go. When the road seems endless and the way uncertain, they will be our guiding lights.

Buen Camino to us all.

Outcasts, Outsiders, and Others

Gypsies are the ultimate outsiders. The only people who have never had a homeland and don't seek one, yet sing unendingly of their yearning for home.

Ambivalent outcasts, they have always lived on the margins, resisting assimilation to the ways of the *gadje* and priding themselves on not being swallowed up by the cultures around them.

But being outcast has its price. Often there is considerable shame, as if it's a reflection of one's essential worth and value. As if one has been judged by collective standards and found wanting and deficient. As if there is some kind of secret norm of successful adaptation one hasn't lived up to. This is how it has felt to me through the years. I want to be free to follow the inner call and not be held hostage to the collective's gods and orthodoxies, to alien values of fame and fortune, power and prestige. My gods have always been elsewhere. Nor do I want to be saddled with rules and generic regulations that recognize nothing of my individual reality and show no regard for my soul. What does this mean for the *gypsy* in me?

Ambivalent outcast indeed. Not heartbroken for not belonging. Not fearful about what has been at times a marginal existence. Where do I want to be—inside, outside, both? Free to follow my soul's promptings and still be part of the community. Not out in the cold on my own, feeling denigrated and shunned. Outcaste, *mahrime*, impure. Part of a lower order, a lower caste. Not deserving of dignity, no honour attached. Without external recognition, affirmation, acceptance, am I real, do I matter? Even then, ambivalent. Still exultant for wide open skies that don't limit my horizons. The freedom that comes with abandonment is precious and painful.

Growing up I felt I didn't belong anywhere. If there is such a thing as a well-adjusted, happy, popular young girl, that was not me. At home, I was too outspoken; at school, I was too smart (and felt too fat); and at church, I asked too many questions. Most of the time I was an internal exile in a realm filled with the magic and beauty I yearned for in waking life, and with beings who could see the magic and beauty in me. Including the *gypsy*, who had already taken root in my soul. *The other that I am and am not, that I don't know how to be, but that I feel passing, that makes me live—that tears me apart, disturbs me, changes me.* The paradox of both being and not being the *gypsy*. Often my outer life was sedentary and predictable, lacking the impetuous surge and bright-eyed sparkle that says, "It's a new day and I'm off to parts unknown." Inwardly I was restless and always ready for adventure.

I think we all carry many others inside us, live many lives at once. Jungian analyst Murray Stein once suggested during a seminar in Zürich that the psyche is like a multiplex cinema and we are always choosing which theatre to walk into. While we are busy living the life that others can see, our other lives are playing out elsewhere, in other cinemas of our being. Maybe fantasy is simply our word for those invisible parallel lives that are always going on within us. Just as real as our outer lives, but lived on a different plane.

Often we dismiss our fantasies as unrealized wish fulfilments. "Just get on with things," we tell ourselves. "*This* is the life you've chosen. Everything you've done has brought you to this moment. Why think about all the roads you didn't take." But my soul recognizes all of those lives, refuses to relinquish them, and loves to enter them from time to time. "Fantasy gives life a glow and a color which the too-rational outlook destroys," says Marie-Louise von Franz. In another room in that multiplex theatre, there is a soprano singing with choirs and orchestras throughout the world. There's a mother of half a dozen children who simmers enormous pots of soup on a wooden stove, sews clothes and quilts, and welcomes grandchildren to the hearth. There's a writer in a cabin deep in the woods, tending her garden and cherishing the green silence; a designer of *gypsy* skirts, each one unique in colour, texture, and design; a lifelong wanderer carrying what she needs on her back as she roams the earth and encounters its creatures. There are so many other others. Some come to light in the outer world while others require secrecy, but I feel their vivid pulse inside me.

How often I have been told that I look like a singer by someone with no knowledge of my love of music, or like a dancer despite my non-dancer's body. Years ago a young woman told me, "I don't know why, but every time I come to your house for a workshop, I feel as if my mother is still alive," smiling as she walked up the stairs in my home at the start of a workshop. Many women have echoed this sentiment over the decades and I know it's the presence of that soup-simmering, quilt-making mother in me.

"You look like a Gypsy," I have heard throughout my life. "Are you sure you don't have Roma blood?" I'm not sure, though there's no evidence that I do, but it's clear that the imaginal *gypsy's* blood pulses through my veins.

I say this not to celebrate myself—although why shouldn't we celebrate the inner others that enrich our lives?—but because it reflects the diaphaneity of inner and outer worlds. In the inner realm I have surely sung and danced my way through the world, mothered children and orphans, and roamed with the Roma. More and more I see that the imaginal world is just as real to the psyche, and sometimes more so, than the outer world. Can there be any doubt, given how often we act on faulty assumptions, project our own stuff onto others, and succumb to the power of emotional complexes that knock us out with their irrational strength? Whether they rejuvenate us or deplete us, those inner others have their own insistent reality that demands to be lived.

And while we may feel ourselves at times cast out by family or community, alone and adrift in the sea of modern life, we also refuse to shelter our own vagrant energies, leaving the unwanted parts without a home, all the while suspecting that they might hold the potential for a richer and fuller life. What and whom have I cast out of myself? Too often, I know, it's the writer. I lacerate her with condemnation when she's paralyzed and afraid to put down words because they might be the wrong ones. I reject her fear and vulnerability, demand an impossible perfection, and subject her to a tyrannical judge who only ever finds her wanting. (He's inside me now, an echo of the patriarchal Judeo-Christian God who demands that Abraham slaughter his beloved son to prove his obedience. "Take me instead!" I would have shouted at Yahweh. "I will never kill my child, you merciless tyrant." Then why can't I argue back to the Serbian bully in my dream who so often threatens my creative child?) How she—the writer—longs to put words down on paper without fear, curious to see what emerges, and able to hold it all without judgment. She used to be able to write that way—relishing the process and excited to see where she'd end up. What happened?

So many mysteries surround those inner others. I grew up in a German Baptist home and was compelled to obey God, church, and parents, so perhaps it's not surprising that the *gypsy* would be so strong in me—compensating for generations of German Baptists in my lineage—but why not a different archetype, *rebel* or *revolutionary*, for example? I don't think the *gypsy* can be understood simply as a compensation for everything that was thrust on me as a child or what I force on myself even now. I was surely other to my parents in many ways and even to myself, to the smart and well-behaved girl I believed myself to be. I was always Mary in the church nativity scene after all, not the glorious angel of the Lord I so longed to be, and surely not a Gypsy. If I'd had any inkling that the Roma refer to their beloved Saint Sara as *Mary the Gypsy* I'd have taken much more delight in my role in the annual Christmas Eve pageant.

"In each of us there is another whom we do not know," Jung wrote, and I will take the liberty of changing the pronouns. "(S)he speaks to us in dreams and tells us how differently (s)he sees us from the way we see ourselves. When, therefore, we find ourselves in a difficult situation to which there is no solution, (s)he can sometimes kindle a light that radically alters our attitude, the very attitude that led us into the difficult situation." I think we all contain these others, each one offering a different viewpoint and tale. The *gypsy* is my outcast, my outsider, my other.

GYPSY FUGUE

Enter on a curving road with nothing
in sight but the curved road itself.
Seven paces forward, you arrive
in the place where you began, but it is not the same.
A new path arises in the clearing like the first,
and then another and another; all seem
to contain the same landmarks. Strange,
these roads that always bring you home
whose scenery is ever changing.

—John Stone

To write is to note down the music of the world, the music of the body,
the music of time.

—Hélène Cixous

They all have gone back to the old ways…scattering and regrouping, like
the flowing of water, adapting itself to all circumstances, endlessly remod-
eling itself but forever remaining true to its essence, the eternal Rom.

—Jan Yoors

From the beginning, I conceived this book as a fugue. During the late
thirteenth century *conceiven* meant "to take (seed) into the womb, become
pregnant." By the middle of the following century, the figurative sense included "to take into the mind and hold." It feels like both to me. I have been
pregnant with this creative child long enough to give birth to not one but
several baby elephants. The actual writing began in Zürich but it had lain in
my body long before that.

Nor Hall says, "It is easy, in a world that does not value the patient work of the womb, to conceive of something and then forget about it.... Mothers often go for years without being able to show anything for all their conceptual effort. But memory finds a channel. Even when you cannot perform or deliver, your body holds on to what it knows and cradles it in the darkness." Throughout its drawn-out gestation the fugal metaphor persisted and I imagined an endless interweaving and overlapping of voices taking up the *gypsy* theme.

Timeless, sinuous, and undulating, the fugue is always a wonder. We sense eternity in the serene unfolding of the theme as it wanders from voice to voice, expanding and transforming in the process. Height and depth are also evoked, with occasional moments of sublime vertical harmony throughout the fluid horizontal movement. Throughout time the fugue has been regarded as a reflection of the *harmonia mundi* or harmony of the spheres.

I love the unpretentious opening statement of the theme, how it's taken up and repeated by a second voice, and then opens into a small eternity of time- and spacelessness. Listening, we are taken deeper into a musical mystery that unfolds and further unfolds, until at last it returns home in a calm and satisfying resolution. Unlike other musical forms that announce themselves with bold emphasis, the fugue insinuates itself into our awareness with stark and graceful simplicity, then gradually expands into something transcendent and marvellous. Takes us on a journey into other dimensions and brings us back enlarged, more spacious somehow, as if, in the words of T.S. Eliot, "the end of all our exploring / Will be to arrive where we started / And know the place for the first time."

In my music history textbook I read that the fugue is based on "a single 'affection' or mood—the subject that dominates the piece." It begins with a short musical theme or subject that serves as the unifying idea or focal point of a contrapuntal web. As it moves from one voice to another, this theme is woven into an intricate musical tapestry where each recurrence reveals new dimensions of its nature and new themes are woven in as well. The fugue unfolds according to the composer's fancy; "caprice, exuberance, surprise— all receive free play within a supple framework." Baroque composers loved the fugue form because they could pour into it "the living substance of their own time" and combine their technical prowess with "imagination, feeling, and exuberant ornamentation." Every fugue is thus a unique musical expression of an archetypal form.

Then I read about *The Art of Fugue*, considered to be the greatest achievement in this form. One of only a few works J.S. Bach wrote for his own pleasure rather than as a commissioned work, *The Art of Fugue* was composed over many years and remained unfinished at the time of his death in 1750. It's even possible that Bach intended to write additional fugues for this collection, beyond the final incomplete one he left behind. Consisting of eighteen fugues in the key of D minor, he wanted to explore all the possible variations, both of a single musical motif and of fugal writing, in this work.

Is it audacious to take as my inspiration for this chapter the most venerated example of the fugue form? Even to its incompleteness, for, as the eminent Bach scholar Christoph Wolff reminds us, "the work is missing its ending." Just as any memoir or autobiography must remain unfinished as its author lives on beyond the story.

My musical imagination leaps again when I read that Einstein associated the key of D minor with counterpoint and chromaticism. Counterpoint in music is "the technique of combining two or more melodic lines in such a way that they establish a harmonic relationship while retaining their linear individuality." But counterpoint is also a style of embroidery in which point is set against point. Embroidered music, again. Chromatic notes (from Greek *chroma*, or "colour") are notes outside the prevailing musical key of a musical work that serve to embellish the melody or harmony, and are referred to as *accidentals*.

The symbolism is intriguing because the Roma do indeed live in counterpoint with the prevailing culture, hoping for a harmonic relationship while retaining their unique identity. Even the notion of *accidentals* is evocative since they clearly live outside the prevailing key of cultural values and are often treated as colourful "chromatic notes" whose place in society is precarious and accidental. The same is true of the archetypal *gypsy*, whose marginal existence is part of her essence. To extend the metaphor a little further, perhaps this entire chapter is written "in the key of D minor," filled with the multiple *gypsy* melodic lines and chromatic notes that have embellished the fugue of my life so far.

Bach, Jung, and the Gypsy

What common threads can there possibly be among J.S. Bach, C.G. Jung, and the archetypal *gypsy*? I ask myself. The music of Bach has carried me through some difficult times and Jung himself proclaimed, "Bach talks to God," suggesting that for him, too, Bach's music was transcendent. Of course Jung talked to God too. The magnificent *Red Book* is the result of his decades-long engagement with *Elijah, Philemon, Salome*, and other numinous, archetypal figures arising out of his own depths and the depths of the collective unconscious. Jung's sustained commitment to encountering his unconscious was surely a labour of love for his soul, and Sonu Shamdasani, the book's editor, claims the book's most important message is "Value your inner life." The *gypsy* is a beloved indwelling presence and an archetype of magnetic attraction for many in these prosaic and technological times. All three—Bach, Jung, and the *gypsy*—are deeply rooted in the unconscious and have the capacity to inspire and reanimate the soul. They have surely done that for me.

Jung had a little more to say about music than about Gypsies during his lifetime, but not much more. In her biography of Jung, Marie-Louise von Franz says he loved the music of Bach and felt it was an expression of the unconscious "unclouded by ego elements." In a letter in 1950, Jung wrote, "The circular character of the unconscious processes is expressed in the musical form; as for example in…the perfect circular arrangement of the *Kunst der Fuge*." Reading this I thought of a musical mandala, then discovered that elsewhere he observed that mandalas can be "formed with the hands, danced, and represented in music, for instance Bach's *Art of Fugue*."

For me, it has always been Bach. Monteverdi and Mozart, Beethoven and Brahms, Debussy and Dvorak thrill and delight, but Bach is bedrock, as if his music were known to me before I was born. When the novelist

Bernard Malamud was asked what writing meant to him he answered, "I'd be too moved to say," and that pretty much describes how I feel about Bach.

⤴

When I am thirteen I purchase a Deutsche Grammophon LP record at A&B Sound in Vancouver for $1.25. It's a sampler of Bach's music with the legendary Dietrich Fischer-Dieskau, Fritz Wunderlich, and Christa Ludwig. But it's the Austrian soprano Gundula Janowitz who takes my breath away with her shimmering solo from Bach's *Christmas Oratorio*. The otherworldly radiance of her voice entrances me, and I fall in love with singing.

Then Sonia Berg—a family friend who arrived from Berlin with her husband with only the clothes on their backs the day I was born—invites my younger sister, Nellie, and me to listen to the entire *Christmas Oratorio* in her living room one cold December evening. I know Sonia loves me because one day she told me, "If I had a daughter I would want her to be just like you." I love her too. Not her husband, Harold, whose eyes linger on the breasts and legs of the girls in the Sunday school class he teaches and who won't let go of our hands during the morning handshake, grasping them tightly and pulling us closer to him. Sonia learned to play the piano only after she was forty and now she is teaching my sister. I know she admires the way I play piano, and takes me seriously as a musician. This is the first time she has invited Nellie and me to her home without our parents and we feel honoured.

"Lie down on the carpet," she urges in German, as we step carefully onto the elegant Persian rug. "Close your eyes, and you'll see, the music fills you up." Her eyes shine with joy. The room is aglow with candlelight and we are charmed by her warmth and unexpected informality. My sister and I curl up next to each other on the thick rug with our coffee cups and a plate of chocolate *Lebkuchen* next to us. In the soft candlelight my life shimmers with promise; maybe one day I will be a singer too.

The three of us listen to the oratorio from start to finish without talking. Joyous angels, eager shepherds, solemn wise men—my imagination is alive with the story and soaring melodies. The tenderness of the Christ child's birth in the stable surrounded by animals moves me like never before and the sheer joy of the music permeates every cell in my body. Even after the jubilant final chorus and trumpet fanfare subside, we stay quiet for a long time. Then Nellie and I get up, hug Sonia, and leave in silence, our hearts lit up like the stars sprinkled across the black December sky.

During my first year at religious college in Edmonton, I am the music professor's personal accompanist. Professor Neufeld loves Bach (and young women accompanists—he has an affair with his next one) and I get to play much of the *Christmas Oratorio* on the piano. I'd rather be singing, but that seems like an impossible dream. My piano teacher, Professor Rose, wonders whether I might possibly be related to Bach. He knows I love Bach's music and thinks I resemble him. As I look at the venerable composer's stout, cherubic features, I am taken aback but flattered by the fantasy that I could possibly be his descendant. I write a poem that begins, "Sometimes, when Bach is happy, we talk. / He tells me that he wrote his happy music just for me."

Later at university back in Vancouver, I listen to the *Violin Concerto in E Major* every morning with my coffee, and it's only fitting that my audition piece for the Vancouver Bach Choir is the beautiful "Echo aria" from the *Christmas Oratorio* that ignited my passion to sing more than a decade earlier.

"Your voice is perfect for Bach and Handel," the conductor says during my audition. "It's clear and resonant, and the vibrato is just right for Bach." He's considered the best voice teacher around, and I hold his words close to my heart like a secret mantra, and carry his written report in my journal for years. "Lovely quality of sound," it says. "Excellent sight-reading. You should do more with it."

When I finally have the chance to study voice in England, the first piece I want to sing after all the tiresome vocal exercises is Bach's soprano cantata *Jauchzet Gott in Allen Landen* (*Exult in God in Every Land*).

"Starting with the easy stuff, are you?" my new singing teacher says, with amusement. I know it's considered one of the most difficult pieces in the soprano repertoire but I don't care. It's what I want to sing. He is surprised when I hit the high C in the final aria. So am I. During Easter break I attend a two-week Bach master class for singers in Aldeburgh. I'd give anything to be one of the singers rather than an auditor, and make detailed notes of soprano Heather Harper's advice to the budding young soloists.

The following year I meet Steve and we go to a performance of the *Mass in B Minor* at London's Royal Festival Hall on our first date. He is as moved by the music as I am, a good sign in my books. In 1988, as I stroll through Gordon Square in Bloomsbury before my doctoral dissertation defence, I quietly sing Bach arias to keep the breath moving through my body and ward off anxiety while waiting to be summoned. And so it has continued through the years, my life with Bach.

᠁

In the *Larousse Encyclopedia of Music*, a gift from Sonia and Harold, I read that more fully than any other composer before or after him, Bach "united the intellectual and emotional drives of the human spirit." Wondering what could possibly link Bach's cosmic harmonies with the volatile and mercurial ways of the *gypsy*, I continue reading and discover that Bach had "a headstrong will and a quick contempt for the stupidity of the official mind." Not surprisingly, he frequently found himself at odds with various authorities in Leipzig and the school in which he taught, and was even embroiled in a skirmish involving drawn swords. Bach was a rebel, it turns out, and not one to suffer fools gladly.

Then I read that one of Bach's sons played with Gypsy musicians. It's a fascinating story and the stuff of legend.

It happened that one day in the mid eighteenth century, amongst a Gypsy tribe camping at the gates of Darmstadt, a young violinist attracted particular attention; his talent, according to music lovers, was so amazing that the Burgermeister took the trouble to question him. The mayor learnt to his great astonishment that the virtuoso was none other than Wilhelm Friedemann Bach, eldest son of Johann Sebastian. Once a teacher of mathematics and organist of Our Lady at Halle, he had left everything a few years previously to follow a tribe of Gypsy musicians. The Burgermeister offered him the position of Choirmaster which W.F. Bach held for several years. But seized by nostalgia in recollecting his freedom in wandering he went back to live with his chance companions.

Even if the tale were only partly true, its point is borne out by other evidence of collaboration between composers of the Baroque period and Gypsy musicians. Georg Philipp Telemann, Bach's friend and the godfather to his second son, was also extremely taken with what he described as the "barbaric beauty" of Gypsy music, and no doubt discussed his interest with Bach.

More recently, the middle of the last century saw the discovery of the Uhrovska Manuscript, created in 1730 and comprising 350 folk tunes and ballads of Polish, Hungarian, and Slovakian origin, and believed to derive largely from Gypsy music. Drawing on the Uhrovska Manuscript, the Montreal-based Ensemble Caprice has made an energetic case for the influence of eastern European Gypsy music on Baroque composers with recordings such as *Vivaldi and the Baroque Gypsies* and *Telemann and the Gypsies*, and with concerts like "Bach and the Bohemian Gypsies."

Django Reinhardt, the famous Gypsy jazz musician, loved Bach, claiming, "His music speaks to my heart and brings tears to my eyes. This is the mother of all music." Recently I discovered a gypsy swing performance of Bach's *Concerto for Two Violins* by Reinhardt, Stéphane Grappelli, and Eddie South on YouTube that works so well it makes me wonder whether Bach too harboured a Dionysian *gypsy* in his Apollonian soul.

And so it seems there are unexpected threads of affinity among Bach, Jung, and the *gypsy* after all. With common roots in the archetypal world of depth and image, they are soulmates indeed.

The School of Fools

I have been writing this book over many years and the writing has been its own kind of journey. During that time I have gone from the middle of middle age to its far side, and things look different from where I stand now. The emotions are no less intense and the colours no less saturated but the horizon is shorter, and the once-distant rumble of my mortality is becoming more audible. There is less of Kore and more of Persephone, along with a glimmer of Hecate. Sometimes I've had to ask myself, "Is that still true and accurate? Shall I leave it as I wrote it five years ago or revisit it from where I am today?"

For some time now I've been wondering what happens to the *gypsy* as I grow older. While the archetypal image may exist outside of time, I most certainly do not. What happens to that primal energy and vitality as the decades pile up, gravity pulls down, and arthritis sets in? Several years ago I had a dream that offered a glimpse of what aging might be like.

> I am at a conference in the north of Spain with Heather (a close friend) and several other women I know. We are in skiing territory and there is snow on the ground. One of the women makes a gesture, as if to begin dancing, and another woman quickly gets up and mirrors her movement. Then a third one joins them, and it has the quality of ritual dance in India, where each gesture has symbolic meaning.
>
> Suddenly I realize there are Gypsies all around us. We walk into a large hall to hear a performance, and I pause in the entranceway to place copies of an essay by Marion Woodman and one of my own on the Dark Goddess on a table. At the front of the hall, an older Gypsy

man is singing, playing guitar and violin, and talking about music. I love listening to him, and I'm very curious to know whether he comes from a place I have heard of called the School of Fools. When the performance is over I walk up to the front and tell him I loved his recital. He seems very interested in talking with me. He says he can tell that I have a good singing voice and begins to tell me about Gypsy culture and music. Much of what he says is familiar to me. Other people come up and listen to our conversation.

He is tall and lean and slightly weather beaten. His dark hair and eyes and expressive face remind me of both Leonard Cohen and Steve, my husband. As I look at him I think—he's a Gypsy and he's very much like me. He's not particularly exotic, and there is something poignant about him. When he bends his head toward me I notice there's a bald spot where his hair is thinning. I ask if he teaches at the School of Fools, and he says yes. He moves me deeply and I am so happy to be with him.

My first thought upon waking was that I wanted to know more about the School of Fools. That day I headed off to an annual Women's Body Soul retreat where I encountered the Gypsy again during a dream enactment. When I asked whether he would still be singing at ninety, he assured me he intended to keep making music as long as he was alive.

His weathered face, aging body, and soulful music move me. He may be past his peak in physical stamina and attractiveness but he's singing his heart and soul out, just like Leonard Cohen during his final world tour, every song a prayer as he fell to his knees. If the Gypsy musician is teaching at the School of Fools, that's where I want to be, and I'm so glad that he seems just as excited to meet me as I am to meet him.

On the last day of the retreat I stopped for coffee before heading home. It was early in the day but three musicians were making live music as I walked into the café and I realized suddenly that they were playing "A Day in the Life of a Fool." The next morning, as I prepared for the evening writing workshop, I saw that our weekly reading was an essay titled "The Joy of the Fool." Helen Luke says the Fool of the Tarot is always dancing in the world and while the dance may look like folly to some, those who live from their own deep centre recognize it as "the dance which is the joy of the universe." She suggests that a far better image for aging than the wise sage would be the "foolish" old man or woman who can finally let go of all convention and the need to do the right thing, and simply be free. These fool-ish synchronicities brought great delight and deepened my sense of being guided on my quest to understand the heart of aging in myself and the *gypsy* within.

In the course of writing workshops I often ask participants to relate a particularly vivid dream as if it were the story of their lives. In that spirit, I would tell the dream as follows.

I'm on a pilgrimage in Spain, searching for insight about how to live as I grow older. It's colder here than I expected, especially up in the mountains, and there is snow on the ground. This is the land of Gypsies, flamenco, and *deep song*, and I'm very hopeful that some inspiration will come as I wander. I am travelling with my soul sisters, and we support each other in the dance of life. There's great love and trust among us, and we laugh and cry together freely. Our ritual dance is both serious and playful, and we feel the presence of the Dark Goddess in our creative work.

Then I meet an older Gypsy musician who has studied and taught in some interesting places. I love his passion and complete ease in performing. I'm powerfully drawn to him and he seems to feel the same way. He says he plans to keep on singing until the day he dies and encourages me to do the same. I want him to tell me more about the School of Fools. He is manly but there is nothing macho about him and I love the gentleness of his attention. I see his soulfulness and the vulnerability of his aging body and feel enormous tenderness toward him, as if I've known and loved him for a long time. I know he is my soulmate and I want to keep him close to me for the rest of my life.

The dream reflects so much of what has mattered most to me in recent decades. The circles of women I belong to and lead. My desire to walk the Camino and travel in Spain. The Dark Goddess of life and death, beloved patron saint of abandoned daughters and the Roma. Marion Woodman, another aging *gypsy*. Music and dance, and the fact that I'm finally singing again. Increasing awareness that I've passed the twin peaks of youth and midlife, and am on the other side of the mountain now, contemplating the aging process that lies ahead and even my own mortality. What a gift to meet this Gypsy musician and to be reassured that growing older doesn't have to mean a fading away of eros and creative passion. That it can bring new depths of soulfulness and ease with who I really am. The poignancy and tenderness of the dream bring back these lines from William Butler Yeats' poem "Sailing to Byzantium."

> An aged man is but a paltry thing,
> A tattered coat upon a stick, unless
> Soul clap its hands and sing, and louder sing
> For every tatter in its mortal dress.

The Gypsy in my dream was singing his heart out. And when I leave the middle ground behind and cross the threshold of old age, I want to clap my hands in fierce flamenco, and sing, and louder sing for every tatter, crease, and wrinkle in my mortal dress.

THE FIVE CHAPATIS

While travelling through Rajasthan in 2007 I heard a story about the Gypsies' origins in the Thar desert. According to this tale, the goddesses Kali and Durga were fighting the devil, who managed to clone himself with every drop of his own spilled blood. Kali gobbled up the cloned demons as quickly as they appeared, while the mortals drank the devil's blood out of coconut shells to prevent him from replicating himself further. Then Kali told the mortals that the devil would scatter them all over the world but promised that wherever they travelled, they would always be fed. As they dispersed, they became the Gypsies.

Then our host in the desert town of Jaiselmer told us an old Indian folk tale about the five chapatis. "The fifth chapati is for the cow," Pradeep said. "The fourth is for the dog; the third one is for the Gypsy; the second, for the street cleaner; and the first one is for the musician. That's why people give Gypsies food left over from the day before," he explained. "One must always feed the Gypsy." Later that same day we saw a young Gypsy girl receive a plate of rice from a family in Jaiselmer and I wondered if they knew the tale of the five chapatis. Made of whole wheat flour, salt, and water, chapatis are the staple food of most of India's people. Affluent or poor, almost anyone can get their hands on chapatis, and the nourishment they offer is basic and wholesome.

The fifth chapati is for the cow. Cattle represent wealth and abundance in many cultures and in Hinduism the cow is the sacred animal. As a symbol of the earth, the cow serves as a surrogate mother, providing humans with food and, in India, with the all-important dung for fuel. The cycle of caring for the cow and receiving her gifts in return is part of the great round of life. In feeding the cow, we honour the sacredness of the earth and ensure our own survival. Cow's milk brings us the gifts of nature and the Great

Mother, primal matrix of our being, but also the milk of human kindness that sustains us on our journey through life.

In feeding the cow I remember my animal nature. Chewing her cud as food passes through the four chambers of her stomach, a lot is happening in that cow. With my innate impatience, how can I honour the part of me that chews and ruminates and chews some more, taking all the time in the world? I know that digestion can't be rushed, even when something inside me jumps up and down shrieking "too little, too late!" How can I allow my life to take its own sweet, organic time?

The fourth chapati is for the dog. The dog may be the animal companion to Shiva and Indra in Hindu mythology but we saw hundreds of stray dogs in India, all of the same nondescript mongrel variety and most of them near starving. In the desert of Rajasthan my friend and travel companion took compassion on one particularly skeletal creature cowering near the entrance to a way station, ever hopeful for kindness. Lael went straight to the kitchen and ordered a chicken sandwich for the poor beast. Incredulous that someone would buy food for a mangy, homeless dog, the cook refused at first to prepare it but my friend prevailed. When she set the food on the parched earth outside, the dog fell on it ravenously and devoured it in an instant, as if terrified it would be taken away. "Just once in its poor miserable life, I want that dog to have a full stomach," Lael said, as we watched.

For us in the West, dogs provide companionship, unconditional love and protection. On a symbolic level, their unfailing devotion and sure nose for the truth make them trustworthy psychopomps, the mythic figures who guide mortals between the worlds and ultimately between the realms of life and death. Dogs represent the instinctual animal body that carries us faithfully through our day-to-day lives, hungry for love and attention and always eager for play.

The dog reminds me of my own capacity for shameless frolicking in the face of propriety and deadlines. When I feed the dog—eat and rest, walk and play—my body responds to that indulgent attention, gravity's weight is suspended, and I feel the child's delight in galumphing again. (How I wish I could do that more often, and what is it that stops me, anyway?)

The third chapati is for the Gypsy. Outcast and wanderer, the Gypsy depends on the generosity of others to survive, reminding us that we are all kin and there is always someone who requires our kindness. That our abundance can sustain others on their journey. The Gypsy reminds us to care for the restless outsider within, as well. In feeding the Gypsy, I care for my own vagrant energies, those that stray outside the frame of my proper life but pull and demand my attention all the same. In writing this book, I offer a giant chapati to the Gypsy.

The street cleaner's humble labour restores cleanliness and order in the world, keeps the road open for travel, and prevents the village from sinking into chaos and filth. It is no surprise that it's members of the lower caste who perform this task in India. In our impatience to get on with loftier tasks, can we remember to save a chapati for the street sweeper who doggedly, faithfully clears away the rubble that impedes our passage?

Through the years I have come to appreciate how crucial this service is. Clogged by clutter, my outer life falters and my inner life chokes. Then it's time to sweep away everything that no longer serves. Old clothing and furnishings. Outworn attitudes and resentments. A big chapati for the street cleaner, for sure.

Finally there's the musician, who nourishes our hearts and souls with deep feeling and aesthetic delight. Every culture, no matter how isolated or impoverished, has made music, as if sharing a common rhythm of breath and sound were as essential as food and water. Which of course it is. Reading and writing, singing and dancing, everything I take in through the senses and imagination, all of it nourishes the musician who carries my soul on the wings of song.

Five chapatis for everything that requires our devoted attention. The cow that grounds us in the earth of our lives, and the dog that awakens instinct and playfulness. The Gypsy whose wandering leads us into the unknown, the street cleaner who restores order, and the musician who brings beauty to our lives. All live within me, each one essential and together making a whole that is the quintessence of my life.

CROSSING BOUNDARIES

Günter Grass says we need the Gypsies because they have crossed many borders and remained European despite all the suffering they've endured. He writes, "As born Europeans, they are, from their centuries of experience, in a position to teach us how to cross borders, indeed, to abolish the borders in and around us and to create the kind of Europe without borders that is not only the subject of empty oratory but an actual state of affairs." For most of us, national boundaries are a universal given except in times of war and the forcible conquest of new lands, but the Roma cross them freely, and experience themselves both at home everywhere and as strangers everywhere.

There are many kinds of boundaries and many ways of crossing them. On the border between the familiar and the unknown, old categories and definitions fail and we are forced, but also free, to reinvent ourselves. "Beyond the boundary lies the unknown, the uncanny, the dangerous, the unconscious," writes Murray Stein. "When markers are created and limits set, however, curiosity and explorativeness are also excited and new spaces for exploration and discovery invite the bold and courageous traveler."

Transgressively and creatively I have crossed many borders throughout my life—between different languages and countries, spiritual traditions, and scholarly disciplines. Baffled by what often seem like arbitrary boundaries and restrictions, I have veered off the beaten path and gone my own way with freedom and loneliness, exhilaration and self-doubt as my companions. My "acorn," as Hillman called the unique spark and *daimon* in each of us, apparently prefers autonomy to security. After a lifetime of wondering why orthodoxies of every kind alarm and alienate me, I've come to accept that the margins are where I feel most at home. Sometimes that can be a lonely, even dangerous place to be.

German was my mother tongue but I've lived my life in English. After leaving my evangelical roots, I joined the Quakers for a time but I feel most at home with Jung's understanding of the symbolic life, and the organic process of the deep feminine. I immersed myself in music during my two years at religious college, then took up the study of literature at university and gradually added depth psychology into the mix. Three distinct disciplines, but to me they seemed cut of a single cloth.

My parents' sporadic education in wartime Germany was limited to elementary school with frequent time out when the Allied bombardment grew too heavy. I was born a decade later in Canada and had opportunities they never could have imagined, including the chance to do graduate work in Europe and the freedom to keep studying throughout my adult years. They'd hoped that after graduating from high school I would teach piano, marry a good Christian man and start a family, and live within walking distance from them in a beautiful house my father would build for us. As it turned out, my husband is an academic and philosopher from New York City whom I met in Cambridge, England. For many years we lived in New York, where the coastal orientation always felt wrong to me and the frequent border crossings never let me forget my marginal status as a "resident alien" in what felt, even then, like a sometimes surprisingly foreign land. Our eleven-year age difference, too, is a kind of boundary. We grew up with different music, movies, and cultural frames of reference; his, a largely secular Jewish world in Brooklyn, and mine, a church-dominated life among immigrants in the Pacific Northwest of Canada.

In my various roles as a university professor, writer, Jungian counsellor, and workshop leader, I have also crossed professional borders. When people ask what I do, I hesitate because it's such a mix. With feet in a number of different camps, I have always been at the margins, never in the inner circle. As a young professor I saw students hungry for embodied knowledge and understanding that would nourish their hearts as well as their intellect. When I expressed this during department meetings there was silence, as if it were somehow unseemly to suggest our students might bring more than their minds to class. And yet it was obvious—imagination and feeling, sweat and tears, anger and outrage—all were present in the college classroom and welcome, too, as far as I was concerned. The warmth that often developed in class had less to do with the curriculum than with the sharing of stories and experiences, and the homemade muffins I brought to class.

My formal Jungian study began with a renegade program whose founders hailed from the worlds of English literature and Jungian studies, dance, theatre, and voice. Working at the margins of academic and Jungian institutions, our fearless Body Soul Rhythms leaders—Marion Woodman, Mary Hamilton, and Ann Skinner—encouraged each woman's quest to move beyond lifelong roles and explore the new reality emerging out of her dreams, body, and soul, quietly subverting conventional notions of healing and therapy. From Ireland to Israel, Brazil to Australia, Canada to South Africa, and many other countries, we gathered and explored, an international community of women travellers. And although there were rigorous program requirements, there was no official degree or diploma at the end; what we took from it is what we got.

In my own workshops I have wanted to provide a space where body, soul, and spirit are all invited to the dance of creative exploration. After many years of focussing on writing I created *Body Soul Writing*, where we weave writing with movement exploration and dance, music and art, dream work and guided meditation. For many participants the joy and freedom of moving freely between writing and other channels of creative expression—embodied writing—is the week's biggest revelation. Out of that evolved *Body Soul Sundays*, a nine-month Jungian program for women that brings together everything I love—literature and writing, depth psychology and myth, music and dance, love of mystery and yearning for soul. With my embroidered altar cloth from Rajasthan and Black Madonna candle from Einsiedeln on the altar table, we study Jung and dance our dreams as we explore the archetypal energies that shape our lives.

"So you are a *father's daughter?*" Marion Woodman said to us on more than one occasion. "Celebrate it!" Accept it as both blessing and burden, in other words. "So you are a fiery, thin-skinned *gypsy*," I tell myself. "Celebrate that too!" And accept the particular suffering that comes with being true to myself including failures and blind spots. There is no doubt I have sometimes crossed boundaries of decorum and tactfulness as my outspoken self attempts to discern what can and cannot be spoken. I come by it honestly; my mother almost always said what was on her mind, and it was not always gentle or kind. But honest it was.

My favourite books usually elude established categories and meander among genres. *Gypsy Fugue* crosses the boundary between memoir and personal essay, blends Jungian scholarship and ethnographic research, blurs the border between concrete and imaginal, discursive and poetic, and between the inner and outer realities that make up our lives. "Breaking boundaries, whether it be of syntax, content, or style, is a peculiarly Dionysian vehicle for the conveyance of new material," says Nor Hall. The Roma people and the *archetypal gypsy* manifest the energy of Dionysus, god of eros, indulgence, and ecstatic revelry. Would it be presumptuous, then, to imagine *archetypal memoir* as a vehicle for the conveyance of new material, and the *gypsy* as its perfect Dionysian examplar?

Gypsy-Scholar /
Scholar-Gypsy

In her wonderful book *Wild: An Elemental Journey*, Jay Griffiths says:

> To be a nomad in one's mind is in our gift: to move and learn, to
> be a student always, to discover new lands, leaving behind some
> rock of certainty, to wonder without doxy, letting the mind wan-
> der till it surprises itself. The mind, let loose, is a walking, asking,
> searching thing, an extra-vagrant of mental journeys, questioning,
> questioning, whose root, of course, is to seek, to go on a quest.

Sometimes this nomadic quest leads me out into the shining world; sometimes it takes me deeper into my own imagination; and sometimes it tempts
me into bibliographies of wonder. So much mystery all around, and so many
dimensions to explore. The fact that I am no longer young and the horizon
ahead no longer limitless tells me I'd better choose wisely. Even shrewdly.

Matthew Arnold's poem "The Scholar-Gipsy" (1853) tells of an Oxford lad who left the hallowed halls of the university and went "to learn
the gipsy-lore, and roam the world with that wild brotherhood." Arnold
could have been describing Walter Starkie (1894–1976), the Irish scholar
and musician who wrote many books about his own double life of teaching
throughout the academic year, then travelling with Gypsies during long
summers of music making. Starkie spoke fluent Romany and claimed some
of the Gypsies as his blood brothers. He writes that Hungarian Gypsies
taught him "there are two kinds of music and poetry in the world, the tame
and the wild. To pick up the wild I had to join the Romanichels in their
tents and caravans, learning the wisdom of the sun, moon, stars, and opening my ears to the music of the wind on the heath."

I wandered (though sadly never with Gypsies) all through my university years, among academic departments, countries, and training programs, not knowing where I'd end up, or whether all those years of study would ever amount to anything like a career or a professional identity. While teaching in New York I wrote, "My adjunct status at the College of Staten Island places me both inside and outside the academy, but being underemployed has its distinct advantages. A gypsy scholar is exempt from the usual round of administrative duties and committee work. I have more control of my time and energy than most people I know." By then I had completed university degrees in three literary fields, and several additional diploma and certificate programs. I'd studied in four countries and taught in five universities in eight departments and programs, all with no fixed academic home, office, or scholarly identity. As a *gypsy scholar*, I taught where I was invited and where I felt drawn. English and world literature, creative writing and women's studies, interdisciplinary and continuing studies programs. Twenty-five different undergraduate and graduate courses in a dozen years.

Academic scholarship is traditionally defined by well-bounded disciplines but much of what I've done has been interdisciplinary in the broadest sense. So I was intrigued to discover an article claiming Arnold's Scholar-Gipsy and the Roma themselves as fitting metaphors for the majority of people engaged in interdisciplinary work, people who often find themselves homeless, in a state of social and intellectual marginality. If boundary crossing has become a defining characteristic of the age and "creativity and breakthroughs are most likely at the intersections of the disciplines," the *gypsy scholar* is a fitting image of both the hardships and generative possibilities of crossing these boundaries.

Clearly the upside of my tenuous and untenured academic lot was a great freedom to do work I loved, and my private writing workshops flourished. Then out of the blue I was offered a high-level administrative position at my college and, for the first time in my life, a generous salary and benefits package. The night before I had to call in my decision I dreamed I'd stepped out of the subway and walked into Bloomingdale's on an impulse, hoping to find something wonderful I could buy. But I soon discovered the exquisite lingerie on display was not my size, decided the Godiva chocolates weren't good for Steve or me, and the green plates beside the escalator were not genuine Depression glass but imitation. At that point I walked out of the store empty-handed with no regrets. I had hoped for a dream to help me decide and the clear symbolism of "not my size," "not good for Steve or me," and "not genuine but imitation" made it easy to decline the position and carry on with my adjunct teaching, independent scholarly work, and beloved workshops.

Independent scholarly work is itself a kind of endless wandering into unknown territory. An exciting and open-ended treasure hunt, where synchronicity points the way. The danger being that I want to "walk the Camino" for every vignette, write a thesis rather than an anecdote or personal reflection. Often I've had to call a halt, remind myself that I can't write a lengthy opus on each variation of the *gypsy* theme, no matter how exciting the connections that emerge.

However, this freedom comes at a considerable cost. For a *gypsy scholar* it means sporadic work and little sense of belonging to a stable or supportive community, negligible pay and professional recognition, no pension, sick leave, or paid holidays. No guarantee of employment from one semester to the next, and no safety net in times of emergency. A marginal existence indeed.

Writing the Gypsy

A way of saying is needed whose failure to identify the ways of the soul
with the certainty of facts or the precision of ideas becomes the measure of
its success. A way of saying is needed whose energy and rhythms, imagery
and animation serve the soul in its vagabond wanderings.

—Robert Romanyshyn

A good word is like bread.

Romany proverb

This book is itself a *gypsy*. A shape-shifter from the start, it has been a restless
and unruly thing, forever eluding my attempts to approach in writing something that remains, at heart, a mystery. Not that I would wish it otherwise
and therein lies a paradox. Perhaps I shouldn't expect to invoke an archetypal
image without suffering its shadow side. Along with the joyous romp and
riot of music and dance, I have experienced considerable chaos and liminality, resistance to order, and rebellion against limitations, especially my own.
Often sentences, paragraphs, and entire sections have (e)migrated from one
chapter to another before ending up somewhere entirely unforeseen. Sometimes I've felt this book is all over the map, and maybe that's exactly where
a *gypsy* book should be. But the truth is I have never written anything so
mercurial, so difficult to grasp hold of and corral into its proper place.

As I noted earlier, *wander* comes from the Latin *vagary*, the root of
vagabond. While writing the *gypsy* I have been a vagabond in a mythic landscape of unknown and immeasurable dimensions. As I write this, two huge
flowering cherry trees are bursting into bloom outside my studio window.
But parts of this book have been written in India, in the south of France and
in Spain, in Switzerland and England, and on various islands in the Pacific

Northwest. A vagabond book, forever on the road. Forever a trickster, one moment showing me its tantalizing face, then disappearing into the shadows, just beyond my grasp. Throughout the months and years of its gestation, fantasy and imaginative association flowed most freely when I was on my feet, walking through the tree-lined avenues of Vancouver or along the shores of Jericho Beach, or dancing. It could hardly hold still.

My first book is a celebration of women's journals, my second, a year-long meditation on simplicity—well-behaved books, both. This one is a wild child. I never know where it will go next, and writing it has been anything but an orderly process. Often I've meandered among vignettes and chapters, adding a few words here, a sentence there, not always sure of where I am, but not lost either. Written by short-term visitation, the chapters have fertilized each other over time as I moved among Roma culture and folklore, dreams and archetypal readings, memories and snippets of autobiography, poetry and music, ethnomusicology and film. One day, it's Isabel Fonseca's tale of living with eastern European Gypsies, the next day, James Hillman's *Healing Fiction,* Leonard Cohen's *Book of Longing,* or Nor Hall's *Dreaming in Red.* All my efforts at steady and consistent productivity have brought nothing but frustration; it has indeed resisted the certainty of facts and perhaps even the precision of ideas that psychologist Robert Romanyshyn describes as antithetical to the ways of the soul.

Frequently I've wandered off the fugal path, down many tempting side roads. There are countless possible variations of the *gypsy* theme and each vignette begs for further fantasy and amplification. But would these meanderings ever amount to a book, I wondered, and if so, what kind of book would it be? Often I felt liminal as I explored the imaginal body of the *gypsy* in writing, and wondered if I was conjuring up a chimera.

Returning to the book after months of teaching, I felt lost. *What is it I'm really writing about?* I asked myself. Not a memoir of my outer life, but not a personal journal either. Something very intimate but also transpersonal, since the *gypsy* is a potent symbol for many others too. How to write about this when I struggle to understand it myself. Everything about this book has felt elusive, like quicksilver.

❧

During my childhood in the fertile farmlands of the Fraser Valley, we often bought milk from friends and made our own butter. When the cream had risen to the top of the gallon jar, my mother carefully skimmed and ladled it into another glass jar. Then we placed the jar between our knees and shook it up and down, back and forth, as vigorously as we could until our arms ached and we began to think nothing would ever happen. Finally someone would notice tiny yellow specks starting to appear, and gradually small blobs of buttery fat, and then larger chunks, until at long last they coalesced into one large, irregularly formed ball of butter floating in a sea of delicious buttermilk that tasted nothing like the store-bought kind. That was always a magical moment.

And that pretty much describes my experience of writing this book, but the butter has been a long time coming! Rocking the alchemical vessel with the hope that something substantial will appear, writing the gypsy has been a process of gradual clumping and accretion. Of gathering associations, amplifications, and fragments of others' writing that sing to me and seduce my promiscuous, polygamous imagination. I have been a *flâneur*, a passionate stroller through other writers' pages. What joy there is in finding the perfect word or phrase, even if it isn't my own; in creating a gypsy bricolage, a quilt of quotes, a choir of voices. Memoir—from the French mémoire, or "memory"—is not usually peppered with quotations but I have woven in other people's words that have im-pressed me, pressed themselves into me, become part of me. Paradox underlies not just the title but the entire book. My hope was to combine solidly grounded research with flights of fancy and personal associations, tender thoughtfulness with reckless audacity. A tall order, to bring these opposites together.

❧

When I began writing this book I dreamed of a woman standing very close to a blackboard. I watched with curiosity and someone explained that she was writing with her breasts in order to create intimacy. I have thought of that dream so often. To write with her breasts is to share her most feminine essence with a roomful of others. Women write with mother's milk, in white ink, says Hélène Cixous. Then I remember that she describes writing as a gesture of love and the feminine writer as "she who looks with the look that recognizes, that studies, respects, doesn't take, doesn't claw, but attentively, with gentle relentlessness, contemplates and reads, caresses, bathes, makes the other gleam. Brings back to light the life that's been buried, fugitive, made too prudent. Illuminates it and sings it its names." That would be *writing with one's breasts*. And it all fits. I do yearn to reclaim the *gypsy*'s fugitive life that has been made too prudent—in myself and in our culture at large—illuminate it, and sing it its names.

Feminine writing—writing in circles, circumambulating the mystery without a blueprint or map, writing associatively and following the soul. "Multiple beginnings are characteristic of archetypal work," I read. "A feminine text starts on all sides at once, starts twenty times, thirty times, over."

✍

Perhaps this is also a love song to all the authors who have "written with their breasts" and whose writing has nourished and inspired me over the years—Hélène Cixous and Marie Cardinal, Virginia Woolf and Christa Wolf, Helen Luke and Marion Woodman—but this is hopeless because the list would run many pages long and include men who wrote with white ink, too. Not to mention the poets, who become more important to me with each passing year. All of them, imaginal *gypsies*, with their nomadic, questing, roaming, trickster imaginations.

✍

Writing out of the imaginal realm I am faced again and again with the realization that I am writing about something invisible, intangible, and mostly beyond words. The discrepancy between my hopes for this book and their imperfect realization on the page can only be acknowledged, never resolved. Perhaps because, as Hillman says, the *daimon* doesn't recognize limitations and can never be satisfied by the accomplishments of mortals.

✍

This is one way to write my story. I could have written it another way.

✍

What I didn't expect to discover was my own reluctance to disclose personal details of my biography. Even though I've taught life-writing workshops for decades, I'd never envisioned writing a memoir myself, and even granting that the desire to hide in order to be safe is characteristic of the *archetypal gypsy*, I found myself looking for cover. I've written a journal since age eleven, no holds barred, but here I've often felt like hiding my story rather than committing it to paper. Often I've written myself around and between the stories. Sometimes I really did feel I was starting twenty, thirty times over, and almost despaired of pulling it all together.

There's also the matter of truth in the autobiographical realm, along with the desire not to betray the soul. *Writing the gypsy* may indeed involve concealing as much as I reveal; perhaps even concealing while seeming to reveal. Tricksterish memoir writing. Now you see me, now you don't; now it's my face you see, now it's your own. So that in reading this, you are looking into a mirror, brought back to your own dark *gypsy* life.

Let the writing be edgy then. Tender and volatile, capricious and raw. Let it echo and incarnate the *gypsy*'s edgy antics. Like a kaleidoscope (from *kalos*/"beautiful," *eidos*/"form," *scopein*/"look at") revealing ever-shifting patterns of colour and form, reflecting all the facets of the *archetypal gypsy*. Let it be lyrical and loving, turbulent and crude. Let it begin twenty times, thirty times, over, each time in a new register.

> The process is after all like music,
> like the development of a piece of music.
> The fugues come back and
>   again and again
> interweave.
> A theme may seem to have been put
> aside,
> but it keeps returning—
> the same thing modulated,
> somewhat changed in form.
> Usually richer.
> And it is very good that this is so.

ZÜRICH DREAMS

Ever since I read Jung's *Memories, Dreams, Reflections* thirty years ago I dreamed of becoming a Jungian analyst. After spending half my adult life as a student, the thought of embarking on what is essentially another doctoral program seemed impractical but the dream persisted. Once Steve and I had settled in Vancouver in the summer of 2000, it occurred to me that perhaps I could, after all, go to Zürich as a matriculated auditor for a semester, with the possibility of training as an analyst.

No doubt it was the *gypsy* who took me to Switzerland. There are training institutes much closer to home but my parents and grandparents stem from Germany, Russia, Poland, and Czechoslovakia, and my ancestral roots lie deep in central Europe. My mother tongue was German, and my parents often conversed in various Slavic dialects when they didn't want the children to understand what they were saying to each other. I'd always dreamed of living in Europe and this seemed a perfect occasion.

Zürich is a gracious and beautiful city of lilacs and roses, where life is lived on a human scale. I loved being a student again, going to lectures and seminars taught by Jungians from all over the world, and then returning to the solitude of my little studio apartment at the foot of Zürichberg. Evenings I read Jung and Marie-Louise von Franz, dined on roast chicken and salad, red wine and chocolate from the nearby Migros market, and danced alone in my studio.

The International School of Analytical Psychology, known as ISAP, draws mature students from many corners of the world, and the fact that I could speak German was a boon. On free afternoons I wandered for hours through the city and up the hill, where I could look down on Lake Zürich glistening in the late-afternoon sunshine. Many churches offered classical music every weekend and a variety of concerts and lectures were available all through the week. I loved living in the heart of Europe, just a few hours' train travel from half a dozen other countries. Steve and I spoke on the telephone daily and exchanged frequent emails. He visited me in Zürich and I flew home between semesters to be with him and the rest of my family, and to earn some money teaching. In many ways, it was a charmed life.

After a number of years during which my writing had taken a back seat to other creative work, I looked forward to completing the essays required of training candidates. I mentioned earlier that *Gypsy Fugue* grew out of the first of these, but my fascination with the *gypsy* continued to grow, and when it came time to write my comparative religion and ethnology essays, the topics had already chosen me: "Dark Sisters: Kali and the Black Madonna," and "The Role of Song in the Lives of Contemporary European Roma."

"You're well on the way with your next book here," my Reader commented. I felt my body and soul pulsing with the colours and rhythms of the *gypsy* and everything I'd discovered about the Roma, and I'd never had so many people ask if I had Gypsy blood. Once again I delighted in wearing my *gypsy* skirts, and singing and dancing in my room to music I'd uploaded onto my trusty laptop. It seemed the *gypsy* had seized hold of me and I was filled with creative fire.

And yet—somewhere along the way I also began to feel uncertain about whether I could continue my studies in Zürich. I'd told myself and those close to me that I would take things one semester at a time, to be sure. But since I relished all aspects of life in Zürich my ambivalence seemed strange, and I searched deep within myself, trying to understand it. The long separations from my husband and aging parents, several new and promising projects awaiting me at home, and a lifelong impatience with institutional structures—all were at play. At times I felt I had one foot in and one foot out. It was disconcerting and I knew I couldn't go on like that forever.

My dreams, meanwhile, were unsettling, to say the least. Again and again I dreamed of being ignored or snubbed by the Jungian community in Zürich and of turning my back on them. Something wasn't working. Finally I had several dreams that seemed to shed some light on my inner predicament. In one, I was instructed by a Jungian interviewer to write my name on my forehead. "I had to do that once before when I was baptized into the Church," I responded. "I'm not going to do it again."

In another dream I found myself in a comfortable sitting area in a spacious and beautiful underground library in Zürich, with my back turned to the room. The walls of the library were covered with rock paintings, figures of humans and animals, and it occurred to me that this place was very old and had been there for a long time. Weathered wooden chairs, tables covered with flowers, and old Persian carpets were tucked into the room's nooks and crannies. Several other students were working quietly in the library and the atmosphere was peaceful and still. Antique bookshelves loaded with books lined the walls, and several large, square cases of CDs and DVDs with music and film stood at the front, next to the checkout counter, along with a tall, rotating stand displaying semi-transparent greeting cards that could be purchased for nine Swiss francs. Far too expensive, I thought as I looked at them. They're beautiful, but I don't want to pay that much for greeting cards when I can make my own, which are just as attractive.

Then I noticed two dimly lit tunnels leading out of the library, ancient underground walkways like catacombs, leading off into the dark unknown. The rough tunnel walls were covered with gold leaf with black stone shimmering through the gold, and there was more cave art visible too. A soft light flickered off the gilded walls in such a way that they appeared almost alive, and suddenly I knew I had to explore those glistening caves and discover where they would lead me. I was fascinated by their primal energy, such a stark contrast to the gracious and civilized atmosphere of the library.

What struck me most as I reflected on the dream afterward was my unwillingness to pay what seemed like an unreasonable price for the transparent greeting cards and the feeling that I absolutely had to walk into those caves. I felt these were clues, and wondered whether my unconscious was urging me toward the dimly lit, mysterious underground tunnels. Away from the scholarly collective represented by the beautiful library, and onto my own individual journey into unknown *gypsy* territory. I had no idea where those tunnels would take me, but I felt compelled to find out.

This possibility seemed to be echoed in a third dream where I showed up for a seminar about the Roma and their horses just to discover I was the only one there. The seminar was to be taught by a Jungian lecturer with whom I had struck up a friendship and who'd previously been married to a Roma man. I knew that horses are important for the Roma, and when I shared the dream with my analyst, he suggested the reason that I was the only one at the seminar was because the *gypsy* symbol was intended only for me.

Throughout that semester a refrain kept playing through my head, despite my best efforts to suppress it. "I think I'm done here," a voice said, over and over again.

"But I came here to become a Jungian analyst," I protested. "I don't want to leave! I love the seminars, the sense of community here, and the people I've met. And I love living in Zürich."

"I think I'm done here," I heard again, quietly in the background. Every day I found myself asking, "When, if not now?" The old *thou shalts* and need to finish what I'd begun no longer seemed to apply. Which didn't make it any easier because if I knew anything, it was how to obey the inner *shoulds*.

One day it struck me that whatever my future in Zürich might be— whether I would stay or leave—henceforth the decisions I made in my life would be based solely on Dreams, Desire, and Delight. In Upper Case Letters. Not Duty, Diligence, nor Dread of failure. Simply Dreams, Desire, and Delight.

<hr />

"Good news," I said to my training analyst as I walked into his office one shining May morning after waking up with a vivid dream. "Singing and dancing have broken out in the German Baptist Church." He knew that the question of whether or not I would continue my studies in Zürich was foremost in my thoughts.

"That's wonderful," he said, with a rare smile. "It doesn't matter then, whether you go or stay. The important work has been done." We had worked hard on what he referred to as my "German Baptist complex."

I took the exams and returned to Vancouver bursting with creative energy. Again I heard, like a constant background refrain, "I think I'm done there." Again I tried to stifle it, but there it was.

Months of uncertainty followed. One dream of dark men and women blocking my way over the Limmat River as I tried to return to my little room next to the institute left me wondering whether this *gypsy* complex was preventing me from achieving my lifetime dream. I felt anguish and a deep sense of loneliness, knowing that no matter how much my family and friends might want to support me, the decision was ultimately mine to make. Liminality, a sense of being adrift, and some small consolation from Gide's caveat, "One does not discover new lands without consenting to lose sight of the shore for a very long time." I repeated those words out loud day after day as I waited, hoping for clarity. Sometimes I second-guessed my understanding of the dreams and wanted to return to Zürich in order to put an end to the painful sense of uncertainty and of being between worlds. Then I happened upon a passage by Marie-Louise von Franz that helped me no end.

> Generally, if one can stand the agony of no decision and go on watching the dreams without making any hasty movement, the situation clarifies and one eventually gets a dream which clearly illustrates the point, or in consciousness one gets a feeling of what to do. Then one can decide without a dream, one has a strong feeling as to what one is going to do and will stick to that, no matter what the unconscious thinks about it; the solution out of the agony of doubt, the solution as a third thing comes into existence. But a certain backbone and inner strength of personality is needed to stand the agony. Haste is of the devil, as the alchemists say, and all hastiness or nervous wanting of a quick decision is a symptom of psychological weakness and childishness. Panic is the one really catastrophic thing in dealing with the unconscious.

And agony there was. Often the old critical voices raged at me with accusations of arrogance—"Who do you think you are to think you can do Jungian work without a diploma?"—and of the most insidious sin of all, self-deception. Two semesters went by and I didn't return. Finally a bureaucratic issue forced my hand, and since I couldn't decide wholeheartedly to return I decided to withdraw, with a very heavy heart.

In the Russian folk tale "The Maiden King," the old crone Baba Yaga asks Ivan, the young hero, "Are you here of your own free will or by compulsion?" Ivan replies, "Largely of my own free will, and twice as much by compulsion," suggesting the question can't be answered on the basis of logic. I think I will never know exactly what led me out of Zürich. Some might say I got caught up in a *gypsy* complex; even I can argue that abandoning a training program midway, after longing to be there for decades, points toward a possession by archetypal energies not answerable to reason. I would prefer to believe that in tracking my dreams as honestly as possible I was responding to something deeper than my desire to become an analyst; something telling me my path was not that of the Jungian collective.

But it took me another long year of heartache to let go of the dream. I took some comfort knowing that among Jungian writers whose work I loved most, both Helen Luke and Robert Johnson had also followed solitary paths and experienced self-doubt and loneliness in being true to their calling. Above my desk I placed the following quote of Jung and I read it every day for months.

> If you want to go your individual way it is the way you make for yourself, which is never prescribed, which you do not know in advance, and which simply comes into being of itself when you put one foot in front of the other. If you always do the next thing that needs to be done, you will go most safely and surefootedly along the path prescribed by your unconscious.

When people ask why I went to Zürich, the obvious answer is to study Jung's work and become an analyst myself. The more vulnerable and honest response is that I wanted to know, as fully as possible, what lies deepest and darkest in me. The good, the bad, and the ugly; the creative and the destructive. Both for myself, and in order not to project my own "stuff" onto others, whether family or friends, clients or workshop participants. What I discovered, or rediscovered on another round of the spiral, is the realm of the deep feminine and my own *dark sisters*: the *gypsy* and her lust for life, the *crone* and her steady, grounding gaze, and the *witch*, ready to pounce on the new creation.

Back in Vancouver, I resolved to bring the *gypsy*'s creative fire into my work as a Jungian counsellor. But what would it mean to bring that energy into what Jungian analyst and writer Murray Stein refers to as the "third space" between counsellor and client? I allowed myself to spin a fantasy of what that might look like.

FANTASIA FOR A GYPSY ANALYST

Jung did not encourage people to become acquiescent members of society but eccentric individuals on their own unique journeys. Presumably that applies to the way analysts and counsellors conduct their work with clients as well. This is how I imagine it.

To bring the *gypsy* into the third space of analysis or counselling is to roam and wander with the client during the therapeutic hour. Not feel beholden to an agenda of fixing anything, of helping the client feel better or achieve adaptation to the status quo. Not bound by any orthodoxy or established technique, but attuned to how the psyche speaks through symptom and symbol, dream and fantasy, desire and aversion, gesture and sound. Free to follow intuition, meander, squat and dwell, and carry on.

To bring the *gypsy* into the third space is to create a common language between analyst and client, a "Romany of the unconscious" arising out of the client's dreams and synchronicities, where recurring themes become incantations. To celebrate the kinship, the Jungian "Romanes," forged by this common language. To acknowledge that their shared devotion to the client's *deep song* and their ongoing commitment of time and energy (including the analyst's expertise and client's financial resources) to non-lucrative pursuits is a radical gesture of faith in an age obsessed with quick-fix remedies. To allow for detours, idiosyncrasies, and the trickster dynamics of Hermes. To appreciate flourish and embellishment in what happens; not be caught by too literal and prosaic a reality, or feel oneself bound by facts that may obscure deeper layers of truth. To express a certain shared recklessness and passionate enthusiasm in their felt connection and desire to make "true speech" together. To embrace liminality, the in-between, where all things are possible and nothing is fixed. The client doesn't know where he or she is headed and neither does the analyst or counsellor, but they are travellers together. *Unterwegs*, on the way, in service to the client's individuation journey. As Jung himself intimated in many different ways, to be on that journey is to be at the goal.

Then analysis becomes a shared pilgrimage, and analyst and client, a caravan of two. A temporary rest station. An oasis on the long journey of life. A *caravanserai* (like the ancient inns along the Silk Road where travellers could rest and recover at day's end) of the inner world, where nomadic analyst and client meet for the sake of safety and nourishment and to discover new springs of living water in the depths of the client's psyche. Knowing their relationship to be both real and something apart from everyday reality, existing on a different plane, in a different dimension. Allowing a rambunctious and unbridled energy to animate the space between them, and together loving the imaginal embellishments and adornments of the journey, the often exquisite "embroidery" of it all. Giving in to *Weltschmerz*, and feeling the archetypal loneliness that Hillman claims is essential to our condition. Turning it into poetry, song, and dance. Together creating the kind of *cante jondo* that Jan Yoors discovered among the Roma, *deep song* that carries their way of life "in its fullness, intensity and dignity," just as the analyst helps mediate the client's sense of wholeness, meaning, and possibility in life. Holds clients in unconditional love while helping them to love their own images and discover the creative force and healing power of their own numinous symbols.

A *gypsy* analyst might take to the road from time to time, occasionally disappear for a month or two, not succumb to entrenched routine, week in and week out. This is how Jung himself worked, after all, and Marion Woodman too, alternating months of intense work with clients with periods of writing and travel, and engagement with the world at large. This rhythm would appeal to clients who are themselves nomadic at heart. *Gypsy* clients. Analysis itself is boundary-crossing work, "a place of paradox, liminality, and in-betweenness," which suggests there are strong *gypsy* and *trickster* elements present in any analysis, as analyst and client sojourn through inner and outer realms of the client's psyche, move back and forth between consciousness and unconsciousness, past and present, ego and Self.

This is how I imagine my work as a Jungian counsellor. Not having completed the formal training program for Jungian analysts, that's how I refer to myself, although I was intrigued to hear rumours of "black analysts," those students of Jung who went on to practise without formal accreditation. Perhaps it's a fantasy, but this is as much a work of my imagination as anything else. And maybe it wouldn't be called analysis anymore but something else, Jungian synthesis, perhaps. A gathering together of shards and fragments, of the broken, shattered, cast-off parts of us into a wholeness that acknowledges and accepts and blesses them all.

CARAVANS

As I was reflecting on what to call my workshop and seminar series some years ago I dreamed of a large, earthy woman who moved slowly around a circle of people, greeting each one with a specific gesture and inviting them to respond with a gesture of their own. When she came around to me she looked deeply into my eyes and said, "Gesture to the left, and imagine that you are joining a caravan." I was moved and delighted. She got it exactly right, I thought. She sees who I am!

Caravan comes from the Persian *karwan* or "group of desert travellers." Its meanings include "covered horse-drawn carriage," "vehicle on wheels for living in—a gypsy caravan," and "a company of travellers, merchants or pilgrims, travelling together for safety, as through a desert." On my website I wrote, "We are all travelers and pilgrims wandering along our journey through life, on the way to somewhere that feels like home—often in solitude, sometimes in loneliness, and occasionally in the blessed company of other travelers. In recognition of the safety and companionship we offer each other along the way and the fact that these workshops and seminars travel wherever they are welcome, I am calling them *Caravan Workshops and Seminars*."

Not long after that I dreamed there were caravans in the park across the street from our home, next to the water. Gypsies on our street! The scene was so vivid that I sprang out of bed and looked out the living room window. In the early morning light the field was empty, but in my imagination, the Gypsies and their caravans lingered. In another dream I was walking down the same street with a friend when suddenly I spotted an ornate, burgundy caravan at the side of the road. "Look," I said excitedly, "there must be Roma nearby!"

While reading about the Roma I came across the fascinating story of Jan Yoors, a young Belgian boy who left his home during the 1930s to travel with a group of Gypsies and was adopted into their tribe. Many years later he recalled the lively sights and sounds of his first encounter—"Fifteen covered wagons were spread out in a wide half circle, partly hiding the Gypsies from the road"—and his sense as a young boy of their mysterious and fleeting appearance. "Tomorrow they would no doubt vanish again, leaving hardly a trace of their presence—a few dark spots where the campfires had burned, some refuse and trampled grass—and only the rumors about them would remain."

The covered wagons of American pioneers moving westward in the nineteenth century provided temporary shelter en route to new territories and homes, but for the Roma, the traditional horse-drawn caravan or *vardo* itself has been home. A moveable home in their moveable country. Ornately painted and decorated, the vardos were embellished with traditional Romany symbols (horses, birds, vine work, floral designs), extensive scrollwork, and gold-leaf ornamentation.

I saw this for myself in 2009 when I visited the Gordon Boswell Romany Museum in England, which claims to have the largest collection of vardos in the world. As Gabi and I wandered through the museum, Mr. Boswell himself invited us to step up into the vardos and take a closer look, and I was struck by their comfort and elegance. We also entered several fully furnished modern caravans where, to my delight, I quickly spotted the Royal Albert Old Country Roses bone china I'd collected as a young woman, its audacious red and yellow roses reflecting Gypsy (and *gypsy*) opulence and love of colour. The modern caravans of the 1970s were much larger and contained more of the creature comforts that sedentary folk deem essential to the good life, but they lacked the exotic charm of their predecessors. In Les Saintes-Maries-de-la-Mer too I had seen vardos with birds and animals carved into their wooden frames but they were far outnumbered by their modern counterparts, long, sleek white vans with roll-down canopies at the sides providing cover for people to sit and visit.

I imagine these modern caravans don't appear and vanish as mysteriously as the covered wagons Jan Yoors saw on the outskirts of Antwerp almost a century ago, but they still bear witness to a people prepared to move on at a moment's notice. Perhaps that's why they continue to hold such appeal for many people today. "The lure of wild and nomadic freedom has never left us, any of us," Jay Griffiths writes. "It is in our lungs, breathing in freedom, in our eyes, hungry for horizons, and in our feet, itching for the open road. Put your boots on."

The desire to be less weighed down with material possessions and responsibilities of ownership in favour of greater mobility may also be behind the impulse of the recent "small house" movement. Some "tiny houses," as they are called, are even built on wheels so they can be hitched to the owner's car and transported down the highway to a new location, like a turtle carrying its home on its back. To say nothing of the recent trend among retirees to take to the road in custom-fitted RVs in pursuit of milder climates and seasons of the year.

Another variation is the trend toward owning yurts. When my friend Sally had to sell her home and adjoining five acres on Vancouver Island, her friends simply dismantled her beloved yurt, then moved and reassembled it at the rear of the small cottage she bought for herself, under the shade of tall Douglas fir trees. Sally doesn't live in the yurt, but she could. It has a huge deck at the front, electrical heating and a full bathroom and spacious storage closet built onto one side. Our friendship sparked over our shared fascination with yurts at a time when most people hadn't even heard of them. It wasn't feasible for me to have one in the city but Sally offered me space on her five acres to build my own yurt as a writing retreat. I had visions of waking up to birdsong and sunshine pouring through the skylight and the fantasy was tantalizing but the five-hour travel time and expensive ferry trip between our homes were daunting, and I regretfully declined.

Instead, we began offering annual *Jung in the Yurt* weekend workshops in Sally's yurt and I was amazed at how different it felt to be in a circular space with a dome-like ceiling and no corners.

A round room offers no place to hide and no one is far from centre. With its wood-burning stove and the nineteenth-century hand-carved wooden doors Sally's father had brought back from Spain, the space feels hallowed and intimate, even with fifty people inside. When we get up to dance it feels like we're moving inside a mandala.

Nor Hall writes, "The gypsy wagon is the best possible way to give an image to the idea of a roving temenos. A *temenos* is a sacred enclosure, a sanctuary, a square or ovular space where individuating or unfolding life is protected. These spaces must be 'roving' now that our orientation toward spirit and the search for meaning are no longer attached to specific sacred stones, groves, mountains, or altars where the god dwells." For Rumi and Hafiz, the caravan was a reminder of human transience and community on the move. "Come, come, whoever you are," Rumi invites us, "Wanderer, worshipper, lover of leaving. / Ours is not a caravan of despair." And Hafiz writes, "every moment camel bells leaving the caravanserai / This is how we wake, with winespills / On the prayer rug." For Saadi, the world is "a caravan, / filled with eccentric beings / telling wondrous stories about God."

The longing at the heart of their poetry echoes in the music of Loreena McKennitt, Canadian songwriter and singer-musician. She doesn't refer specifically to the Roma but themes of exile and transience run through her music and extensive liner notes, as she travels through the world, exploring the roots and affinities of Eastern and Western spirituality and music. The haunting melodies, exotic instrumentation and blending of diverse musical traditions capture the nomadic impulse and the yearning for a home that is not of this world. In the deepest sense, all her music is *gypsy* music, as in these lines from "Caravanserai," one of her most beautiful songs.

> This glancing life is like a morning star
> A setting sun, or rolling waves at sea
> A gentle breeze or lightning in a storm
> A dancing dream of all eternity...
> What is this life that pulls me far away
> What is this home where we cannot reside
> What is this life that pulls me far away
> My heart is full when you are by my side.

An inn with a central courtyard where many languages are spoken by travellers from distant lands, the *caravanserai* is where the bazaar is held; where silks, spices, and many other goods are bought, sold, and traded, and human community is practised. Perhaps we are all part of the great *caravanserai* of humans, animals, and nature at large, making our way through life on this beautiful, imperilled planet that we call home.

O Lungo Drom

Happy the man with an open road before him.

Romany proverb

During my time in Zürich it began to dawn on me that what I'd taken as a quixotic lifelong fascination with the *gypsy* has shaped my life at the deepest levels. I have previously described waking up from a dream and hearing the words *The Journey of the Roma, with its Passion, Reality, and Essence* and knowing in my bones that the journey of the Roma was also my own. *O lungo drom*—the long road of the Roma—is an evocative image of the journey through life that Jung referred to as the process of individuation. All our lives we travel through an unknown landscape on a long road filled with endless twists and turns and unforeseeable detours.

According to Jung we are all spiritual *gypsies*. There is no collective road map for individuation. We simply put one foot in front of the other, trusting that our meandering is purposeful even without knowing where the road will take us. The Roma don't speak of individuation but Jan Yoors recounts a conversation he had with his adoptive father.

"One day as we were tending the horses, Pulika asked me abruptly, 'Which is greater, the oak or the dandelion?' The correct Romany solution was 'whichever one of the two achieves fulfillment.' A matured dandelion would be greater than a stunted oak, irrespective of its size or usefulness. The ultimate measure, the fulfillment of one's potentialities, was the valuation: the truthfulness to one's own seed and nature."

During my mid-twenties I took myself to Europe on an open-ended ticket with Pan American Airlines. I'd received a scholarship from the Goethe Institute for advanced German language study in Staufen im Breisgau, a picturesque town on the edge of the Black Forest. I loved the little town with its quaint bakeries and cafés but my native German proficiency put me ahead of the game, so I packed my bags and set out to wander across the continent. For the next five months I travelled by train, bus, and plane through Italy and Austria, Hungary and Yugoslavia, Greece and Israel, with no real plan except to follow my nose, take in as much as I could, and stretch out my limited funds for as long as possible.

In Florence I met Caroline from Boston who had a similar plan, and we decided to travel together. Caroline looked like a cross between Brooke Shields and Margaux Hemingway. Her fair colouring and fresh-faced prettiness identified her as American wherever we went. Not so with me. My brown hair and hazel eyes blended in everywhere, and people generally thought I was one of them. In Italy and Hungary, Greece and Israel, they addressed me in the local language and looked surprised when I stared back in blank incomprehension.

For more than three months Caroline and I wandered through Europe and Israel, hungry for the sights and sounds of cultures we knew little about but attributed with nobler and more romantic values than our own. And yet, not having been born in Europe seemed like a fluke to me; my parents could just as easily have left for Canada a few years later after my birth, or not at all. In many ways, I felt more at home in Europe than in Canada.

Then, just in time for Christmas, I flew home with less than a hundred dollars in my wallet. This was 1979 and near the end of the great wave of hippies backpacking through Europe and Asia. Like the hippies, I was on a quest for cross-cultural adventure and some kind of deeper truth about myself and the larger world than I thought I could find at home. I was never a thrill seeker or even much of a risk taker but I hungered for new experiences—landscapes, customs, food, music, men—with a foreign flavour. No doubt I was hoping to find a broader vision for my life than the evangelical perspective I'd grown up with and abandoned several years earlier. It was during those long months of travel that I encountered Gypsies for the first time. And though my six months of travel through Europe and Israel were tame compared with Jay Griffiths' intrepid expeditions to the farthest corners of the world, I was not the same person when I arrived back home. My *lungo drom* had left its mark and I knew myself to be a traveller.

The lengthy process of writing this book has been its own *lungo drom*. The long road of the archetypal *gypsy* has taken me down unexpected paths in unforeseen directions toward crossroads I never could have anticipated. May the journey continue for as long as I live...

NOCTURNE

DREAMING THE GYPSY

The time will come
When, with elation
You will greet yourself arriving
At your own door, in your own mirror
And each will smile at the other's welcome,

and say, sit here. Eat.
You will love again the stranger who was your self.
Give wine. Give bread. Give back your heart
to itself, to the stranger who has loved you

all your life, whom you ignored
for another, who knows you by heart.
Take down the love letters from the bookshelf,

the photographs, the desperate notes,
peel your own image from the mirror.
Sit. Feast on your life.

—Derek Walcott

And always the dreams. So many dreams of Gypsies over the years. Dreams that have left me with a profound sense of being recognized and known. Nocturne or *night song* reflects the soul's lunar life, invisible in the bright light of daytime. Sometimes I feel my dreams greet me from the underworld and show me my face before I was born. Their *gypsy* wildness energizes my orderly waking life. Then again, as Hillman suggests, maybe it's actually the other way around, and the predictable rhythm of daily life balances out the dark rumblings of my dreams.

Either way, it's hard to miss the vivid *gypsy* thread that runs through them. Richly coloured caravans sitting at the water's edge. Haunting melodies echoing the Gypsy scale. Raven-haired women wearing long floral skirts and dark-skinned men in embroidered vests, playing guitar. Infant girls with huge dark eyes and brown-skinned urchins whose joyful mischief and forlorn abandonment linger long after I wake up. Textiles and tapestries, violins and mandolins, tricksters and vagabonds abound in the stories my psyche tells while I sleep. During the day I work hard to keep a stable identity, but at night the dreams show me the whole range of characters that inhabit my soul, and what a motley crew they are!

According to Marie-Louise von Franz, isolated dreams may seem to be strange and fragmented, but over time "our dream life creates a meandering pattern in which individual strands or tendencies become visible, then vanish, then return again." If we pay attention we can gradually notice "a sort of hidden regulating or directing tendency at work, creating a slow, imperceptible process of psychic growth—the process of individuation." With this in mind I have gathered some of the forty-plus dreams that show the *gypsy* strand weaving through my life during the past decades. For the most part I don't relate them to my personal psychology or what was happening in my waking life at the time. I'm more interested in tracking the evolution of the *gypsy* image itself over the years.

Not surprisingly the main theme is always my identification with Gypsies. In one dream (1998), I have to fill in my ethnic background on an official form. *Traveller/Gypsy* is one of the options and I feel that's the correct one for me. In another (2004), a young musician is playing guitar outdoors in a public square and a crowd gathers around him, dancing and singing along. Someone shows us how to spell our names with sesame seeds and I write *Gypsy*. In a third dream (2003), I am lying on a grassy hillside with several friends from childhood when two European men approach and tell us we aren't attractive to them because we're too much like Gypsies. I get the feeling they mean me because I have the darkest hair and most colourful clothes, but I don't believe them. I think they are just teasing us.

Another thread through the years has been my growing closeness to Gypsies. In my earlier dream of Gypsy women in the English countryside I longed to jump off the pickup truck and join them, and in this one it seems I'm getting closer.

(2002)

I am in Romania with a friend who wants to study the breastfeeding practices of Gypsies. I'm fascinated to see how they live, and wander down a dark and crowded street looking at all the wares for sale. I have been spending time with two women in particular, and I'm living in the home of one of them. The other one tells me she wishes she could run a market stall so she could introduce me to some young men. She has tears in her eyes and I'm touched that it means so much to her, as if meeting a Gypsy man might help keep me there.

I look for an overhead walkway to cross the busy market street but when I climb up the ladder I see it leads only to a high attic-like room full of textiles. I can't easily get in because piles of fabric block the doorway. The room is open on one side and I see a large group of Gypsy women in there. They all wave at me and I feel they have accepted me as one of them.

It appears they're quite poor and it occurs to me that the next time I come, I should bring gifts, although I'm not sure what to bring. They seem to have enough food and there are boxes of fancy soap around, but maybe I can bring them something larger like an appliance, although I'm not sure they even have electricity. I see a Gypsy man wearing a brocade vest with rich colours and I tell them that I have many beautiful brocades at home and sew similar vests myself.

I feel empathy and belonging here. I know the Gypsies are curious about me and have welcomed me into their group. I wasn't born here and I'm not officially one of them, but I feel that they are my people.

This dream was richly atmospheric. I can still see the dark, crowded market street in sepia tones and the attic stacked high with colourful textiles, so much like my own collection of fabrics gathered over the years. I remember the joy of living with Gypsies rather than eyeing them from far away. In the dream it was clear that they wanted me to stay with them, and I no longer felt on the outside hoping to be included.

Some dreams have reflected my physical appearance as a Gypsy and others include Gypsy clothing and closets full of Gypsy garments. In one dream (2007), a Polish woman touches my hair and tells me she loves it. I see myself in a mirror and my hair is long and loose and wavy. I look like a Gypsy. Several other dreams follow below.

(2006)

An older woman with great dignity is making herself clothing out of jewel-toned fabrics. She puts some dark green lace up to her right ear to show me that she can make earrings too. Then she turns into a black woman, and we meet in a store that has many gorgeous Indian gypsy skirts covered with colourful embroidery. The black woman is looking at the skirts with me. She is absolutely and authentically herself, and I love her.

(2008)

There's an open closet with my things in it, and I think, "It's pretty clear this is the closet of a Gypsy." The clothes are all made of dark, floral fabric with lots of flamboyant colour. It's not at all what's in fashion, but I look at it and think, "Yes, that's me." Then I hear a melody, slightly Celtic in flavour, and I wake up humming this melody.

(2008)

A group of friends and I walk to the home of one of my relatives, and we're talking to Gypsies. The Gypsies walk into the bedroom where there's an open closet full of clothes that look just like mine. An older Gypsy helps himself to a colourful skirt that he wants to give to the woman. The man who owns the house is indignant and says, "You can't take that!" The Gypsy throws it on the bed, but then the host relents and says, "All right, take it," and the Gypsy takes it and leaves. There seems to be an understanding that if Gypsies want to take something, you should just let them take it. I'm glad they haven't taken any of my favourites! But mostly I'm just delighted to have spoken with the Gypsies.

When I woke up from this dream I felt great happiness at cavorting and having fun with Gypsy men, since most of my dreams were about women.

Gypsy music is another recurring theme, as in my two earlier dreams of five singing lessons and of the older Gypsy musician in Spain. In another dream I'm looking for CDs of Indian music when I come across scrapbooks of poetry and my own sketches of horses and elephants, animals associated with the Roma.

Often the dreams express joy at sharing time with Gypsies and their happiness to have me with them as well. In one, I am in Les Saintes-Maries-de-la-Mer after the annual gathering of Roma from across the world. In another (2010), I see a vibrant woman with dark, curly hair, and when someone tells me she's a Gypsy, I think, "No wonder I feel such an affinity with her!"

(2008)

I'm in a grocery store with friends, and two women and two men walk in. One woman seems to be British or American, while the other one and the two men are Gypsies. The Gypsy woman, middle-aged, large, and comfortable in her skin, is wearing a floral skirt and blouse. The men look like some of the Gypsies in "Latcho Drom." They are wearing western clothes, shabby and stained.

There are long lineups at the checkouts. I find an express lane that is shorter, and we have just under twelve items, all of us together. As we wait in the lineup I ask them where they are from, and the western woman responds but I don't understand her. The men have merry, laughing faces and the younger one says he is Romny. I feel very happy and tell him, "I thought so—I thought you were Gypsies."

Over the years several dreams contained information that my waking self did not have, instances of what Jung called synchronicity. I had no idea, for example, that the Roma's language is called Romany or that they refer to themselves as Romny, but my unconscious knew. The most dramatic instance of this appears in the following dream.

(2010)

I am in an outdoor market in Italy with a young hippie woman and her little girl. There are five or six Gypsies nearby and the young woman walks up to them and asks, "Are you part of a kumpa?" They nod yes. "Can we talk?" she asks them. Again they say yes, and gesture toward the lone woman in their group as if to say, she's the one to talk to. The men are a little guarded but they look kind and gentle. I sense that they have suffered a lot, and feel empathy for them. I notice that one has clear hazel eyes exactly the same colour as my own. It's that simple, I think. I could join the Gypsies too.

On waking I had no idea whether *kumpa* was even a word but later discovered that a *kumpania* is a Romany caravan group or clan of Gypsies who travel together. In his lyrical fashion, Jan Yoors describes it as "a loose, temporary association, forever kept fluid, scattering and regrouping as new patterns of interests developed, alliances shifted and old relationships waned...endlessly remolding itself but forever remaining true to its own essence."

There are also dreams that show the trickster at play. In one that I mentioned earlier, a group of aggressive dark-skinned men and women block my way on the bridge across the Limmat River in Zürich. Here is another one.

(2009)

A young male trickster stands inside a large, dark brown cone-like structure. I don't even realize there's a real live person in there until someone tells me. There is a little hole around eye level where a worm appears. Apparently this young guy is quite an unruly teenager. It's not clear that he is malicious, but several other women and I feel we have to keep an eye out because we suspect he may have sociopathic tendencies. A kind of gypsy figure appearing out of a mound like a beehive or a huge molehill.

The *gypsy*'s shadow side, too, has appeared, both as victim and persecutor. The following dream haunted me for weeks.

(2002)

I am in a desolate landscape on a bus full of refugees in an atmosphere of great fear. Famine has struck and many people have had no food for weeks other than a few dried-up parsnips. There is a sense of utter devastation everywhere—of starvation and terror and violence ready to erupt at any moment. On the bus there's an uneasy semblance of goodwill, but everyone knows they could be killed at any moment. One middle-aged man near the front seems especially brutal. I am watching things unfold, and wondering if we can get to our destination without any ugliness breaking out.

Halfway back on the left side of the bus, a strong, attractive Gypsy woman in a sari is sitting with her young daughter of eleven or twelve years. For some reason, I fear for them. The woman gets up out of her seat and approaches the nasty man at the front and asks to speak to him.

"I know you are the chief in command and I have a request," she says. She is straightforward and direct, and I fear that he may not like that.

"You are new around here, aren't you?" she says. "We very much need to get some tea. Could we get some tea for my daughter? Our custom here is that when a young girl begins to menstruate we take care of her in that way."

He takes offence at her frank and unapologetic request. At his command, two other men take the terrified young girl out of the bus and throw her over a ravine. Her body forms an arc through the air and I'm sure she will be smashed to death on the rocks below, but she lands on some branches on the top of a tree, and instinctively grabs on to them. She is small and light, and miraculously she is still alive.

I watch it all in shock and horror and don't know how to help her. How will she get safely down? Will she be allowed to live, or will she fall to her death? I wake up deeply shaken.

The dream left me quite shaken emotionally because I identified with the Gypsy mother who was helpless to protect her young daughter from the brutal thugs.

One day I reflected in my journal, "Does the shadow of the *gypsy* gnaw at my soul, containing chaos and perhaps even violence? I need to bring that into my writing and look more closely at the *gypsy's* dark energies." The following morning I woke up with a startling dream of a murderous old witch.

(2008)

A crazy old woman is murdering people. I am terrified because she has just killed somebody. Somehow I manage to scoop her onto a wheelbarrow from behind and then onto a couch. I throw a blanket over her, and don't want anything more to do with her. It seems she has done terrible things in the past. A man named "Lungi" says she murdered his mother during the Holocaust. Suddenly the old woman gets off the couch and starts to head back in my direction.

What can I do? I think in panic. I'll change the locks—I'm bigger than she is so I can probably fight her. I feel she is really evil.

The man is holding a tiny black African boy, not more than two years old, whom he has adopted, in his lap. He gets up and approaches the old woman from behind. She is bent over, and he stabs her in the back. I am so relieved. Good! That's the end of her, once and for all. He says something more and sits down again with his tiny black son peacefully on his lap.

There was the shadow, a crooked old witch lacking physical strength but nonetheless able to kill people through her evil emanation and trickery. Curious about the man's name, I discovered *lungi* is Hindi for a length of cotton or silk worn as a sash or turban, suggesting his Gypsy connection with India.

Many dreams have involved being on the road, on a path, on a journey. Whether I'm riding in the back of a pickup truck, travelling to Romania or Les Saintes-Maries-de-la-Mer, strolling down a street lined with caravans or a trail through the woods, I'm always wandering.

Sometimes the dreams are more oblique: I am discussing Gypsies with friends or reading about them. In one I'm reading a weekly newspaper titled *Romany National News* in a café, and when someone accidentally spills liquid on it, I quickly blot the newspaper so I can finish reading it. In another dream, Marion Woodman appears at my friend's house in the south of France. I struggle to open the front door in order to let her in and she tells me she has brought me a gift. I say, "There are more people interested in Gypsies now than in the past. It used to be just you and I, but now there are others as well." She nods.

In recent years I've dreamed of writing about Gypsies, culminating in the "book of secrets" at the beginning of this book. Here are some earlier variations.

(2007)

I am in the library of the Jung Institute in Küsnacht and a German man picks up an open book about the Roma that I have been looking at. He and his two children are very interested, and I tell them they can get the book from the librarian when I'm done. I mention that I'm writing a book about Gypsies myself, but I'm glad they don't ask me for more information because I wouldn't know how to describe what kind of book it is. I tell them about Ian Hancock's book, *We Are the Romani People*, and write down some other titles for them too.

(2009)

I am outside in a field and I see a group of young Gypsies on a hilly green incline. I've been reading a book about the Roma, and making notes for my own writing. The Gypsies come down and gesture to me to join them, then go back up the hill and begin to dance. I also start dancing, off to the side. A man I know is drumming, and then everyone is dancing. The Gypsies are laughing and amused that we have joined them, and there is a joyous feeling in the air.

(2010)

I am recording a dream about Gypsies when a man approaches and tries to engage me in conversation. I desperately want to write but he is persistent and there's too much commotion, and I can't concentrate. I feel frustrated and angry because I must get the dream written down.

As I wrote this dream into my journal I wondered if the disruptive man in the dream symbolized the inner critic who is forever getting in the way of me *writing the gypsy*.

But even among so many dreams of gypsies, one stands out for its clear and unequivocal affirmation.

(October 24, 2006)

I am walking along a country path with a young man and woman on a beautiful sunny day. The man seems quite interested in me although I don't understand what he is saying. He is speaking Spanish and also using sign language. The young woman seems concerned with establishing her prior claim on him but he persists, and I find myself returning his sparkling glances. Suddenly we come up to a large life-size mirror on the right side of the path. It's set firmly on the grassy earth, and I see my reflection in it.

I am a Gypsy. My hair is long and dark, tied back with a crimson scarf. I'm wearing a yellow peasant blouse and long black skirt with another scarf around my waist, and large gold earrings. I am a Gypsy, and I am beautiful. No wonder that young man is interested in me!

Upon waking it occurred to me that red, yellow, black, and gold are the colours of alchemy. The dream felt like an image of wholeness and completion, like the culmination of a process of transformation. I was very taken with the large mirror on the *right side* of the country path, a mirror that showed me a *life-size* reflection of myself in my *true colours*. With this dream, the last whisper of doubt that I might be conjuring a romantic self-idealization was put to rest. "From the palace of mirrors send me my old, lost self," writes the poet Lisel Mueller in "Spell for a Traveler." This dream gave me back my old, lost self. The night before, while ruminating on the relentless stream of self-criticism that had been haunting me for weeks, I'd written in my journal how much I longed for a dream of loving support. During the weeks that followed, I felt affirmed in the deepest core of my being.

"Whenever we encounter in dreams an image which undergoes such numerous transformations, we can be sure we are dealing with a particularly potent and dynamic symbol," says Jungian analyst Edward Edinger. Sometimes the dreams were filled with emotion that lingered throughout the following day; after waking up with the dream of five singing lessons, I wept for an hour and the exam complex melted away for good. Other dreams unfolded like stories or films I'd stepped into. What seems clear is the increasing intimacy and rapport with the *gypsy* through the years. From my yearning to join the Gypsy women in the English countryside to the feeling of being welcomed by Romanian Gypsies; from the black woman who makes *gypsy* skirts like my own to the Gypsies who rummage through my closets and take what they want; from learning to sing the Gypsy scale to joining a caravan; from wanting to learn the Romany language to conversing freely with Gypsies everywhere; and from seeing my Gypsy reflection in a life-size mirror to my joy at holding the "book of secrets" in my hands at last—the arc of the dreams is toward closeness, empathy, and connection.

Jung said that if we look closely at our dreams over time we can often observe a developmental process under way. "I have called this unconscious process spontaneously expressing itself in the symbolism of a long dream-series the individuation process," he wrote. As I look back at my dreams I see how the *gypsy* has lived her life in me through the years. May her nocturnal visitations continue as long as I live.

FOLLOWING THE GYPSY

The feminine style of transformation is to seek the spirit in the hidden
meaning of concrete happenings, to go down deep into personal events
and into the dark unknown places of our own emotions, where we find
abundance of life in an intensity of our inward responses.

—Ann Ulanov

As soon as you let yourself be led beyond codes, your body filled with fear
and joy, the words diverge, you are no longer enclosed in the maps of social
constructions, you no longer walk between walls, meanings flow.

—Hélène Cixous

Perhaps we all have renegade landscapes in our souls, secret territories that
haunt us with glimpses of denser textures than our daily lives provide. Why
mine should be a *gypsy* landscape remains a mystery. As far as I know I don't
have any Roma blood, although my ancestors surely did their own kind of
wandering as they criss-crossed the ever-shifting borders of central Europe.
Someone once suggested that perhaps I'd been a Gypsy in a past life. I
suppose it's possible, but it doesn't interest me very much; this life, with its
inexplicable synchronicities of time and space, holds wonder enough for me.
Rather than past or future lives, it's psyche's life that enthralls me. In that
inner terrain, my *gypsy* sister runs through open fields in a whirl of flying
skirts and scarves, tambourine in hand. I have done my best to follow her
in these pages; this book has been her dancing place, her canvas, her song.

It doesn't seem far-fetched to imagine that my evangelical Christian
upbringing, with its vertical absolutes of right and wrong, might invite a
compensatory swing in the direction of horizontal freedom and spaciousness, or that years spent in the ivory tower of the academy would propel me

toward greener, earthier territories. I think the *gypsy* was there from the be-ginning, in the mischief on my infant face, in the restlessness for travel and stories and songs I composed during my childhood, in the directness and quicksilver impatience of my temperament. In his *Berlin Chronicle* Walter Benjamin wrote about the "fan of memory" in whose folds and segments the truth resides. I see her there, the *gypsy*, hiding in those folds, forever evading me and seeking me.

For Jung, the symbolic life was the only life worth living. "Spirit that demands a symbol for its expression is a psychic complex that contains the seeds of incalculable possibilities," he wrote. *Following the gypsy* is following the soul, and like the *gypsy*, the soul doesn't have a logical itinerary, doesn't care about success or failure but wanders where it will. It peregrinates, cir-cumambulates, leaps, meanders, rejoices, and mourns. One moment we may feel ourselves attuned to life's deepest wellsprings, and the next, adrift in a sea of ennui. I've come to think the soul is not a pure and pristine realm of airy perfection, but filled with everything that makes us uniquely ourselves, including our wounds and emotional complexes. To *follow the gypsy* is to follow the soul's deepest promptings with devotion and joyous spontaneity, and with anguished uncertainty when the ego's desires are thwarted. Led by imagination and instinct, intuition and desire, and in this sense anyone who writes archetypal memoir would be *following the gypsy*, tracking his or her own archetypal images and allowing them to infuse the writing.

To *follow the gypsy* is to be on a journey that never ends. A journey that allows time to saunter, to turn around and circle back for a second look, to savour the moment with curious eyes. The very lilt and cadence of the words—*following the gypsy*—suggest a springing, swinging, dancing gait, languorous yet fully alert to what's happening in the environment. I feel it in my body.

But the music has just begun. Other vignettes swirl through my imag-ination: siren songs of the *gypsy*'s other *dark sisters* and of Mercurius the magician, *deep songs* of *gypsy* shadowlands and endarkenment, of yearning, *nastos*, and archetypal loneliness, and other *gypsy* chants and dirges. "The soul is ceaselessly talking about itself in ever-recurring motifs in ever-new variations, like music," Hillman writes, and everything in me knows it's so. Yet, for now, I must call a halt.

⚜

But not before reprising the dream with which I began these peregrinations, the dream of the Gypsy woman's book of secrets. It marked the start of this journey and also marks its culmination.

There is a young Gypsy woman whose diary is held under lock and key. She is calm and quiet but it seems she's a survivor of some kind of concentration camp and torture, and I am deeply moved by her story. I see the open diary. It is a "book of secrets." I recognize a few words in it but much of it is written in a language I don't understand.

There are other people in the room and I watch as a man locks her diary in a wooden box, then puts the box away. Then Steve, my husband, tries to fit a key into the lock on the broad side of the box but the key doesn't fit. He tries a different lock on the bottom of the box and this time the key fits, so he opens the box and takes out the book. We are all very happy and relieved to have it in our hands and gently open it. It seems to be written in a mixture of different languages and includes hieroglyphics and some colours. It's clear to everyone present that this is a precious document and we are very grateful. I have the sense that we cherish it.

The young woman is watching us quietly and I ask if this is her diary. She says yes. I begin to weep with deep emotion and she does too. There's a feeling among us all that this diary is a long-lost treasure that will provide insights and answers to some important historical questions.

Then I am walking outside with the Gypsy woman and a little girl who seems to be her daughter. We come to the end of a path and embrace each other tightly. I thank her again and again. We are both crying. She takes the little girl's hand and they turn to the left and walk up into the forest. I walk down in the opposite direction, away from them. The Gypsy woman seems peaceful and content that her book of secrets is in good hands and will be read by people who treasure her story. Then I wake up.

Having lived with this dream through the years of writing *Gypsy Fugue*, here is my fantasy about it now. The *gypsy's* life has appeared in the pages of my journal, my own "book of secrets," for decades. While writing this book, I did indeed keep it under metaphorical lock and key; I didn't discuss it with anyone other than my husband for years. In the dream, the diary is written in a mixture of languages just as Romany itself is; in *Gypsy Fugue*, I have hoped to bring all of my own voices together. The colourful hieroglyphics reflect my fantasy of including images and colours, fancy lettering and special fonts in the book's production. Hieroglyphs (from the Greek *hierogluphikos* for "sacred carving," and from Egyptian "god's words") hearken back to earlier pictorial forms of language that resemble archetypal images. Perhaps we are weeping, the Gypsy woman and I, because we know that the book of secrets contains the story of her inner life, her *deep song*. It is her diary after all, and she has suffered and survived. Calm and serene, she is not troubled in the least that her book of secrets has been found, because she knows it's in the hands of grateful, appreciative readers who cherish it.

At first I wondered whether I should "open the diary" but now I know it will remain a book of secrets, even once it has been read. The fact that we can't decipher or decode its many languages protects its numinosity. The hieroglyphs suggest that the *gypsy's* numinous essence remains veiled in the realm of images. And the book of secrets contains a knowledge lost to modern culture. Ancient knowledge of blood and instinct, of something only darkly divined but so essential in our cerebral, disembodied times. Locked inside the wooden box, it reminds me of Psyche's quest to bring back the treasure box containing the beauty of the knowledge of life and death from the underworld. This is my fantasy but I don't want to pin Psyche, the butterfly, to the wall.

At the end of the dream, we go our separate ways, the Gypsy woman and I, both of us weeping over what has taken place in this ritual handing-over of the diary. Having offered her book of secrets to people who welcome it, she slips back into the Forest of Invisibles where she resides. Carrying the book with deep gratitude I go my own way, in turn.

And then I wake up with the memory of those pages filled with colours and symbols and many languages vibrating within. Even now I am humming the melody of the dream. The *gypsy* landscape stretches out before me, calls me toward an ever-receding horizon. So much left to say and sing, so much unexplored territory that beckons still. For now this is a stopping place. Tomorrow I will carry on.

When the soul wishes to experience something,
she throws an image of the experience out before her,
and then enters into her own image.

—Meister Eckhart

Coda

Musings on Archetypal Autobiography
and Memoir

Whatever image you take within you deeply…
see how it reveals the whole—the great tapestry.

—Rainer Maria Rilke

Other-Love is writing's first name.

—Hélène Cixous

When we write about our lives we tell one of many possible stories. The narrative we create may be one of adversity fought and overcome, of a long-held dream achieved at last, of an unusual adventure from which we return transformed. But it's always a particular story that shapes our writing, and we follow its thread by selecting the moments and anecdotes that best embody and illustrate it. What is the tale I choose to tell? What is yours?

There are so many ways to write our story. With autobiography and memoir no longer defined by linear narrative or chronological unfolding, we can write about our lives in whatever form we choose. Poems and essays, short stories and fairy tales, letters and dreams, lists and recipes—all are grist for the autobiographic mill. The way we tell our stories is limited only by the scope and daring of our own imaginations. "Form too is archetypal," writes Hillman. "Were the story written in another way, by another hand, from another perspective, it would sound different and therefore *be a different story*."

Through the years I've come to realize people enrol in autobiography workshops in order to write about their lives, but often what they're really hoping for is to discover who they are. Workshops offer time and space away from the demands and busyness of everyday life in which to reflect on where life has brought them and what is most important to them. As this has grown clearer to me I've begun speaking about it openly with the participants. Their response is always immediate. Many nod their heads in agreement and relief that this can be openly acknowledged.

Who am I, and what matters most to me? Where have I come from, and where am I going? *Who is it* that wants to write my story? Reflecting on these questions is preparing the ground because before we can write honestly about our lives, we need to know who it is that's doing the writing. Sometimes the most powerful moment in a week-long workshop is an unexpected insight or small epiphany that leads to a whole new story, one that the writer had no idea existed and never expected to tell. The gold is always in those deeper stories, the stories beneath and inside the stories we were planning to write.

Gradually the focus moves from external events to the symbols and images that capture the meaningful moments of our lives and reveal their essence. A serendipitous conversation with a stranger, a book discovered on a deserted beach, a dream that has always haunted us, a long forgotten photograph that suddenly reappears, a melody that continues to resound in our inner ear—any of these can lead into unexpected depths that give rise to a new story of our lives. Sometimes I ask people to bring small objects they love to class, and those too can open memory's doors and windows. Images seem to hold infinite possibilities of association and meaning. Concepts may stimulate the intellect and excite our minds, but images arouse the imagination and resonate through our bodies until our entire being vibrates with *Yes!*

⚬⚬⚬

How do memory and imagination weave the seemingly random threads of our inner and outer lives into a meaningful tapestry in which a distinguishable pattern gradually becomes visible? "The pattern in the glory," as Helen Luke referred to it.

Some years ago (in 2007) I had the following dream.

We are given a paper mesh or grid to write our stories in. There is a beautiful insect in the middle of mine. Not exactly a dragonfly, perhaps a scarab beetle. It's an iridescent royal blue colour and quite beautiful.

I write all around it in wavy, concentric circles and fill the page with my writing. There are other smaller symbols too, including flowers. I realize I've done a lot of drawing and used many colours in my journal. I'm a bit surprised, but it's a good feeling.

When I attempted to draw this image in my journal the large insect in the centre did in fact look like a cross between dragonfly and scarab beetle. The dragonfly is one of the fastest flying insects in the world and carries the winds of change on its transparent wings. Symbolically it reawakens us to the magic and mystery of life and guides us to a true and mature understanding of ourselves. For the ancient Egyptians, the scarab or dung beetle was an image of the sun god and a symbol of creation and resurrection. It was considered sacred because dung beetles rise out of eggs laid under the earth, as if reborn. In the dream the two had merged, uniting heaven and earth and reconciling dung and decay with rebirth and creation. Around the insect I had drawn concentric spiralling circles of blue ink on the crisscrossed page. When I looked at what I'd drawn, I saw a mandala.

As I puzzled over the dream, it suddenly struck me as a harbinger of what I'd begun to think of as *archetypal autobiography and memoir*. In the dream "we" find an image in the centre of the page, set against the warp and woof of our lives, as suggested by the grid. I write around the image in a spiral moving from left to right and eventually back to the left, suggesting the uninterrupted flow between unconscious and conscious realms. "Unconsciousness needs the eye of consciousness; consciousness needs the energy of the unconscious," writes Marion Woodman. I'd imagined *archetypal memoir* as a process of circumambulating numinous images that hold our life energy, images that help us get closer to the myth we are living. The writing that circles out from the centre of the page in the dream also reminded me of how our personal images and stories connect us with others and with the archetypal dimension of life itself.

A story that circles around an image is not a linear tale. Unlike much of Western literature with its basic underlying plot line of "who does what to whom," it's a story of tending and gestating the image, a story written in language "saturated with love," as a dream suggested years ago. It's a story whose meaning arises from deep within and invites the images of others.

Who's to say that the outer facts of our lives are more important than the images that glow in our imagination and dreams? James Hillman asks us to look at our lives with fresh eyes in order to gain a renewed sense of their beauty. "Restless inquiry is not the only kind of knowledge, self-examination not the only kind of awareness," he writes. "Appreciation of an image, your life story as studded with images since early childhood, and a deepening into them slows the restlessness of inquiry, laying to rest the fever and the fret of finding out."

What if deepening into the images that move us throughout our lifetimes is also a valid way of writing autobiography and memoir? Couldn't we take Hillman's words as inspiration for a mode of writing in which our stories would emerge out of those images? Such imaginative tracking of the soul's life would expand autobiography's usual focus on an individual's experience in a particular time and place into a larger transpersonal dimension where all our stories overlap in imaginal space and *kairos* time. The Greek word *kairos* refers to the right or opportune moment, a moment of undetermined length in which something special happens. *Chronos* time is sequential and measurable but *kairos* time is qualitative; it is time of a different order. This is the time we enter in creative work, feminine time, "a conception or pregnancy of the moment, a sudden birth of feeling."

Attending to dreams, fantasies, and irrational associations would lead us to the underlying themes of our lives and reveal how they shape our story. Archetypal memoir would be *depth memoir*, the many layers of our experience rather than variety or drama would be its purview. Exploring the images that enthrall us and haunt us would provide glimpses of the *daimones,* the invisible animating spirits that accompany us on our journey, reflected fleetingly in the mirror of our writing. It would reacquaint us with our mother tongue, and remind us that myth not only resides in ancient Egypt and Greece but is alive in us now, shaping our dreams and destinies and daily lives.

Archetypal memoir—following imagination's flights of fancy—would take us into a space "that connects the upper world with the underworld, the world of shades and dreams, the unconscious." Neither an objective account of my outer life nor a personal journal of my subjective experience, archetypal memoir would offer the *third space* in which outer and inner realms converge and are transmuted into something new.

When memoir reaches into the archetypal realm, my story merges with the stories of others who love this image—perhaps with yours. And if we live in the *anima mundi*, the ensouled world, this is not only my story of the *gypsy*, but just as much the *gypsy*'s story of incarnating in me.

Archetypal memoir would allow us to explore the larger forces at play in our lives. Like Jung, in *Memories, Dreams, Reflections*, it would place greater value on the inner arc of our lives than on their outer events. Our imaginal landscapes would be as significant as our daily comings and goings, and the soul's vagabond wanderings would be reflected in the cadence and style of the writing. If someone were to write about the archetypal bear, the writing might be *bearlike*—fierce and bold, maternal and protective, lumbering and powerful. Only the individual could say what that would mean for his or her story. Another's writing might be *elephantine* or *labyrinthine*, *starlike* or *horselike*. Each would explore and embody an image in his or her own way.

❧

Viewed through this lens, some of my favourite books through the years could be described as archetypal memoirs. Christine Downing's *The Goddess* and *Journey through Menopause* explore her personal experience with archetypal feminine mysteries during different stages of her life. *Traveling with Pomegranates* follows the deepening relationship between Sue Monk Kidd and her daughter, Ann Kidd Taylor, against the mythic backdrop of their shared pilgrimage to Eleusis, the ancient Greek mystery site of the archetypal mother and daughter, Demeter and Persephone. In *The Sister from Below*, Naomi Ruth Lowinsky explores her lifelong relationship with the muse, while Patty de Llosa's *Taming Your Inner Tyrant* describes her ongoing dialogue with a bullying inner animus, and Linda Leonard's *Meeting the Madwoman* considers the many faces of the archetypal "crazy lady."

In *What Her Body Thought*, Susan Griffin weaves together an account of her autoimmune illness over the years with her aching desire to recover her mother's lost bodily presence and the story of Marie Duplessis, known as the mythic courtesan Camille, whose story inspired Verdi's *La Traviata*. Hers is an archetypal memoir of longing for a communal body in which all would be cared for and no one forgotten. Marion Milner's *Eternity's Sunrise* is a memoir of wandering and pilgrimage, and Helen Luke brings to light the rites of conscious aging and becoming crone, in *Such Stuff as Dreams Are Made On*. At the age of 85 she wrote, "The great images of my life speak with increasing power and beauty, and when I live with them I feel no need to ask for more."

None of these writers have described their writing as archetypal memoir, but the mythic underpinnings of their personal stories are everywhere evident. Christine Downing weaves together her own experience and archetypal reflection so seamlessly that each illuminates the other. She describes her realization while writing about the Greek goddesses as images of feminine potential that she was creating a kind of autobiography made up of "childhood memories, dreams from many different periods, and a complex history of identifications." I think our books may be cousins.

⁑

"Transformative images are engaging and even arresting metaphors," writes Murray Stein. "If these powerful archetypal images are strong and impressive enough, the whole fabric of a person's life can be transformed. Their effects are not only momentary. Over time they become irreversible. This is because these images reflect psychological content that is emerging in a person's life and give it shape. They are metaphors with profound underlying structural support and meaning."

But how do we find the images that can transform our lives? Often it seems as though they choose us, appearing over time and revealing themselves through our persistent fascinations, recurring dreams, and waking fantasies. We can *notice what we are noticing*. Be attentive to what draws our attention and energy in both inner and outer worlds, particularly the synchronicities that bring the two worlds together. When we encounter the homeless man or wild-eyed cat in last night's dream coming toward us on our morning walk, pay attention; when a scene or melody from a movie stays with us for weeks, ask ourselves what has taken us captive.

When a particular image seizes hold of us, we can turn to it with wonder and gratitude, ponder its place in our personal myth, explore its role in our ancestral heritage and the psychic legacy of our family line. Get curious about its archetypal roots and look for it in myths and fairy tales, in literature, art, and film, noting where the outer world meets us halfway on our imaginal journey. We can draw it, sculpt it, or shape it in clay, dance it or sing it, and note where we feel it most alive in our bodies. Like Jung, we can carry it around with us and ask questions of it until a meaningful web of associations begins to emerge over time.

In writing *archetypal memoir* we might begin each chapter with a dream or anecdote or reflection, then spin out archetypal associations and bring in a relevant myth or fairy tale, or cultural folklore. We can weave fantasies, questions, and further imaginings into our writing until gradually the tapestry of our inner landscape begins to reveal itself.

For more than four decades, my husband, phenomenological philosopher Steven M. Rosen, has been exploring the symbolic mysteries of a paradoxical mathematical structure called the *Klein bottle* in which inside and outside run fluidly together along a single surface. For Steve, the Klein bottle is a modern incarnation of alchemy's hermetic vessel in which transformation occurs. He has published six books and countless articles on this theme and it has often occurred to me that the Klein bottle is an archetypal image of his lifelong desire to unite inner and outer dimensions in order to transcend the dualities at the heart of our perception. His latest book, *Dreams, Death, Rebirth* contains elements of memoir—personal dreams, photographs, and sketches—and the electronic multimedia version includes brief audio and video clips of him speaking, along with art, music, and film clips. In the course of this modern alchemical text, phenomenological philosophy, mathematics, and personal material merge in a narrative that invites the reader's active participation and what Steve refers to as the reader's own parallel text. What would it mean to write a Kleinian "inside out" philosophical text?

❧

Other voices on writing, love, and archetypal images:

Only the images by which we live can bring transformation. Each of us has a well of images within which are the saving reality and from which may be born the individual myth carrying the meaning of a life.

The creative process, so far as we are able to follow it at all, consists in the unconscious activation of an archetypal image, and in elaborating and shaping this image into the finished work. By giving it shape, the artist translates it into the language of the present, and so makes it possible for us to find our way back to the deepest springs of life.

Our inherent natures and the individual circumstances of our childhood put us in touch with particular archetypal patterns; these are the tapestries within which our lives are woven. How we relate to them is our choice. We can succumb to a pattern, identify with a pattern, resent our apparent destiny or we can acknowledge our personal parameters and celebrate the mystery of who we are....Knowing who we are, celebrating who we are, is individuating the archetype.

From my previous writing about archetypes I know that for readers, having words and images for what they have only known subjectively is like seeing themselves in a mirror for the first time. There is the possibility of reflection, and with it, the memory of events and feelings.

I am not merely what I have thought, as Descartes proposed, nor simply what I have done, as the existentialists claim, but also, as Gaston Bachelard has so powerfully shown, what I have imagined and remembered.

When we experience the symbol, we simultaneously experience the complex, the archetype, the inner psychic entity that is represented by the symbol. When the image speaks, it is with one of our own inner voices. When we answer back, it is the unseen inner part of our own self that listens and registers.

If you are in search of soul, go first to your fantasy images, for that is how the psyche presents itself directly. All consciousness depends upon fantasy images.

Work of the eyes is done, now
go and do heart-work
on all the images imprisoned within you.

We cannot get to the heart of the image without love for the image.

〰

This is one way to tell my story. I could have told it another way, but as a lover of soul and teacher of personal writing workshops in which I'm forever encouraging participants to attend to their own images, the archetypal *gypsy* seized hold of me and wouldn't let me go. *It's my story,* she insisted. *Tell my story.*

Reflecting on the period of psychic upheaval that followed his break with Freud, Jung wrote, "All my works, all my creative activity, has come from those initial fantasies and dreams which began in 1912, almost fifty years ago....The years when I was pursuing my inner images were the most important in my life—in them everything essential was decided." Jung's profound and painstaking engagement with the figures of his own unconscious marked the beginning of what he came to refer to as active imagination, and, over time, culminated in the *Red Book*. Gradually he encouraged his patients to explore their own fantasy images as well, and describes that process as follows.

> [I] took up a dream-image or an association of the patient's, and, with this as a point of departure, set him the task of elaborating or developing his theme by giving free rein to his fantasy. This, according to individual taste and talent, could be done in any number of ways, dramatic, dialectic, visual, acoustic, or in the form of dancing, painting, or modelling.

We're fortunate that Jung gave us a way of communicating with our inner world. Through attending to our waking fantasies we catch a glimmer of what is hidden in the shadow of our daytime solar consciousness and begin to sense that there is a vast substratum of life buried in our psyches. By dialoguing with the images in our dreams and letting them voice the deepest truths of tissue and bone, we get to know those unknown aspects of ourselves. With excitement and sometimes with trepidation we acquaint ourselves with "the inner family of souls," as Marie-Louise von Franz referred to them.

Gypsy Fugue itself is an extended active imagination. Perhaps all autobiographical writing is, as we engage with the ghostly presences and images of our past and present lives. Years ago I stumbled across a reference to a new kind of research "based on the conjunction of dream, experience, and scholarship." I imagine weaving those three strands into a glossy, dark braid like the one I dreamed of in Zürich (the dream contained just the single image of a thick and lustrous dark-brown braid). The fluid conjunction of dream, experience, and scholarship could just as well describe what I'm calling *archetypal memoir*. My *gypsy* dreams both sleeping and waking, my own experience and that of the Roma, and scholarly reading in related fields come together in a braided narrative containing loose ends, I am sure, yet comprising, I hope, one harmonious whole.

ᔈᕒ

"Other-Love is writing's first name," says Hélène Cixous. If love of the other is what prompts us to write, what happens when the other is within and it's a part of ourselves we're invited to love? While conducting filmed interviews with Marion Woodman some time ago, I asked her what she would say to people who have difficulty remembering their dreams. She was quiet for a moment. "I would ask them, 'Do you *love* your dreams?'"

Perhaps the inner others are just as eager to be known and loved as the outer ones in our lives, just as responsive to being attended to and cherished. Perhaps they love us in return, have been quietly loving us all along, as Derek Walcott promises in his beautiful poem: "You will love again the stranger who was yourself / Give wine. Give bread. Give back your heart / to itself, to the stranger who has loved you / all your life." If loving our dreams is required for remembering them, perhaps love for the image and the other inside us is necessary to writing archetypal memoir as well.

Sit. Feast on your life.

—Derek Walcott

ENDNOTES

A Book of Secrets

Page 11. C.G. Jung, *Memories, Dreams, Reflections*, p. 19.

Page 15. A Note on Terminology: Among Roma writers who have addressed the issue of nomenclature, Dr. Ian Hancock writes, "When lower case, gypsy has come to stand for the person most often found in literature—not a member of an ethnic population (which would require upper case) but an individual so labeled because of his or her behavior and appearance. Although publishers are being persuaded to capitalize the word, it is in fact being slowly replaced by the more accurate Roma or (preferably) Romanies." Introduction to *The Heroic Present: Life among the Gypsies*, by Jan Yoors, p. 26. Many poets in *The Roads of the Roma* use the terms interchangeably, while others reject the use of "gypsy" claiming it has pejorative associations. "Rom" simply means "man," and "Roma" is plural, though some Roma advocates prefer "Rrom," which more accurately represents the correct pronunciation of the word. There are various accounts of its etymology; one suggests "Roma" is derived from "domba," or "man living by singing and music" in classical Sanskrit.

Shimmering Darkly

Page 21. Eva Hoffman, *After Such Knowledge: Memory, History and the Aftermath of the Holocaust*, p. 66. This Leadership Training Program was taught by Jungian analyst and writer Marion Woodman, dance and movement professor Mary Hamilton, and voice and theatre specialist Ann Skinner, from 2000 to 2009. It was based on their thirty-year collaboration teaching week-long Body Soul Rhythms Intensives for women internationally.

Page 21. C.G. Jung, *The Collected Works* (hereafter cited as *CW*), vol. 8, para. 618.

Page 23. C.G. Jung, *CW*, vol. 8, para. 644.

Mother India's Forgotten Child

Page 25. Elsewhere Grass wrote, "If we don't want united Europe to become just a vast bureaucratic creature lumbering to extinction, we who are each caught up in the grip of our national shackles, should note that the Roma, who live throughout Europe, are Europeans in the true and full meaning of the word. Those we call the Gypsies are a long way ahead of us in at least one respect: they are the natural inhabitants of a 'Europe without frontiers'. It is vital that they are given a passport that allows them to live anywhere in Europe, from Romania to Portugal. But we are a long way from such a vision." Günter Grass, "True Europeans," *Index on Censorship, Gypsies: Life on the Edge* 27 (July 1998): pp. 51–53.

Page 26. In an interview Tony Gatlif has described *Latcho Drom* as "a hymn to the universal gypsy condition." archive.is/20130128230027/www.mondomix. com/en/news/freedom. Film critic Jonathan Romney described *Latcho Drom* as an "impassioned manifesto for a freer cinema and a freer life," in "The Incredible Journey," *The Guardian*, May 3, 2000. Gatlif's other films about the Roma include *Gadjo Dilo, Vengo, Mondo*, and *Korkoro*, which portrays French Roma under the Nazis.

Page 27. Ben Seidler and Simon Marks, "Gypsy Style, in the Harsh Light of Day," *New York Times*, October 3, 2008. The following year the *Vancouver Sun* published an article titled "Bohemian Rhapsody" describing the contemporary "couturier interpretation of the non-traditional blithe-spirit garb worn by the vagabonds, gypsies and nomads who roamed Europe in the 19th and 20th centuries." Shelley Fralic concludes that Bohemian style "is all about wearing your freedom on your sleeve." *Vancouver Sun*, June 11, 2009.

Page 27. Isabel Fonseca, *Bury Me Standing: The Gypsies and Their Journey*, p. 239.

Page 28. Ian Hancock, *The Pariah Syndrome: An Account of Gypsy Slavery and Persecution*, p. 126.

Page 28. Noble savage. Charles Leland, for example, described Gypsies as "the last rags of the old romance which connected man with nature." In David Malvinni, *The Gypsy Caravan: From Real Roma to Imaginary Gypsies in Western Music*, p. 17.

Page 29. Vibrant new adventure. Perhaps, as Toby F. Sonneman suggests, "When people long to break the ideological chains of government, politics, economics and law, of stagnation, routines, and expectations—even the confines of time itself—they look toward the images of Gypsies to represent the illusion of freedom, to offer them hope." "Dark Mysterious Wanderers: The Migrating Metaphor of the Gypsy," *Journal of Popular Culture* 32, no. 4 (Spring 1999): p. 132.

Page 30. For one magical moment. In her discussion of synchronicity between inner and outer worlds, Marie-Louise von Franz wrote, "If one observes a series of dreams and unconscious processes in an individual over a considerable period of time, one sees that with some frequency, but sporadically and irregularly, a dream motif or an unexpected fantasy will appear in the material environment also, as an outer event." *C.G. Jung: His Myth in Our Time*, pp. 236–37.

Page 33. You will never learn our language. Fonseca, *Bury Me Standing*, p. 13.

Page 34. Until the ethnologists began. Margery Silver, introduction to *Gypsy Sorcery & Fortune Telling*, by Charles Godfrey Leland, pp. vii-viii. There are now several riveting accounts of Roma origins and history by both Roma and non-Roma writers, among them Ian Hancock's *We Are the Romani People* and Donald Kenrick's *Gypsies: From the Ganges to the Thames*.

Page 35. You are Mother India's forgotten child. J.S. Pathania, cited in Donald Kenrick, *Gypsies: From the Ganges to the Thames*, p. 3.

Page 35. Jigsaw puzzle. Kenrick, *Gypsies*, p. 10. I have relied substantially on Kenrick's and Ian Hancock's accounts of Roma history and origins in the overview that follows.

Page 35. Ralph L. Turner, in Bart McDowell, *Gypsies: Wanderers of the World*, p. 191.

Page 36. Twenty million in India. The 2011 documentary *A People Uncounted* cites 12–15 million Roma in Europe alone.

Page 37. The Europeans are organizing. Hancock, *The Pariah Syndrome*, p. 33.

Page 37. Had this ignominious episode. Fonseca, *Bury Me Standing*, p. 175.

Page 37. Numbers of Gypsies murdered. Estimates range from 300,000 to

1.5 million, but the most frequently cited number is 500,000.

Page 37. Donald Kenrick, *Gypsies Under the Swastika*, p. 17.

Page 38. According to this film. Through the years there have been many films and television series about the Holocaust; however, until recently the only film about Roma suffering under Nazi Germany was *And the Violins Stopped Playing*, made in 1988. Tony Gatlif's 2010 film *Korkoro* (Freedom) focussed on French Roma during World War II. There may be other recent films that I am not aware of. *A People Uncounted* is reminiscent of Claude Lanzmann's *Shoah*, 1985, with their stark personal testimony of Roma and Jewish survivors of Hitler's death camps. Jan Yoors wrote a riveting account of Gypsy involvement in the Resistance and, ultimately, the death of most members of his Gypsy family and *kumpania* or clan: *Crossing: A Journal of Survival and Resistance in World War II*.

Page 39. A renewed wave of racist violence: https://www.theguardian.com/commentisfree/2008/jul/10/race.humanrights.

Page 39. Amnesty 2016–2017 Annual Report on Human Rights. https://www.amnesty.org/en/latest/research/2017/02/amnesty-international-annual-report-201617/. The renewed vilification of European Roma has put the plight of today's Gypsies in the spotlight of public attention, invoking the ire of celebrities like Madonna. In August 2009 she was booed in Romania for speaking out on behalf of equal rights for Gypsies by the very same crowd who had eagerly applauded her band of Roma musicians earlier that evening.

Page 39. Aidan McGarry, *Romaphobia: The Last Acceptable Form of Racism*.

Page 39. Although the word "Gypsy." Ian Hancock, *We Are the Romani People*, p. 2.

Page 40. Gypsies use their language and core-culture. Hancock, *The Pariah Syndrome*, p. 128.

Page 41. Passion and temperament. Liszt, cited in N.B. Tomasevic and R. Djuric, *Gypsies of the World*, p. 176.

Page 41. Imitate the sounds of nature. Daphne Maurice, "Yehudi Menuhin and the Gypsy Violinists," *Journal of the Gypsy Lore Society* 52, no. 3 and 4 (1973): p. 93.

Page 42. Wobbly rhythms. Garth Cartwright, *Princes among Men*, p. 11.

Page 42. Fevered, soaring, tempestuous. Jarko Jovanovic, cited in Bernard Leblon, *Gypsies and Flamenco*, p. 8. Despite the reciprocal influences, there are characteristics unique to Roma music that transcend local music traditions. To begin with, there are traditionally three voices, which can either be sung, as in the large Russian choruses, or simulated by instruments. A tendency to start slightly after the beat, a particular rhythmic pattern, and a prevalence of minor chords also feature largely, and singing is characterized by a particular use of the voice, which is natural and often even rough. In Lev Tcherenkov and Stephane Laederich, *The Rroma. Volume 2: Traditions and Texts*, pp. 704–05.

Page 42. Masters of innovation. T.P. Vukanovic, "Musical Culture among Gypsies of Yugoslavia," *Journal of the Gypsy Lore Society* 41, no. 1 and 2 (1962): p. 51.

Page 43. You can also sing it to your children. Carl-Herman Tillhagen, "The Songs of the Swedish Nomadic Gypsies," *Journal of the Gypsy Lore Society* 30 (1951): pp. 87–88.

Page 43. Fonseca, *Bury Me Standing*, p. 5.

Page 44. Walter Starkie, cited in Diane Tong, *Gypsy Folktales*, p. 9.

Page 44. During the *Mulatsago*. Michael Stewart, *The Time of the Gypsies*, pp. 183–88.

Page 45. We don't live for tomorrow. Garth Cartwright, *Princes among Men*, p. 10.

Page 45. In truth, no one knows. http://www.reocities.com/~patrin/stsm01.htm. The Patrin website hosts many fascinating essays and articles about the Roma. http://www.oocities.org/~patrin/.

Page 46. Kali Sara is now finally. Ronald Lee, "The Romani Goddess Kali Sara," https://kopachi.com/articles/the-romani-goddess-kali-sara-ronald-lee/.

Page 48. C.G. Jung, *CW*, vol. 10, para. 395.

Wanderers on This Earth

Page 51. A set of variations. C.G. Jung, *CW*, vol. 8, para. 270, 417.

Page 51. Archetypes are complexes of experience. C.G. Jung, *CW*, vol. 9/1, para. 62, 266.

Page 51. Nuclear centers which give the drive. Marie-Louise von Franz, *The Way of the Dream: Conversations on Jungian Dream Interpretation with Fraser Boa*, p. 23.

Page 52. C.G. Jung, *CW*, vol. 10, para. 395.

Page 52. Marion Woodman, *Conscious Femininity: Interviews with Marion Woodman*, p. 125.

Page 52. James Hillman, *Re-Visioning Psychology*, p. xix.

Page 52. Christine Downing, ed., *Mirrors of the Self: Archetypal Images That Shape Your Life*, p. xv.

Page 52. Murray Stein, "Hermes and the Creation of Space," online article, http://www.jungatlanta.com/articles/Hermes-and-the-Creation-of-Space.pdf, p. 3.

Page 53. Marie-Louise von Franz, *The Interpretation of Fairy Tales*, p. 10.

Page 53. C.G. Jung, *CW*, vol. 9/1, para. 99, 302; *CW*, vol. 14, para. 463. For a more detailed exploration of how archetypal images manifest in our lives see Downing's *Mirrors of the Self*.

Page 53. The harsh conditions of life. Hancock, *The Pariah Syndrome*, p. 123.

Page 54. Sprang from a component of the personality. C.G. Jung, *CW*, vol. 6, para. 454.

Page 54. Fernanda Eberstadt, author interview with Summer Block, May 29, 2006, http://www.identitytheory.com/fernanda-eberstadt/ (link live in May 2017).

Page 55. Eva Hoffman, *Lost in Translation: A Life in a New Language*, p. 280.

Page 56. Ann Ulanov, *Spiritual Aspects of Clinical Work*, pp. 78–79.

Page 56. Anaïs Nin, *The Diary of Anaïs Nin, Vol. 5: 1947–1955*, p. 207.

Page 56. Carriers of our collective shadow. Alexandra Fidyk, "'Gypsy' Fate:

Carriers of Our Collective Shadow," *JUNG: the e-Journal of the Jungian Society for Scholarly Studies* 4, no. 1 (December 2008): p. 18.

Page 58. Wildly sensuous, chaotic. Robert Johnson, *Lying with the Heavenly Woman: Understanding and Integrating the Feminine Archetypes in Men's Lives*, pp. 46–47.

Page 58. Esther Harding, *Woman's Mysteries*, p. 125.

Page 58. Marion Woodman, *The Pregnant Virgin: A Study in Psychological Transformation*, p. 112.

Page 58. Her own rejected self. Marion Woodman, *The Ravaged Bridegroom: Masculinity in Women*, pp. 162–67.

Page 58. She is my survivor. Marion Woodman, *Bone: Dying into Life*, pp. 48, 49.

Page 59. There's the Gypsy. Marion Woodman, private telephone conversation, October 25, 2007.

Page 59. I feel the archetypal energy. Woodman, *Bone*, p. 241.

Page 59. David R. Kinsley, *The Sword and the Flute: Kali and Krsna, Dark Visions of the Terrible and the Sublime in Hindu Mythology*, p. 77.

Page 59. Irving Brown, *Deep Song*, p. 111.

Page 60. Jan Yoors, *The Heroic Present: Life among the Gypsies*, p. 69.

Page 60. Ann Belford Ulanov, *The Feminine in Jungian Psychology and in Christian Theology*, p. 172.

Page 61. Ulanov, *The Feminine*, p. 175.

Page 62. Whore of Babylon. Jung discusses the red of instinct and purple of spirit as the two poles of the psychic spectrum, which would make fuchsia a blend of instinct and spirit. *CW*, vol, 8, para. 414, 420.

Page 62. C.G. Jung, "On the Psychology of the Trickster-Figure," in *CW*, vol. 9/1, para. 457.

Page 62. Very often it is the older folk-elements. C.G. Jung, *CW*, vol. 6, para. 316. Although Jung didn't write explicitly about Gypsies he wrote extensively of India, the land of their origin. Profoundly moved by what he saw and experienced during his first trip in 1933, he reflected, "It is quite possible that India is the real world, and that the white man lives in a madhouse of abstractions....Life in India has not yet withdrawn into the capsule of the head. It is still the whole body that lives." *CW*, vol. 10, para. 988.

Page 63. The burst of fire. W.R. Rishi, *Roma* (Patiala, India: Punjabi University, 1996). Cited online at www.romani.org (this link is no longer active).

Page 63. C.G. Jung, *CW*, vol. 9/2, para. 261.

Fugue

Page 66. Writing is the passageway. Hélène Cixous and Catherine Clément, *The Newly Born Woman*, pp. 85, 86.

Page 67. Ulanov, *The Feminine*, p. 171.

Page 67. Implying a flight of fancy. Joseph Machlis, *The Enjoyment of Music*, p. 296.

Page 68. Open up the space. Hélène Cixous, *The Newly Born Woman*, p. 91.

Page 69. James Hillman, *The Dream and the Underworld*, p. 62.

Page 71. The week-long Body Soul Rhythms Intensives combined Jungian lectures with experiential processes including dream work, movement and voice work, art and mask making, and various improvisational exercises.

Page 71. According to Ian Hancock. Hancock, *The Pariah Syndrome*, p. 107.

Page 72. I found / my body / on red velvet. Mariella Mehr, "A Red Foundling Strolls into This Dream," in *The Roads of the Roma*, p. 61.

Page 72. The reanimation of fresh spirit. Monika Wikman, *Pregnant Darkness: Alchemy and the Rebirth of Consciousness*, p. 8.

Page 72. Linda Fierz-David and Nor Hall, *Dreaming in Red: The Women's Dionysian Initiation Chamber in Pompeii*, p. v.

Page 76. Marlene Schiwy, *Simple Days: A Journal on What Really Matters*, pp. 196–98.

Page 77. Edward Lucie-Smith, *The Story of Craft: The Craftsman's Role in Society*, pp. 135–36.

Page 78. Marie-Louise von Franz, *The Feminine in Fairy Tales*, p. 40.

Page 78. The arabesques. Irving Brown, *Deep Song*, p. 14.

Page 80. Ulanov, *The Feminine*, p. 177.

Page 81. C.G. Jung, *Letters, Volume 1*, p. 542.

Page 81. Bach talks to God. C.G. Jung, "Men, Women and God," in *C.G. Jung Speaking: Interviews and Encounters*, p. 240.

Page 81. Margaret Tilly, "The Therapy of Music," in *C.G. Jung Speaking*, p. 263.

Page 82. Marion Woodman with Jill Mellick, *Coming Home to Myself*, p. 173.

Page 87. Cartwright, *Princes among Men*, pp. 12, 111.

Page 87. Charles Godfrey Leland, *Gypsy Sorcery & Fortune Telling*, p. 98.

Page 87. Anna Akhmatova, "Listening to Singing," in *Poems*, p. 90.

Page 90. Marie-Louise von Franz, *Number and Time*, pp. 120–21, 123.

Page 91. Marie-Louise von Franz, *Dreams*, p. 23.

Page 91. Hélène Cixous, *The Newly Born Woman*, p. 93.

Page 93. You *are* flamenco. *Gypsy Caravans: When the Road Bends* (documentary film), 2007.

Page 93. D.E. Pohren, *The Art of Flamenco*, p. 51.

Page 94. In his preface to Federico García Lorca's *In Search of Duende*, Christopher Maurer says that Lorca's vision of *duende* is characterized by four elements: "irrationality, earthiness, a heightened awareness of death, and a dash of the diabolical" (p. ix).

Page 95. Woodman, *The Owl Was a Baker's Daughter: Obesity, Anorexia Nervosa and the Repressed Feminine*, p. 113.

Page 96. Federico García Lorca, *Deep Song and Other Prose*, pp. 25, 28.

Page 96. The essence of human feeling. Irving Brown, *Deep Song*, pp. 277–293. Fascinating accounts of the history of *cante jondo* can be found in Lorca, Brown, Leblon, etc. A more contemporary comment comes from Pedro Peña, who writes: "The *soleá* is the song from midnight to one in the morning, when you feel good, when your spirit is still calm and the tears aren't yet brimming at the corners of your eyes. The *soleá* is for feeling fine! The *seguiriya*, by contrast, is for two or three in the morning. Your pain is right up at the surface, you've got to lance it. It's a confession." Cited in Bernard Leblon, *Gypsies and Flamenco*, p. 56.

Page 96. The true poems of deep song. Federico García Lorca, *Deep Song and Other Prose*, p. 33.

Page 97. The first sob and first kiss. Federico García Lorca, *Deep Song and Other Prose*, p. 30.

Page 97. Federico García Lorca, "Ballad of the Spanish Civil Guard," online at http://www.poesi.as/index214uk.htm.

Page 98. Leonard Cohen's acceptance speech for the Prince of Asturias Award for Literature in Spain, October 21, 2011. Like other *cantaores* of *deep song*, Cohen was poet, songwriter, and singer in equal measure and he was awarded this prize for literature, not for music. http://cohencentric.com/leonard-cohen-the-prince-of-asturias-awards-speech-with-annotations-commentary/ (link live in June 2017).

Page 101. Susan Griffin, *What Her Body Thought*, p. 313.

Page 104. C.G. Jung, "The Psychological Aspects of the Kore" (1951), in *CW*, vol. 9, para. 316.

Page 107. Ulanov, *The Feminine*, p. 171.

Page 108. Ronald Schenk, *The Soul of Beauty*, pp. 41, 42.

Page 108. James Hillman, *The Force of Character and the Lasting Life*, p. 116.

Page 108. James Hillman, *A Blue Fire*, p. 299.

Page 109. Sociability is expressed. Ada I. Engebrigtsen, *Exploring Gypsiness: Power, Exchange and Interdependence in a Transylvanian Village*, p. 137. The author goes so far as to say that the practice of beauty is an expression of *romanes* and a moral act.

Page 115. Woodman, *The Pregnant Virgin*, p. 81.

Page 116. James Hillman, "On the Necessity of Abnormal Psychology: Ananke and Athene," in *Facing the Gods*, pp. 17, 18.

Page 118. Michael Stewart, *The Time of the Gypsies*, p. xiii.

Page 119. Woodman, *The Pregnant Virgin*, pp. 10, 122.

Page 119. The gold is in the dung. Jung writes of "the intimate connection between excrement and gold in alchemy, the lowest value allies itself to the highest." C.G. Jung, *CW*, vol. 5, para. 276.

Page 121. C.G. Jung, *CW*, vol. 9/1, para. 291.

Page 123. Nor Hall, excerpts from "Channel a Muse: Notes Toward the Construction of a Mother-Daughter Biography," originally published in *Spring Journal* (Spring 2004). http://www.mythicjourneys.org/passages/august2005/channel_a_muse.pdf.

Page 123. Nor Hall, *The Moon and the Virgin: Reflections on the Archetypal Feminine*, p. 32. As Virginia Woolf famously wrote in *Three Guineas*, "As a woman I have no country. As a woman I want no country. As a woman my country is the whole world."

Page 124. Women's very bodies are nomadic. Jay Griffiths, *Wild*, p. 253.

Page 131. C.G. Jung, *CW*, vol. 5, para. 299.

Page 131. All wandering is from the mother. Hall, *The Moon and the Virgin*, p. 36.

Page 137. Hall, *The Moon and the Virgin*, p. 85. Jung referred to this process as the individuation journey.

Page 137. A congregation of women. Linda Fierz-David and Nor Hall, *Dreaming in Red*, p. 220.

Page 139. The other that I am and am not. Hélène Cixous, *The Newly Born Woman*, p. 86.

Page 139. Marie-Louise von Franz, *The Interpretation of Fairy Tales*, p. 103.

Page 141. C.G. Jung, *CW*, vol. 10, para. 325.

Page 142. The elephant has the longest gestation period of any mammal, lasting from eighteen to twenty-two months. Perhaps that's why it is often thought of as a symbol of the Self.

Page 143. Hall, "Channel a Muse," online excerpt.

Page 143. Joseph Machlis, *The Enjoyment of Music*, pp. 297–98.

Page 144. *The Art of Fugue*. Bach scholar Christoph Wolff says *The Art of Fugue* is conceptually unique as the only "exploration in depth of the contrapuntal possibilities inherent in a single musical subject." https://www.youtube.com/watch?v=jphFYgijiuI (link live July 2017).

Page 145. Marie-Louise von Franz, *C.G. Jung: His Myth in Our Time*, p. 284. Von Franz wrote that for Jung, "Bach, like Shakespeare, was one of the very few geniuses who lived from the creative depths in a wholly unreflecting way. The work of Bach and Shakespeare were for him expressions of the unconscious unclouded by ego elements."

Page 145. C.G. Jung, "Letter to Serge Moreux, January 1950," in *Letters, Volume 1*, p. 542.

Page 145. C.G. Jung, *Letters, Volume 2*, p. xlvi.

Page 148. *Larousse Encyclopedia of Music*, p. 198. John Eliot Gardiner gives a compelling account of Bach's rebellious nature in a chapter titled "The Incorrigible Cantor," in *Music in the Castle of Heaven*.

Page 148. It happened one day. Online translated quote from Jean-Paul Clébert, *The Gypsies*. This story is also told in Bart McDowell's *Gypsies: Wanderers of the World*, p. 61.

Page 149. Bach and the Bohemian Gypsies. Michael Beckerman, "Exploring Bach for His Gypsy Side," *New York Times*, November 6, 2009.

Page 149. Django Reinhardt, cited in Michael Dregni, *Django: The Life and Music of a Gypsy Legend*, p. 137. Online recording by Django Reinhardt, Stéphane Grappelli, and Eddie South. https://www.youtube.com/watch?v=gQZw3nema0Q and https://www.youtube.com/watch?v=_TRjTeQ-sIM.

Page 152. Helen Luke, "The Joy of the Fool," in *Kaleidoscope*, p. 137.

Page 152. Luke, "The Sense of Humour," in *Kaleidoscope*, p. 131.

Page 157. Günter Grass, foreword to *The Roma Journeys*, by Joakim Eskildsen and Cia Rinne, p. 7.

Page 157. Murray Stein, "Hermes and the Creation of Space," p. 3.

Page 159. To the best of my knowledge *Body Soul Writing* was the first writing course of its kind at a Canadian university and began in 2003.

Page 160. Fierz-David and Hall, *Dreaming in Red*, p. 172.

Page 161. Griffiths, *Wild*, p. 260.

Page 161. Walter Starkie, *Scholars and Gypsies: An Autobiography*, p. xi. I was intrigued to discover that Starkie also employs a musical structure; the book's three sections are titled *Prelude*, *Adagio*, and *Allegro*.

Page 162. Marlene Schiwy, "Saturating Language with Love," in *Wise Women: Reflections of Teachers at Midlife*, p. 33.

Page 162. Creativity and breakthroughs. Regenia Gagnier, "Cultural Philanthropy, Gypsies, and Interdisciplinary Scholars: Dream of a Common Language," online article in *19: Interdisciplinary Studies in the Long Nineteenth Century* 1 (2005): p. 18.

Page 167. Hélène Cixous, *Coming to Writing and Other Essays*, p. 51.

Page 167. Multiple beginnings. Estella Lauter and Carol Rupprecht, *Feminist Archetypal Theory*, p. 233.

Page 167. A feminine text starts on all sides. Hélène Cixous, "Castration or Decapitation?" *Signs* 7 (Autumn 1981): p. 53.

Page 168. Muriel Rukeyser, "Käthe Kollwitz," in *The Norton Anthology of Literature by Women*. Edited by Sandra M. Gilbert and Susan Gubar. New York: Norton, 1985.

Page 170. The blog that I wrote for my friends during my time in Zürich provides more detail and is archived at www.marlene-schiwy.blogspot.ca.

Page 173. Marie-Louise von Franz, *Individuation in Fairy Tales*, pp. 62, 63.

Page 173. Robert Bly and Marion Woodman, *The Maiden King: The Reunion of Masculine and Feminine*, p. 249.

Page 174. C.G. Jung, *Letters, Volume 1*, p. 133.

Page 174. Stein describes this third space as a psychic world "created by the mutual interplay of the psyches within it, which represent two other worlds, two persons with full lives outside of this new space." Since Hermes is the messenger god between worlds and between consciousness and unconscious realms, Stein refers to this as "a Hermes space." "Hermes and the Creation of Space," p. 6.

Page 176. Similarly, Jan Yoors cites the Roma's belief that "the road leading to a goal does not separate you from the destination; it is essentially a part of it." *The Gypsies*, p. 123.

Page 176. Yoors, *The Gypsies*, p. 94.

Page 176. Ann Ulanov, *Spiritual Aspects of Clinical Work*, pp. 240, 254.

Page 179. Yoors, *The Gypsies*, pp. 13, 14.

Page 179. Griffiths, *Wild*, p. 257. Since the mid-1980s, a loosely assembled alliance of young people calling themselves "the new gypsies" in the UK have adopted the nomadic lifestyle of horse-drawn caravan, travelling throughout much of the year and then settling in for the winter.

Page 181. Hall, *The Moon and the Virgin*, p. 168. Most of us will never live in a gypsy wagon or movable yurt, but I wonder if our own "roving temenos" might be our journals, another kind of square space and sacred enclosure for the unfolding of our lives.

Page 182. Yoors, *The Gypsies*, p. 160.

Page 186. Marie-Louise von Franz, "The Pattern of Psychic Growth," in Jung's *Man and His Symbols*, p. 161. Elsewhere von Franz writes, "By attending to one's dreams for a long time and by really taking them into consideration, the unconscious of modern man can rebuild a symbolic life...living with the ego embedded in a flow of psychic life which expresses itself in symbolic form and requires symbolic action. We have to see what our own living psyche proposes as a symbolic life form in which we can live....When a dream symbol comes up in a dominating form, one should take the trouble to reproduce it in a picture...and relate to it in some real manner....One should stay with the symbols of one's dreams the whole day and try to see where they want to enter the reality of one's life. This is what Jung means when he speaks of living the symbolic life." *The Interpretation of Fairy Tales*, pp. 96, 97.

Page 190. *Kumpania*. Yoors, *The Gypsies*, p. 121.

Page 195. Edward Edinger, *Ego and Archetype: Individuation and the Religious Function of the Psyche*, p. 121.

Page 195. C.G. Jung, *CW*, vol. 8, para. 550. I recently rediscovered Sheila Moon's *Dreams of a Woman*, in which she writes that her first experience of the unconscious was a dream of a dwarf who told her to listen to gypsy music. For her, too, the *gypsy* was a symbol of "the dark feminine as the keeper of wisdom." Among my friends, clients, and workshop participants dreams of gypsies are not infrequent. In one dream, a group of rebels led by a Gypsy woman broke into the dreamer's office at work and made it clear that she was to move on. She quit her job a month later. In another dream an older Gypsy woman provided wise counsel during a time of crisis in the dreamer's life. These dream variations on a theme point again toward the power of the archetypal gypsy image as a carrier of inner freedom and earthy wisdom.

Page 197. C.G. Jung, *CW*, vol. 8, para. 336.

Page 197. James Hillman, *Re-Visioning Psychology*, p. xxii.

Coda

Page 201. James Hillman, *Healing Fiction*, p. 21.

Page 202. Helen Luke, *Such Stuff as Dreams are Made On: The Autobiography and Journals of Helen M. Luke*, p. 214.

Page 203. Marion Woodman, *Addiction to Perfection*, p. 104.

Page 204. James Hillman, *The Soul's Code*, p. 38.

Page 204. A sudden birth of feeling. Ulanov, *The Feminine*, p. 177. Similarly Nor Hall describes matriarchal time as "qualitative, subjective, experiencing the length of a moment according to feelings. It is heart centered rather than head centered." *The Moon and the Virgin*, p. 97.

Page 204. That connects the upper world. Murray Stein, "Hermes and the Creation of Space," p. 6.

Page 206. Helen Luke, *Such Stuff as Dreams are Made On*, p. 248.

Page 206. Christine Downing, *The Goddess*, p. 1.

Page 206. Murray Stein, *Transformation*, p. 41.

Page 207. Steven M. Rosen, *Dreams, Death, Rebirth: A Topological Odyssey into Alchemy's Hidden Dimensions*.

Page 207. Only the images. Luke, *Kaleidoscope*, 15.

Page 207. The creative process. C.G. Jung, *CW*, vol. 15, para. 130.

Page 208. Our inherent natures. Woodman, *The Pregnant Virgin*, p. 154.

Page 208. From my previous writing. Jean Shinoda Bolen, *Crossing to Avalon: A Woman's Midlife Pilgrimage*, p. 52.

Page 208. I am not merely what I have thought. Downing, *Mirrors of the Self*, p. xiii.

Page 208. When we experience the symbol. Robert Johnson, *Inner Work*, p. 26.

Page 208. If you are in search of soul. James Hillman, "Peaks and Vales," in *Working with Images*, p. 117.

Page 208. Work of the eyes is done. Rainer Maria Rilke, "Turning-Point," in *The Selected Poetry of Rainer Maria Rilke*, ed. and trans. Stephen Mitchell, p. 135.

Page 208. We cannot get to the heart of the image. James Hillman, *Blue Fire*, p. 25.

Page 209. C.G. Jung, *Memories, Dreams, Reflections*, pp. 217, 225.

Page 209. C.G. Jung, *CW*, vol. 8, para. 202.

Page 209. Marie-Louise von Franz, *The Way of the Dream*, p. 160.

Page 210. Based on the conjunction. Lauter and Rupprecht, *Feminist Archetypal Theory*, p. 232. When I puzzled over the dream, my training analyst said, "It's a beautiful image, just enjoy it." I tried to sketch the dream braid in my journal but couldn't capture its shining vitality.

Page 210. Hélène Cixous, "Sorties," in *The Newly Born Woman*, p. 99.

BIBLIOGRAPHY

Akhmatova, Anna. "Listening to Singing." In *Poems*. Translated by Lyn Coffin. New York: W.W. Norton, 1983.

Beckerman, Michael. "Exploring Bach for His Gypsy Side." *New York Times*, November 6, 2009.

Begg, Ean. *The Cult of the Black Virgin*. London: Penguin, 1985.

Bly, Robert, and Marion Woodman. *The Maiden King: The Reunion of Masculine and Feminine*. New York: Henry Holt, 1998.

Bolen, Jean Shinoda. *Crossing to Avalon: A Woman's Midlife Pilgrimage*. New York: HarperCollins, 1994.

Brown, Irving. *Deep Song: Adventures with Gypsy Songs and Singers in Andalusia and Other Lands with Original Translations*. New York: Harper & Brothers, 1929.

Cartwright, Garth. *Princes among Men: Journeys with Gypsy Musicians*. London: Serpent's Tail, 2005.

Cixous, Hélène. "Castration or Decapitation?" *Signs: Journal of Women in Culture and Society* 7, no. 1 (Autumn 1981): 41–55.

——. *"Coming to Writing" and Other Essays*. Edited by Deborah Jenson. Cambridge, MA: Harvard University Press, 1991.

——. "The Laugh of the Medusa." In *New French Feminisms: An Anthology*. Edited by Elaine Marks and Isabelle de Courtivron. Brighton, UK: Harvester Press, 1981.

Cixous, Hélène, and Catherine Clément. *The Newly Born Woman*. Minneapolis: University of Minnesota Press, 1986.

Cixous, Hélène, and Mireille Calle-Gruber. *Rootprints: Memory and Life Writing*. Translated by Eric Prenowitz. New York: Routledge, 1997.

Cohen, Leonard. http://cohencentric.com/leonard-cohen-the-prince-of-asturias-awards-speech-with-annotations-commentary/ (link live in June 2017).

Downing, Christine. *The Goddess: Mythological Images of the Feminine.* New York: Crossroad, 1988.

Downing, Christine, ed. *Mirrors of the Self: Archetypal Images That Shape Your Life.* Los Angeles: Jeremy P. Tarcher, 1991.

Dregni, Michael. *Django: The Life and Music of a Gypsy Legend.* Oxford: Oxford University Press, 2006.

Eberstadt, Fernanda. Author interview with Summer Block, May 29, 2006. http://www.identitytheory.com/fernanda-eberstadt/.

____. *Little Money Street: In Search of Gypsies and Their Music in the South of France.* New York: Alfred A. Knopf, 2006.

Edinger, Edward. F. *Ego and Archetype: Individuation and the Religious Function of the Psyche.* Baltimore: Penguin Books, 1972.

Engebrigtsen, Ada I. *Exploring Gypsiness: Power, Exchange and Interdependence in a Transylvanian Village.* New York: Berghahn Books, 2007.

Eskildsen, Joakim, and Cia Rinne. *The Roma Journeys.* Göttingen: Steidl Publishers, 2007.

Fidyk, Alexandra. "'Gypsy' Fate: Carriers of Our Collective Shadow." *JUNG: the e-Journal of the Jungian Society for Scholarly Studies* 4, no. 1 (December 2008): 1–28.

____. "On Home and Identity: Following the Way of the Roma." *Spring: A Journal of Archetype and Culture* 85 (Spring 2011): 75–102.

Fierz-David, Linda, and Nor Hall. *Dreaming in Red: The Women's Dionysian Initiation Chamber in Pompeii.* Putnam, CT: Spring Publications, 2005.

Fonseca, Isabel. *Bury Me Standing: The Gypsies and Their Journey.* New York: Alfred A. Knopf, 1995.

Von Franz, Marie-Louise. *C.G. Jung: His Myth in Our Time.* Translated by William H. Kennedy. Boston: Little, Brown, 1975.

____. *Dreams.* Boston: Shambhala, 1998.

____. *The Feminine in Fairy Tales*. Zürich: Spring Publications, 1972.

____. *Individuation in Fairy Tales*. Boston: Shambhala, 1990.

____. *The Interpretation of Fairy Tales*. Boston: Shambhala, 1996.

____. *Number and Time*. Evanston, IL: Northwestern University Press, 1974.

____. *The Way of the Dream: Conversations on Jungian Dream Interpretation with Fraser Boa*. Boston: Shambhala, 1994.

Freeman, Phyllis R., and Jan Zlotnik Schmidt, eds. *Wise Women: Reflections of Teachers at Midlife*. New York: Routledge, 2000.

Gagnier, Regenia. "Cultural Philanthropy, Gypsies, and Interdisciplinary Scholars: Dream of a Common Language." *19: The Interdisciplinary Studies in the Long Nineteenth Century* 1 (2005). http://doi.org/10.16995/ntn.433.

Gardiner, John Eliot. *Music in the Castle of Heaven*. New York: Alfred A. Knopf, 2013.

Gatlif, Tony. Interview at archive.is/20130128230027/www.mondomix.com/en/news/freedom.

____. *Latcho Drom*, 1993.

Gopnik, Adam. "The People Who Pass." *New Yorker*, January 13, 2014, 22–28.

Grass, Günter. "True Europeans." *Index on Censorship, Gypsies: Life on the Edge* 27 (July 1998): 51–53.

Griffin, Susan. *What Her Body Thought: A Journey into the Shadows*. San Francisco: Harper SF, 1999.

Griffiths, Jay. *Wild: An Elemental Journey*. New York: Tarcher/Penguin, 2006.

Grobbel, Michaela. "Contemporary Romany Autobiography as Performance." *German Quarterly* 76, no. 2 (Spring 2003): 140–154.

Hall, Nor. *The Moon and the Virgin: Reflections on the Archetypal Feminine*. New York: Harper & Row, 1980.

____. Muse excerpts from "Channel a Muse: Notes Toward the Construction of a Mother-Daughter Biography." Originally published in *Spring Journal*,

Spring 2004. http://www.mythicjourneys.org/passages/august2005/channel_a_muse.pdf.

Hancock, Ian. *The Pariah Syndrome: An Account of Gypsy Slavery and Persecution*. Ann Arbor: Karoma Publishers, 1987.

____. *We Are the Romani People*. Hertfordshire: University of Hertfordshire Press, 2002.

Hancock, Ian, Siobhan Dowd, and Rajko Djuric, eds. *The Roads of the Roma: A PEN Anthology of Gypsy Writers*. Hertfordshire: University of Hertfordshire Press, 1998/2004.

Harding, Esther. *Woman's Mysteries*. London: Rider, 1991.

Hava-Robbins, Nadia. "Gypsy Soul," in *The Roads of the Roma*. Edited by Ian Hancock, Siobhan Dowd, and Rajko Djuric. Hertfordshire: University of Hertfordshire Press, 1998/2004.

Hillman, James. *A Blue Fire: Selected Writings by James Hillman*. Edited by Thomas Moore. New York: HarperCollins, 1989.

____. *The Dream and the Underworld*. New York: Harper & Row, 1979.

____, ed. *Facing the Gods*. Dallas: Spring Books, 1980.

____. *The Force of Character and the Lasting Life*. New York: Ballantine Books, 1999.

____. *Healing Fiction*. Putnam, CT: Spring Publications, 1983.

Hillman, James. "Peaks and Vales." In *Working with Images: The Theoretical Base of Archetypal Psychology*. Edited by Benjamin Sells. Woodstock, CT: Spring Publications, 2000.

____. *Re-Visioning Psychology*. New York: HarperCollins, 1975.

____. *The Soul's Code: In Search of Character and Calling*. New York: Random House, 1996.

Hoffman, Eva. *After Such Knowledge: Memory, History and the Aftermath of the Holocaust*. New York: Public Affairs, 2004.

____. *Lost in Translation: A Life in a New Language*. New York: Penguin Books, 1989.

Johnson, Robert. *Inner Work: Working with Dreams and Active Imagination.* New York: HarperCollins, 1986.

_____. *Lying with the Heavenly Woman: Understanding and Integrating the Feminine Archetypes in Men's Lives.* New York: HarperCollins, 1994.

Jung, C.G. *Aion.* Vol. 9/2 of *The Collected Works of C.G. Jung.* Translated by R.F.C. Hull. Princeton, NJ: Princeton University Press, 1968.

_____. *The Archetypes and the Collective Unconscious.* Vol. 9/1 of *The Collected Works of C.G. Jung.* Translated by R.F.C. Hull. Princeton, NJ: Princeton University Press, 1968.

_____. *C.G. Jung Speaking: Interviews and Encounters.* Edited by William Mc-Guire and R.F.C. Hull. Princeton, NJ: Princeton University Press, 1978.

_____. *Civilization in Transition.* Vol. 10 of *The Collected Works of C.G. Jung.* Translated by R.F.C. Hull. Princeton, NJ: Princeton University Press, 1970.

_____. *Letters, Vol. 1 (1906-1950).* Edited by Gerhard Adler and Aniela Jaffé. Translated by R.F.C. Hull. Princeton, NJ: Princeton University Press, 1973.

_____. *Letters, Vol. 2 (1951-1961).* Edited by Gerhard Adler and Aniela Jaffé. Translated by R.F.C. Hull. Princeton, NJ: Princeton University Press, 1976.

_____. *Memories, Dreams, Reflections.* Edited by Aniela Jaffé. Translated by Richard and Clara Winston. London: Fontana, 1983.

_____. *Mysterium Coniunctionis.* Vol. 14 of *The Collected Works of C.G. Jung.* Translated by R.F.C. Hull. Princeton, NJ: Princeton University Press, 1970.

_____. *Psychological Types.* Vol. 5 of *The Collected Works of C.G. Jung.* Translated by R.F.C. Hull. Princeton, NJ: Princeton University Press, 1971.

_____. *Psychology and Alchemy.* Vol. 12 of *The Collected Works of C.G. Jung.* Translated by R.F.C. Hull. Princeton, NJ: Princeton University Press, 1968.

_____. *The Red Book.* Edited by Sonu Shamdasani. New York: W.W. Norton, 2009.

____. *The Spirit in Man, Art, and Literature*. Vol. 15 of *The Collected Works of C.G. Jung*. Translated by R.F.C. Hull. Princeton, NJ: Princeton University Press, 1966.

____. *The Structure and Dynamics of the Psyche*. Vol. 8 of *The Collected Works of C.G. Jung*. Translated by R.F.C. Hull. Princeton, NJ: Princeton University Press, 1969.

____. *Symbols of Transformation*. Vol. 5 of *The Collected Works of C.G. Jung*. Translated by R.F.C. Hull. Princeton, NJ: Princeton University Press, 1967.

Kenrick, Donald. *Gypsies: From the Ganges to the Thames*. Hertfordshire: University of Hertfordshire Press, 2004.

____. *Gypsies under the Swastika*. Hertfordshire: University of Hertfordshire Press, 2009.

Kinsley, David R. *The Sword and the Flute: Kali and Krsna, Dark Visions of the Terrible and the Sublime in Hindu Mythology*. Berkeley: University of California Press, 1977.

Lacková, Ilona. *A False Dawn: My Life as a Gypsy Woman in Slovakia*. Hertfordshire: University of Hertfordshire Press, 2000.

Larousse Encyclopedia of Music. Edited by Geoffrey Hindley. New York: Hamlyn Publishing, 1975.

Lawrence, D.H. *The Virgin and the Gipsy*. Harmondsworth, UK: Penguin Books, 1970.

Leblon, Bernard. *Gypsies and Flamenco*. Translated by Sinéad ní Shuinéar. Hertfordshire: University of Hertfordshire Press, 1994.

Lee, Ronald. "The Romani Goddess Kali Sara." https://kopachi.com/articles/the-romani-goddess-kali-sara-ronald-lee/.

Leland, Charles Godfrey. *Gypsy Sorcery and Fortune Telling*. Edison, NJ: Castle Books, 1995.

Lorca, Federico García. "Ballad of the Spanish Civil Guard." Online at http://www.poesi.as/index214uk.htm.

____. *Deep Song and Other Prose*. Edited and translated by Christopher Maurer. London: Marion Boyars Publishers, 1980.

_____. *In Search of Duende*. Edited and translated by Christopher Maurer. New York: New Directions Books, 2010.

Lucie-Smith, Edward. *The Story of Craft: The Craftsman's Role in Society*. Oxford: Phaidon Press, 1981.

Luke, Helen. *Kaleidoscope: The Way of Woman and Other Essays*. New York: Parabola Books, 1992.

_____. *Such Stuff as Dreams Are Made On: The Autobiography and Journals of Helen M. Luke*. Edited by Barbara Mowat. New York: Parabola Books, 2000.

Machlis, Joseph. *The Enjoyment of Music: An Introduction to Perceptive Listening*. New York: W.W. Norton, 1963.

Malvinni, David. *The Gypsy Caravan: From Real Roma to Imaginary Gypsies in Western Music*. Abingdon, UK: Routledge, 2004.

Maurice, Daphne. "Yehudi Menuhin and the Gypsy Violinists." *Journal of the Gypsy Lore Society* 52, no. 3 and 4 (1973): 93.

McDowell, Bart. *Gypsies: Wanderers of the World*. Washington, DC: National Geographic Society, 1970.

McGarry, Aidan. *Romaphobia: The Last Acceptable Form of Racism*. London: Zed Books, 2017.

Mehr, Mariella. "A Red Foundling Strolls into This Dream," in *The Roads of the Roma*. Edited by Ian Hancock, Siobhan Dowd, and Rajko Djuric. Hertfordshire: University of Hertfordshire Press, 1998/2004.

Nin, Anaïs. *The Diary of Anaïs Nin, Vol. 5: 1947–1955*. Edited by Gunther Stuhlmann. New York: Harcourt Brace Jovanovich, 1974.

Patrin Roma website: http://www.oocities.org/~patrin/.

Pohren, D.E. *The Art of Flamenco*. Westport, CT: Bold Strummer, 1962/2005.

Reinhardt, Django, Stéphane Grappelli, and Eddie South. https://www.youtube.com/watch?v=gQZw3nema0Q and https://www.youtube.com/watch?v=_TRjTeQ-sIM.

Rilke, Rainer Maria. *The Selected Poetry of Rainer Maria Rilke*. Edited and translated by Stephen Mitchell. New York: Random House, 1989.

Rishi, W.R. *Roma*. Patiala, India: Punjabi University, 1976/1996. Cited online at www.romani.org (link no longer active).

Romanyshyn, Robert. "Poetry: Dark Light." www.online.pacifica.edu/romanyshyn (link no longer active).

Rosen, Steven Marc. *Dreams, Death, Rebirth: A Topological Odyssey into Alchemy's Hidden Dimensions*. Asheville, NC: Chiron, 2015.

Rukeyser, Muriel. "Käthe Kollwitz," in *The Norton Anthology of Literature by Women*. Edited by Sandra M. Gilbert and Susan Gubar. New York: Norton, 1985.

Schenk, Ronald. *The Soul of Beauty: A Psychological Investigation of Appearance*. Cranbury, NJ: Associated University Presses, 1992.

Schiwy, Marlene. "Saturating Language with Love: Variations on a Dream," in *Wise Women: Reflections of Teachers at Midlife*. Edited by Phyllis R. Freeman and Jan Zlotnik Schmidt. New York: Routledge, 2000, 27–36.

____. *Simple Days: A Journal on What Really Matters*. Indiana: Sorin Books, 2002.

____. *A Voice of Her Own: Women and the Journal Writing Journey*. New York: Simon & Schuster, 1996.

Seidler, Ben, and Simon Marks. "Gypsy Style, in the Harsh Light of Day." *New York Times*, October 3, 2008.

Södergran, Edith. *Complete Poems*. Newcastle upon Tyne: Bloodaxe Books, 1984.

Sonneman, Toby F. "Dark Mysterious Wanderers: The Migrating Metaphor of the Gypsy." *Journal of Popular Culture* 32, no. 4 (Spring 1999): 119–139.

Starkie, Walter. *Scholars and Gypsies: An Autobiography*. Oakland: University of California Press, 1963.

Stein, Murray. "Hermes and the Creation of Space." Online article at http://www.jungatlanta.com/articles/Hermes-and-the-Creation-of-Space.pdf.

____. *Transformation: Emergence of the Self*. College Station, TX: Texas A&M University Press, 1998.

Stewart, Michael. *The Time of the Gypsies.* Boulder, CO: Westview Press, 1997.

Stone, John. http://www.kunstderfuge.com/theory/stone/roadmap.htm (link no longer active).

Story, Jimmy. "New Rom," in *The Roads of the Roma.* Edited by Ian Hancock, Siobhan Dowd, and Rajko Djuric. Hertfordshire: University of Hertfordshire Press, 1998/2004.

Tcherenkov, Lev, and Stephane Laederich. *The Rroma. Volume 2: Traditions and Texts.* Basel: Schwabe Verlag, 2004.

Tillhagen, Carl-Herman. "The Songs of the Swedish Nomadic Gypsies." *Journal of the Gypsy Lore Society* 30 (1951): 84–96.

Tomasevic, N.B., and R. Djuric. *Gypsies of the World.* London: Flint River Press, 1988.

Tong, Diane. *Gypsy Folk Tales.* New York: Harcourt Brace Jovanovich, 1989.

Ulanov, Ann Belford. *The Feminine in Jungian Psychology and Christian Theology.* Evanston, IL: Northwestern University Press, 1971.

_____. *Spiritual Aspects of Clinical Work.* Einsiedeln, Switzerland: Daimon, 2004.

Vukanovic, T.P. "Musical Culture among Gypsies of Yugoslavia." *Journal of Gypsy Lore Society* 41 (1962): 41–60.

Walcott, Derek. *Collected Poems 1948–1984.* New York: Farrar, Straus and Giroux, 1986.

Webster, Jason. *Duende: A Journey into the Heart of Flamenco.* New York: Broadway Books, 2002.

Wikman, Monika. *Pregnant Darkness: Alchemy and the Rebirth of Consciousness.* Berwick, ME: Nicolas-Hays, 2004.

Wolff, Christoph. *The Art of Fugue.* https://www.youtube.com/watch?v=-jphFYgijiuI.

Woodman, Marion. *Bone: Dying into Life.* New York: Viking/Penguin, 2000.

____. *Conscious Femininity: Interviews with Marion Woodman*. Toronto: Inner City Books, 1993.

____. *The Owl Was a Baker's Daughter: Obesity, Anorexia Nervosa and the Repressed Feminine*. Toronto: Inner City Books, 1980.

____. *The Pregnant Virgin: A Process of Psychological Transformation*. Toronto: Inner City Books, 1985.

____. *The Ravaged Bridegroom: Masculinity in Women*. Toronto: Inner City Books. 1990.

Woodman, Marion, et al. *Leaving My Father's House: A Journey to Conscious Femininity*. Boston: Shambhala, 1992.

Woodman, Marion, and Elinor Dickson. *Dancing in the Flames: The Dark Goddess in the Transformation of Consciousness*. Boston: Shambhala, 1996.

Woodman, Marion, with Jill Mellick. *Coming Home to Myself: Reflections for Nurturing a Woman's Body & Soul*. Berkeley: Conari Press, 1998.

Yeger, Aaron. *A People Uncounted*, 2014.

Yoors, Jan. *Crossing: A Journal of Survival and Resistance in World War II*. New York: Simon & Schuster, 1971.

____. *The Gypsies*. Prospect Heights, IL: Waveland Press, 1967.

____. *The Heroic Present: Life among the Gypsies*. New York: Monacelli Press, 2004.